Colonel Sion S. Bass, of Fort Wayne, mortally wounded at the Battle of Shiloh.

Memorial Record
of
Allen County Soldiers, War of the Rebellion,
1861-65

A reprint
with
a new index and introduction
by
Charles F. Bragg
and
Mark E. Neely, Jr.

Louis A. Warren
Lincoln Library and Museum
Fort Wayne, Indiana
1989

INTRODUCTION
ALLEN COUNTY IN THE CIVIL WAR

The *Memorial Record of Allen County Soldiers, War of the Rebellion, 1861-1865* was perhaps the last public memorial of Civil War service in this Indiana county. It was published in 1905 or 1906, before the ugly wars of the twentieth century forever changed the attitude toward combat assumed by most thoughtful people in the western world. Although the specific origins of its publication remain obscure, the motives behind the volume seem simple to explain.

The men of Allen County who served in the Civil War deserved memorials, and Allen County celebrated them with the memorial volume reprinted here. But there are larger questions lurking in these lists that escape the moral or sentimental categories of patriotism and service. By publishing this volume, Allen County also celebrated itself a little. Was this deserved? Did Allen County, as the slang of later wars would express it, do its bit? When compared with the rest of the state, how did Allen County's record measure up?

Indiana as a whole turned in an outstanding performance. The state furnished 197,141 men from its slightly more than 300,000 men of military age. It ranked second among the northern states in percentage of manpower mobilized.[1] But how did Allen County rank among the other counties in Indiana?

Local historian B.J. Griswold assessed Allen County's contribution with typical pride:

The great mass of the people of Allen County rallied with enthusiasm about the national government, regardless of party affiliations. The best evidence of this loyalty is the record of the county in the great struggle for the preservation of the union. During the period of the war the county sent 4,103 men to fields of battle; of this number 489 lost their lives in the defense of their country. The county paid $550,145 in war bounties, gave $73,863 for the relief of the families of the soldiers, and to this added $2,000 for miscellaneous expenses, making a total of over $630,000 -- truly a magnificent substantial evidence of the truest patriotism.[2]

The amount of money paid in bounties, relief, and other such expenses (actually $625,998.72) ranked third in the state, behind Marion County's $1,677,199.14 and Tippecanoe County's $894,436.33. Rounding out the top five were Wayne County, at $563,443.35, and Montgomery County, at $537,206.78.[3]

By total population, Allen County was also the third largest in the state.[4] With the other four counties ranking highest in war expenditures, it stood thus:

County	(White) Male	Female	Black	Total
Marion	20,048	18,982	825	39,855
Wayne	14,646	14,042	870	29,558
Allen	15,349	13,916	63	29,328
Tippecanoe	13,542	12,041	143	25,726
Montgomery	10,732	10,006	150	20,888

Perhaps the more "truly...magnificent" patriotic effort came in Montgomery County, whose population was exceeded by Jefferson (25,036), Dearborn (24,406), Laporte (22,919), Vigo (22,517), and Elkhart (20,986) Counties. These five counties, though larger than Montgomery, spent less on their war efforts.

An obvious explanation for such relative differences might lie in the political complexion of the different counties. Here are the 1864 election returns[5] for the ten counties in question:

| | 1864 | | | | 1860 | |
| | Governor | | President | | President | |
	Union	Democrat	Union	Democrat	Repub.	Democrat
Allen	2251	4610	2244	4932	2252	3298
Dearborn	2151	2354	2420	2127	2127	2593
Elkhart	2307	2964	2253	2000	2471	1966
Jefferson	2890	1815	2758	1777	2661	1860
Laporte	2772	2247	2766	2145	3167	2009
Marion	9554	3221	10952	3486	5024	3732
Montgomery	2302	2238	2228	2260	2367	2326
Tippecanoe	3392	2669	3438	9277	5348	0242
Vigo	2872	2211	2887	2167	2429	2382
Wayne	4651	1777	4238	1529	4234	2047

What these statistics reveal is that there is no obvious relationship between loyalty, as measured by county expenditures for the war effort, and political party.

The level of county expenditure is not necessarily the best measure of patriotism or sacrifice. The Adjutant General of the state regarded the disparities in bounties offered as an injustice and rightly characterized some of these expenditures as a means of allowing men of the local county to escape the burden of service (by luring men from other counties with promises of greater bounty payments).

Numbers of enlistments by county are difficult to ascertain. The standard source, the Adjutant General's final report, lists Indiana's soldiers by regiment. Although place of residence is supplied, the nearly 200,000 names make a county by county determination a herculean task. Moreover, sophisticated comparisons of war efforts require taking into account length of service. The earliest efforts to compare recruitment in the Civil War state by state converted the numbers into equivalents of three years' service, and any mere head count would be virtually meaningless. Finally, the nineteenth-century fixation on states as the significant units for comparison makes difficult any measurement by other politico-geographical unit. Hoosiers, for example, did not necessarily serve only in Indiana regiments, but also in regiments from neighboring and even distant states.

A comparison of Allen County's war effort with that of Wayne County is instructive. The two counties, though nearly equal in total population (Wayne, 29,558; Allen, 29,328), included demographic differences that mattered for military mobilization. Wayne held a larger total population by 230 persons, but it had 703 fewer white males. This was partly because Allen County's population was disproportionately male: 1,433 more white males than females; whereas Wayne held only 604 more males than females. Allen County was also disproportionately white. There were only 63 black people in Allen County, as compared to Wayne's 870 (among the largest concentrations of black people in this overwhelmingly white state).

Like Allen County, Wayne was near the eastern border of the state, and a substantial number of Wayne County's youth joined Ohio regiments. Wayne County men served as well in regiments from Iowa, Kentucky, Illinois, Maryland, and other states. The county's black population also meant that some of her sons served in famous regiments credited to states far from Indiana, the 54th Massachusetts Infantry or the 14th Rhode Island Heavy Artillery, black regiments whose soldiers came from all over the country. The same may have been true of Allen County, but figures are not readily available.[6]

Using the figures provided in the unusually inclusive 1884 *History of Wayne County*, one finds 2,392 soldiers listed from the second most populous county in Indiana. Allen County, with a slightly smaller population but with perhaps a few more males altogether, sent a far greater number of men to the service of their country. Allen also contributed more in bounties and relief than Wayne. Yet the two counties could hardly have been less alike politically. Wayne, the home county of the Republican Governor, Oliver P. Morton, contained more than twice as many Republicans as Democrats. It was represented in Congress by the prominent antislavery Republican, George Washington Julian. Allen County, a Democratic stronghold, nevertheless sent far more men to the war.

In fact, Allen County gave almost exactly its share to the Union cause from Indiana. Proportionate to total population of the state, Allen County's share of the 197,141 soldiers sent by Indiana would have been 4281. She sent, according to Griswold, 4103.

In truth, Allen County did not exactly "send" these 4,000-odd men. Most of them volunteered to go, and explaining Allen County's record of service in the Civil War fully would require explaining some 4,000 individual decisions to serve. This war was fought overwhelmingly by volunteers.

Why did they go? History will never know for certain. Historians cannot be sure of the motivations of even the most articulate members of society, like the politicians and generals who leave behind substantial documentation in letters, diaries, and memoirs. Understanding the inarticulate, the common soldiers who left behind a less complete written record, is even more difficult.

Yet some conjectures are possible. Although each individual decided to volunteer on his own, recruitment was nevertheless a mass phenomenon, relying in part on techniques used to sway crowds. Shortly after the news of the firing on Fort Sumter reached Fort Wayne, for example, a large meeting was held on short notice at Colerick Hall. The mayor, F.P. Randall, and numerous local political leaders from both parties, men like Democrat Allen Hamilton and Republican Jesse Williams, were present. Treason and rebellion were denounced, and a committee drafted a resolution, unanimously passed, that said the attack on Fort Sumter justified the president's call for militia volunteers to save the Union. It was also resolved "that in the present crisis of our national affairs, there should be but one party in the State of Indiana, and that this party should stand pledged before the country, to upholding...the National Administration...." Another resolution put it more succinctly and stirringly, "...we will know no party but Union...." "Raptuous applause" greeted the singing of the *Star Spangled Banner*, and at the end of the meeting William H. Link, George Humphrey, and William Segur enrolled volunteers.[7]

Examining the early parts of regimental histories, where the recruiting of the units is described, also reveals the usefulness of enthusiasm-building mass rallies. Surgeon John H. Rerick, of the 44th Indiana Volunteer Infantry, organized in Fort Wayne in the late summer and early autumn of 1861, described the process this way:

> The companies were recruited by patriotic citizens in different localities, who felt it their duty to assist in suppressing the rebellion. These would prepare an enlistment agreement, circulate it among their neighbors for signatures--sometimes canvassing their respective counties--call public meetings, make patriotic speeches, awakening the people to an appreciation of the perils of the Government. When a sufficient number of volunteers had been secured for the nucleus of a company, they were called together at some convenient point in their county, and an election would then be held for company officers. ...The officers

at once marched their men into camp, and when the ranks were not entirely full, some one or more would obtain leave of absence, to return home and continue the recruiting.[8]

Dr. Rerick gave his readers a rather dry account of this process, with but a hint of its resemblance to the exciting political campaigns of the era.

Other histories provide more vivid accounts of the events that created a crowd psychology favorable to enlistment. It is not difficult, for example, to imagine the excitement of the boys in an Indiana village like the one described here, in 1861:

When Company K...returned..., after its ninety days of service in West Virginia, the citizens turned out to receive it. Across Main street was hung a banner emblazoned with the words "Welcome to the Brave." Such an ovation was never surpassed before in enthusiasm in the county. As the boys marched down the street, the multitude enveloped them on every side and shouts of "welcome" rent the air, and from the noisy, patriotic throng could be heard the commanding voice of...the marshal of the day. "Stand back and give the brave boys air!"

It was a great day and the starting-point of enlistments generally throughout...[the] county.[9]

Bands, brass buttons, blue uniforms, banners, and--especially--crowds worked their magic. Their effect was the more pronounced because of the nature of the likely recruit. As one Indiana regimental historian pointed out, his unit "was composed principally of young men who had never seen a greater excitement than that afforded by a camp meeting, or a husking bee, whose wildest dissipation had been a horse race or a circus...."[10]

Another early rally in Allen County reveals the weight of society's institutions brought to bear on the problem of enlistment. At tiny Maysville, on April 20, 1861, a Union meeting "composed of men of all parties" (as the newspaper account was careful to point out twice in the space of five paragraphs) used a choir, a patriotic orator, and--another nearly ubiquitous factor--a minister of religion to stir enthusiasm for enlistment. The choir sang the national anthem and the divine gave a patriotic address. Afterward, eight young men signified their intention to enlist.[11]

War meetings, as they were called, became frequent, and the attendance of politicians became *de rigueur*. In 1862 Democrats were forced to defend their congressional candidate, Joseph Edgerton, from Republican charges that he was a rebel sympathizer:

Mr. Edgerton is not a man who thrusts himself upon, or seeks to make himself conspicious in public meetings, and if he has not attended every war meeting that has been called here, some of them as much to make capital for the abolition party, as to promote enlistment, he has shown his devotion to the government in far better and more substantial ways; that is, by endeavoring to show to the people the true purposes of the war, and the necessity of strict adherence to Constitutional means in its prosecution--as well as by contributing of his means. But a few weeks ago Mr. Edgerton donated one hundred dollars in cash to aid in raising a company for the 12th Regiment....[12]

Some of the earliest companies organized in Fort Wayne carried colorful and idiosyncratic names. Their recruiters were George Humphrey, William H. Link. O.D. Hurd, and William Segur, the first three named being veterans of the Mexican War. Segur's company was called the Wayne Rifles, and they departed for camp in Indianapolis on April 27, less than two weeks after Sumter's surrender. Hurd called his unit the Fort Wayne Union Guards. Link's unit was the Hoosier Guards and Humphrey's, the Mad Anthony Guards.[13]

Departure for camp for organization into regiments and real training provided another emotion-filled event to stir those young men not already eager to enlist. In Fort Wayne, a crowd gathered at the railroad station, where a politician gave a patriotic address, before the departure of Segur's Wayne Rifles, 124-men strong. The proprietor of the Depot Eating-House, E. F. Colerick, furnished the entire company free breakfasts. The night before, the company had been presented a Bible in a ceremony. Cheers sent the men on their way as the train pulled out of the station. Speeches, crowds, cheers, and all were turned out for a 3:30 a.m. departure![14]

Before long, however, the units, which loomed so large in the eyes of their local admirers, became but small parts of a vast and numerically anonymous army, assigned regimental numbers rather than colorful nicknames. They were typical of the mass warfare of the post-eighteenth century era. One will look in vain for the exploits of the Mad Anthony Guards; they apparently became a company of the 12th Indiana Volunteer Infantry, one of 152 such regiments of foot soldiers and one among 195 military units altogether, raised in Indiana during the Civil War.[15]

Mobilization of such numerous forces to save the nation retained a strangely states-rights atmosphere about it. The federal government's authority to raise armies in a hurry was limited. Only Congress could increase the size of the regular army, and Congress was not in session when Fort Sumter was fired upon. To supplement the tiny 1600-man regular army, President Lincoln had to fall back on two hoary statutes, one dating from the previous century. The militia act of February 28, 1795, authorized the president to call out the militia from any state when the laws of the United States were opposed or obstructed by combinations too powerful for a posse or marshals to control. No militiaman could be compelled to such service for more than three months in a year or thirty days after the commencement of the next session of Congress. The other relevant act, the militia law of March 3, 1803, permitted the calling out of the militia to preserve law and order in the District of Columbia. Lincoln issued a proclamation calling for 75,000 men from the militias of the states on April 15, 1861.[16]

Indiana was willing to supply nearly half that number by herself, and other individual states could doubtless have supplied the whole 75,000. On May 3, Lincoln called for 42,034 volunteers, 22,714 regulars, and 18,000 sailors to serve for three years or the duration of the war--this despite the fact that Congress had not yet convened.[17]

Since the states controlled this mobilization until the soldiers were sworn into the service of the United States, commissioned officers were appointed by the governors. The act of July 22, 1861, fixed this system for the duration of the war, calling for 500,000 volunteers, the governors to "commission the field, staff, and company officers requisite for the said volunteers." As Fred A. Shannon, the premier student of the administration of the army in the Civil War, expressed it, "The principle of state rights, as applied to the raising of the army, had prevailed. The federal government might call for the troops and assign the quotas, but the states would raise the men, organize the regiments, and, to a great extent, control their destinies."[18]

Sentiment moved rather quickly from enthusiasm for volunteering to doubts, hesitation, reluctance, and second thoughts. As early as July 1861 the ordinary emotional appeals to patriotism did not always suffice. D.W.C. Rugg advertised for recruits for his zouave regiment by promising $100 in gold and 160 acres of land at the expiration of the term of enlistment. At the same time, Captain Segur of the 9th Indiana Volunteer Infantry was seeking 101 men for three years or the duration of the war, $100 in gold to be paid each recruit at the expiration of his term.[19] By September 1861 the Democratic newspaper in Fort Wayne was calling for a draft as a more equitable system, complaining that the western states had already filled their quotas while the New England states had not. By November there were apparently complaints being heard that recruiting for the 44th Indiana was going slowly, though the local press denied that it was true.[20]

Some of the problems of organizing military units later in the Civil War were described by the chaplain of an Indiana regiment raised late in the summer of 1862:

When these men came together to become soldiers they were ignorant of the duties of a soldier's life, but they were not ignorant of the dangers and hardships of the service. For more than a year the struggle had already prevailed, great battles had been fought, tens of thousands had already lost their lives, and to enlist in the army meant years of hard service for all, and death to many, but still they did not hesitate. They were not hirelings, for many of them had homes and farms and were making money at home, and had they been hirelings there they would remain, for it was the hireling that stayed at home. It was with them a question of patriotism pure and simple.[21]

Patriotism played its part, but some were beginning to hesitate and the money involved in soldiering did matter.

Another call for volunteers was deemed necessary in the summer of 1862, and 300,000 were summoned in orders issued on July 2. The quotas proved harder to fill, and Congress, foreseeing this, passed the militia act of July 17, 1862, authorizing the president to call up state militiamen for nine months and to provide regulations for raising the militia if any state failed to meet its quota. This, in fact, authorized national conscription without mentioning the dread term or the very concept of drafting.[22]

Astonishingly, Democrats in Fort Wayne applauded the move. Although later in the war opposition to conscription would become a touchstone of Democratic party loyalty, at this early stage the party's leaders had not yet formulated their opposition doctrine. The *Sentinel* then characterized "drafting" as "perhaps the only available way" by which the new men could be recruited. "It is also a fair way," the Democratic newspaper commented, "and reaches all classes equally alike. The rich must stand their chance as well as the poor."[23]

Not much time elapsed before the Democrats changed their tune, the proximity of the off-year congressional elections no doubt having some effect toward accelerating policy formulation. On September 20, 1862, the *Sentinel* reported a "strong feeling of opposition to the draft...beginning to manifest itself here," a feeling "pretty generally spread throughout the county ...and...in several other parts of the State." The Democratic newspaper elaborated, saying, "There is something repugnant to the American feeling of liberty and self-control in being thus arbitrarily compelled to leave their families and business and forced to enter the army; and the repugnance is heightened by the doubts generally entertained, that unfairness will be resorted to in drafting."

In the end, probably no policy of the Lincoln administration was more detested than conscription. Yet its principal effect was not to put the government's arm directly on the reluctant draftee but to cause young men to volunteer in order to avoid being drafted. Whole communities participated in this strange spirit of endeavoring to avoid the imposition of conscription locally. As the deadline for meeting quotas drew near, the newspapers monitored the prospects for success and mass meetings were held, like the one in Fort Wayne on the night of September 30, 1862, "to take steps for avoiding a draft in this city."[25]

In general, the draft was avoided by encouraging volunteers with offers of money over and above the army pay they would receive (the pay was already generous, by European standards, as were the soldiers' rations). The bounty system was as old as raising American armies, and it was employed in the Civil War, in some states, with the first call for troops. The federal government made in general as early as May 4, 1861, with a War Department order offering a bounty of $100 for a three years' enlistment, to be paid at the time of discharge after at least two years' service or the termination of the war. Real incentive lay only in the offer of cash in advance, however, and in the summer of 1862 the states dived into the maelstrom of competition for recruits, offering large cash bounties in advance. Counties did the same. In the end, an average of $300 bounty was paid for every single man who enlisted in the Union army. Of course, some garnered much more than that, and others, especially early recruits, much less. The expenditure was astounding-- roughly equivalent to all the pay given soldiers for the entire war, a sort of doubling of wages. But, of course, it was inequitably distributed, and that was, in the end, more condemned than the outrageous total cost, far more.[26]

Fraud grew rampant, but even the legitimate workings of this mercenary system were tragically unfair. As the assistant provost marshal for the eleventh district reported at war's end, it was especially hard on poor areas:

...if the government shall again have occasion to raise troops, ...a strict account should be kept with all the Subdistricts, giving credit to that Subdistrict where the volunteer or drafted man...may, in good faith, reside, at the time of entering the service--and to no others under any circumstances. Such a rule does exact justice to all--requiring every Subdist[rict]s from taking advantage of the poverty of others--by paying large local bounties as an inducement to the young men residing in districts unable to compete successfully for the credit to be obtained--leaving the draft, if one shall become necessary, to fill the quota of the Subdistrict thus shorn of its young men--to be made from heads of families,--men of settled habits of life, not so well suited in many respects for soldiers--but being the principal producers of the country --their presence therefore indispensable to the welfare of the community where they live, and the government--in a word they are the very bone and muscle of the land....

This provost marshal thus accurately described the threefold inequity of the bounty system. Rich counties filled their quotas with men from poor counties. Then the draft hit the poor counties for unfilled quotas. And then, the men drafted were more likely than the young volunteers to be the older, more solid, and productive persons from the poor county. This pathetic plea came from the district *neighboring* Allen County. Fort Wayne and Allen County probably benefited from the inequitable system.[27]

Eventually, hatred of conscription became a central plank in the Democratic party platform everywhere. As Congress debated a real conscription bill early in 1863 (in the end the politicians in Washington would avoid using the odious term even in that bill and called it instead the "Enroll-ment Act"), the *Sentinel* denounced it bitterly:

The Odious Conscription Act is....a death blow to all state rights, and leaves us no better than serfs under a military despotism....It is already estimated that 600,000 to 800,000 men are to be dragged from their families to fight for the negro, as soon as the bill becomes law.[28]

As the above mention in the Democratic press of fighting "for the negro" reminds us, war aims seemed to change during the Civil War, and the announcement of the Emancipation Pro-clamation on September 22, 1862, made abolition as well as restoration of the Union an almost certain outcome of a successful war effort.

But the tempo of enlisting had already fallen off--as early as the summer of 1861--before con-scription and emancipation, and it is difficult to relate the myriad of individual choices for service to specific political policies or events of the Civil War.

In the 1862 militia draft for the July call, Indiana conscripted 337 men. Allen County had the highest deficiency in the state. In the 1863 draft under the Enrollment Act, all of Indiana prov-ed exempt because of a surplus of volunteers. But that was not true of the three draft calls of 1864.[29]

Nationwide, the response to the draft proved thunderously evasive. Of the 776,000 men call-ed in four drafts under the Enrollment Act, over 20%--161,000--failed to report. Figures on eva-sion for Allen County are not readily available, but Indiana as a whole had a creditable record.

In a recent statistical study of Civil War draft evasion that identified the 27 most evasion-prone congressional districts in the North, Indiana had not a one, though three were located in Michigan and one in Ohio.[30]

All the same, conscription hardly can be said to have gone without a hitch in Allen County. Again, records by county are not available, but there are reports for the district of which the county was a part, the tenth congressional district. For example, under the draft call of July 18, 1864, 905 men called in the tenth district failed to report. Under law, such men were deserters and thus technically liable to severe punishment. In fact, most were never caught, and those who were, were simply forwarded to the draft rendezvous to be sent into service. The Provost Marshal for the 10th district, Captain Hiram Iddings, who had an office in Kendallville, reported at war's end that "A very large number of Deserters have been arrested in this District...but by far the larger portion of them were from other states and other districts in this state. It is a fact rather remarkable that but a small portion of them belonged to this district...." Iddings attributed most desertions in his own district to the evil influences of politically malign relatives and friends of the misguided deserters and said that most, when sent back to their regiments after arrest, went on to become good soldiers.[31]

Captain Iddings' report on deserters provides a useful reminder of the intensity of political feeling in Allen County and throughout America in the nineteenth century. Given that deeply partisan spirit, it is perhaps remarkable that Civil War enlistment and conscription worked as well as they did. For after the first few weeks of war, the "one party" spirit evidenced in the earliest Union mass rallies in Allen County entirely disappeared, and intense partisan bickering resumed.

The provost marshals, who were appointed by a political system, were given to altogether political interpretations of their difficulties in administering the draft. Captain Iddings recalled:

> The 10th District was regarded as the point in the state where formidable opposition would be made to the enforcement of the draft and for a time it was feared that the disloyal elements would seriously obstruct the execution of the law. Organizations, whose avowed purpose was to interpose obstacles to the enforcement of the draft, existed in every county of the District. The Opposition Press in the District taught the people that it was their duty to resist the draft unto death.... Politicians instilled into the masses, that most pernicious and dangerous doctrine of state rights....

This interpretation came straight from the Republican lexicon. The Chicago *Tribune*, perhaps Illinois' banner Republican paper, characterized Allen County as "the copperhead stronghold of Northern Indiana" and Fort Wayne as "the county seat." "The bulk of the [copperhead] population," it reported, "is of the Celtic tribe, but a considerable sprinkling of secessionists from the South also reside there." Indiana's premier Republican organ, the *Indiana State Journal*, published in Indianapolis, called Allen County "the stronghold of Copperhead Democracy, where every third man is a traitor." "They protect deserters, resist officers, and give very large democratic majorities in Allen." Indeed, the Provost Marshal for the neighboring eleventh district reported more serious difficulties, including bands of deserters living in the woods in "disloyal areas" of his district. This officer thought that the *majority* of the people in four counties of the eleventh, Adams, Wells, Huntington, and Blackford were "of the persuasion denominated Copperheads Sons of Liberty &c." But there were few incidents of serious violent resistance in Allen County.[32]

Historians have been at a loss to find documentary proof of the existence of such widespread disloyal organizations as these Provost Marshals alleged. And certainly every responsible historian today believes that the Democratic party formed a loyal opposition during the Civil War. In a speech in the spring of 1863, Congressman Joseph K. Edgerton said, as the press reported, that "the necessity of the conscript law, and the odium attached to it, were the fault of Mr. Lincoln's policy. That many democrats were forced to believe that the law was able to be made the instrument of carrying on an abolition crusade, under the dictation of such men as Wendell Phillips, Sumner, Lovejoy, Thaddeus Stevens and B.F. Butler, and of an attempt to subvert constitution government. The law was, therefore, hateful to many, but it would nevertheless be constitutionally obeyed." This was loyal but hardly enthusiastic, and it is easy to see how deep misunderstandings over loyalty and disloyalty arose between the likes of Captain Iddings and Congressman Edgerton.[33]

In fact, the Provost Marshals themselves had to admit that they did not encounter nearly as much trouble as expected. Iddings said that, "though in some instances *illiterate* and *misguided* men made show of resistance [to the draft], yet no serious outbreak occurred [in the 10th District], and the drafts were quietly submitted to, and those conscripted reported, except those who skedaddled, which class was very numerous among certain nationalities; and some took foreign protection papers." Despite the ring of bigotry in this statement, Captain Iddings here reported accurately. Modern statistical studies find some correlation between draft evasion and incidence of foreign-born, Catholic, and Democratic population, though this correlation fell off steadily after the first conscription, and evasion eventually became "chronic" among many classes and types of Americans.[34]

For those Allen County men who complied, the indignities were much the same then as now. All were stripped naked and carefully examined by a doctor to be certain that their health would not make them a burden on the army and the government hospitals. Careful examinations were also necessary, as Captain Iddings put it, because "As a general thing, Conscripts were unwilling to go into the Service, and hence would feign all manner of diseases, and it required great care to guard against imposition." For the draft call of July 18, 1864, 1,085 men in the 10th District were exempted because of physical disability. So disgusted was the Provost Marshal in the 11th District, that in the end he could say, "I am quite certain that I am within the bounds of truth when I assert that seven ei[gh]ths of all the men drafted, complained of some physical disability, or other, that, they insisted, disqualified them for the service. In addition to their own complaints, the Board were constantly beset by the friends of the drafted man--in their persistent appeals for his exemption."[35]

Poor health and shamming proved serious problems everywhere. Of the men who reported for examination after conscription, fully 60% were rejected because of ill health or because they were the sole support of a widow or an orphan sibling or presented a similar case of hardship.[36]

Captain Iddings asserted that "a very large proportion of drafted men, perhaps more than half, furnished substitutes." From the available evidence, this must not have been true. More than half proved medical unfitness, but in the July 18, 1864, call, for example, only 486 provided substitutes and 106 paid the $300 commutation fee. These 602 were considerably less than half of the number drafted: in fact, 866 drafted men reported to the rendezvous from the 10th District that summer. Substitutes loomed large in the eyes of Provost Marshals because they were so troublesome. In fact, they may well have provided the greatest headache for draft enforcement, because these individuals--usually strangers to the community--proved sometimes to be bounty jumpers, who went from district to district collecting the lucrative bounties and then deserting. The system was, Iddings said, "Fraught with much annoyance to the Board."[37]

And certain aspects of the system became grist for the mill of political partisanship. Late in 1863 the Allen County Commissioners, Democrats of course, resisted a move to offer a $50 bounty to volunteers from the county. The local Democratic press commented, "In this we think they have acted judiciously. In the eagerness to escape the draft there is an excitement that interferes with a cool judgment.... The present bounty of $300 is sufficiently high to tempt any man who would enlist for money." Democrats thought of myriad ways of criticizing conscription. Noting that Allen County was far short of its quota in January 1865, the *Sentinel* argued:

...the men who have been so clamorous for a vigorous prosecution of the war have failed in their duty of entering the ranks, to sustain the policy they insisted upon; and apparently nothing can induce them to volunteer. Unless they can be persuaded within the next seven days to show their faith by their works, nothing remains but to submit to the draft, and compel democrats to engage in a war they are not responsible for, and which they conscientiously believe could have been, and ought to have been, brought to a close without resorting a merciless conscription.

If not blaming Republicans for failing to volunteer to fight the war they caused, Democrats in Fort Wayne were excusing their political brethren for reluctance to fight. "While the war was prosecuted for its legitimate objects," the *Sentinel* clucked, "there was no difficulty in procuring all the men needed, without conscription or heavy bounty; but now that it is degenerated into a partisan struggle, the people no longer feel an interest in it, and the demands made by the administration for additional human lives, are reluctantly filled, even when backed by immense bounties and the terrors of the draft."[38]

The draft was a political problem for the Republicans. Dislike of it was bipartisan, and few Republicans could muster Lincoln's enthusiasm for the system. Instead, Allen County Republicans depicted Governor Oliver P. Morton as a saviour of Indiana from the draft (by recruiting freedmen vigorously in Alabama, for example). Pleading for volunteers, the local Republican newspaper, the *Gazette*, said, "It is unnecessary that merciless conscription here should sweep everything before it, as it does in the rebel states." And they blamed the Democratic County Commissioners: "The refusal of our county commissioners to pay any county bounty for volunteering, has left Allen County greatly deficient in its quotas, and thrown a heavier draft upon the county now than otherwise would have been."[39]

In the end, the system worked well enough and encountered little significant organized opposition in northeastern Indiana, though there, as almost everywhere else, the greatest opposition came in the form of a myriad of individual cases who chose to "vote with their feet" against conscription and disappear from the district. Enlistments somehow always more than made up for the deficiencies. The willingness of nineteenth-century men to sacrifice for military service has never been equalled by twentieth-century industrial nations in the Western world. For better or worse, those patriotic times are past.

Memorializing this remarkable sacrifice began early. There was little impulse in the North to forget about the war, however unpleasant the experience for many and however high the casualty rate. Instead, there was an impulse to forget the political divisiveness over it. In 1865 the Indiana state legislature passed a law authorizing Boards of County Commissioners to receive subscriptions from citizens and to make appropriations for the erection of soldiers' monuments and to purchase sites for them near the court house in the county seat. "This Act," the State Adjutant General reported, "is founded on the assumption that the objects attained by the war are a common and precious heritage." And so they proved to be, though the monument process went slowly, in part because of the burden of debt so many counties carried from their efforts at raising bounties for recruits and relief for soldiers' families.[40]

Allen County proved to be among the earliest to erect a memorial, an unusual one, to Mrs. Eliza E. George, a Union army nurse, in 1866. The soldiers' monument, dedicated in 1894 as "A tribute from Patriotic Citizens to the Heroic Sons of Allen County Who Fell in Defense of the Union, 1861-1865," made its appearance in the heyday of such monument building across the country.

The *Memorial Record of Allen County Soldiers, War of the Rebellion, 1861-1865* constituted a later effort. The volume bears no date, but the names of the county commissioners printed on the title page reveal that it must have been published in 1905 or 1906, a time of keen local interest in Civil War history. The Indiana Department of the Grand Army of the republic was to hold its reunion encampment in Fort Wayne in 1907.[41]

The volume the county commissioners produced remains something of a mystery. No one is certain why it was produced when it was, or why only one copy is known to exist. No one knows how it was done nor how complete its listings are. It does not include servicemen in the regular army, the marines, or the navy. It mentions no black soldiers.

Yet it constitutes the most convenient single source for finding men of Allen County who served in Indiana regiments. Its pages are here copied photographically. Whatever errors were made in the original are thus duplicated. It seems obvious that the spelling of some soldiers' names varies from place to place in the book, but one cannot be sure without checking dozens of individual service records in the National Archives. Time and money did not allow the chance to do that.

That original volume contained no index, and the index is the major contribution made by this edition. Since the index serves the pages of the original book, the spellings there--erroneous or not--correspond the spellings in the *Memorial Record*.

We wish to thank the following people for their help: Michael B. Lange for assistance in computer indexing; Jeffrey Krull and Curt Witcher, of the Allen County Public Library, for making the *Memorial Record* available and for many other services; Michael Hawfield, of the Allen County-Fort Wayne Historical Society, for answers cheerfully given to many questions; Gloria Goeglein, for searching county commissioners records; and the Allen County Genealogical Society.

1. These are the figures accepted in the most recent history of the state: James H. Madison, *The Indiana Way: A State History* (Bloomington and Indianapolis: Indiana University Press and Indiana Historical Society, 1986), p. 197.

2. B.J. Griswold, *The Pictorial History of Fort Wayne Indiana* (Chicago: Robert O. Law Company, 1917), p. 453.

3. W.H.H. Terrell, *Indiana in the War of the Rebellion: Report of the Adjutant General, Volume I* (orig. pub. 1869; Indianapolis: Indiana Historical Society, 1960), pp. 109-110.

4. *Preliminary Report on the Eighth Census* ([Washington]: U.S. Census Office, 1862), pp. 254-256.

5. *The Tribune Almanac for the Years 1838 to 1868...* (2 vols.; New York: New York Tribune, 1868), II, 58.

6. *History of Wayne County, Indiana....* (2 vols.; Chicago: Inter-State Publishing, 1884), I, 668-734.

7. Fort Wayne *Weekly Sentinel*, April 20, 1861.

8. John H. Rerick, *The Forty-fourth Indiana Volunteer Infantry: History of Its Services in the War of the Rebellion....* (LaGrange, Indiana: privately published, 1880), pp. 8-9.

9. John R. McBride, *History of the Thirty-third Indiana Veteran Volunteer Infantry....* (Indianapolis: Wm. B. Burford, Printer, 1900), pp. 7-8.

10. William E. McLean, *The Forty-third Regiment of Indiana Volunteers: An Historic Sketch of Its Career and Services* (Terre Haute: C.W. Brown, Printer, 1903), pp. 7-8.

11. Fort Wayne *Weekly Sentinel*, April 27, 1861.

12. Fort Wayne *Weekly Sentinel*, September 20, 1862.

13. Fort Wayne *Weekly Sentinel*, May 4, 1861.

14. Fort Wayne *Weekly Sentinel*, April 27, 1861.

15. Fort Wayne *Weekly Sentinel*, July 6, 1861; Frederick H. Dyer, *A Compendium of the War of the Rebellion*, (3 vols.; New York: Thomas Yoseloff, 1959), I, 37.

16. Fred Albert Shannon, *The Organization and Administration of the Union Army, 1861-1865* (2 vols.; Cleveland: Arthur H. Clark, 1928), I, 27, 29-30.

17. Ibid., I, 36.

18. Ibid., I, 46.

19. Fort Wayne *Weekly Sentinel*, July 6, 1861.

20. Fort Wayne *Weekly Sentinel*, September 21, 1861, November 9, 1861. The Democratic report was only half true. New Hampshire, Massachusetts, Connecticut, and New Jersey failed to meet their quotas, but so too did the border slave states of Delaware, Maryland, and Missouri. Shannon, *Organization and Administration of the Union Army*, I, 259.

21. D.R. Lucas, *New History of the Ninety-Ninth Indiana Infantry* (n.p., 1900), p. 14.

22. Shannon, *Organization and Administration of the Union Army*, I, 276.

23. Fort Wayne *Weekly Sentinel*, August 9, 1862.

24. Fort Wayne *Weekly Sentinel*, September 20, 1862.

25. Fort Wayne *Weekly Sentinel*, October 1, 1862.

26. Shannon, *Organization and Administration of the Union Army*, II, 52-53, 80.

27. Historical Reports of the State Acting Assistant Provost Marshals General and District Provost Marshals, 1865, Records of the Provost Marshal General's Bureau, RG110, National Archives (microfilm edition, reel 1).

28. Fort Wayne *Weekly Sentinel*, February 28, 1863.

29. W.H.H. Terrell, *Indiana in the War of the Rebellion: Report of the Adjutant General, Volume I*, pp. 49, 58-59; Shannon provides the 337 figure (I, 290).

30. Peter Levine, "Draft Evasion in the North during the Civil War, 1863-1865," *Journal of American History*, LXVII (March 1981), 822n.

31. Historical Reports of the State Acting Assistant Provost Marshals General.

32. Ibid; Chicago *Tribune* quoted in Fort Wayne *Daily Gazette*, August 17, 1864; *Indiana State Journal* quoted in Fort Wayne *Sentinel*, August 1, 1863.

33. Fort Wayne *Weekly Sentinel*, April 18, 1863.

34. Historical Reports of the State Acting Assistant Provost Marshals General; Levine, "Draft Evasion in the North," pp. 826-828.

35. Historical Reports of the State Acting Assistant Provost Marshals General.

36. James M. McPherson, *Battle Cry of Freedom: The Civil War Era* (New York: Oxford University Press, 1988), p. 601.

37. Historical Reports of the State Acting Assistant Provost Marshals General.

38. Fort Wayne *Weekly Sentinel*, December 19, 1863; January 2, 1865; May 7, 1864.

39. Fort Wayne *Daily Gazette*, July 18, 1964; July 19, 1864; August 9, 1864 (also September 19, 1864).

40. Terrell, *Indiana in the War of the Rebellion...Volume I*, pp. 378-379.

41. B.J. Griswold, *The Pictorial History of Fort Wayne, Indiana*, p. 528.

The 5th Indiana Battery in action in Georgia in 1864.

The 44th Indiana Volunteer Infantry in combat at Shiloh.

Men of the 44th Indiana Volunteer Infantry, organized in Fort Wayne in the autumn, 1861.

MEMORIAL RECORD

OF

ALLEN COUNTY SOLDIERS, WAR OF THE REBELLION, 1861-65

A mark of respect to those who fought with valor throughout
the period of strife from eighteen hundred and sixty-
one to eighteen hundred and sixty-five

Committees:

Union Veteran Legion, No. 51

    H. C. Zollinger
    H. W. Dickman
    Wm. Glenn
    Samuel Kelker

Lawton Post, G. A. R. No. 590

    Charles Ehrman
    William B. McMakin

Sion S. Bass Post, No. 40, G. A. R.

    George W. Brower
    William Kinnerk
    John N. Kress
    Samuel M. Hench
    James Ligget
    Alfred Dougherty

Anthony Wayne Post, G. A. R.

    Amos R. Walters
    R. S. Robertson

Secretary of Committees, H. WAVELAND KERR

Board of County Commissioners:

CHARLES G. GRIEBEL, President
JOSEPH TONKEL, Vice President
WILLIAM HOCKEMEYER, Secretary

Officers Commissioned by President

Major and Brevet-Colonel—Judson A. Bingham
Captain—Clarence Bailey
Captain—E. P. Ewers
Captain—Henry W. Lawton
First Lieutenant—Pendelton Borden
First Lieutenant—Hobart Bailey
First Lieutenant——— Hinkle

Naval Service

Second Lieutenant of Marines—Edmund P. Banning, United States Ship "Powhatan"
Lieutenant Commander United States Navy—Florence Schmitz
Lieutenant United States Navy—Henry B. Rumsey

Nineteenth United States Infantry

(REGULAR ARMY)

Company A

PRIVATES

John Houser
Edward Harrigan
Aaron Luther

William Miller
George Houser
Wesley Johnson
———— Hall

Charles James
———— Manning
———— Quinn

Peter Spillman
———— Schermire
———— Smith

Company B

PRIVATES

D. Springer   Matthew Garren

Company E

PRIVATES

Edward Bufford

Eighth Regiment Infantry

(THREE YEARS' SERVICE)

The Eighth Regiment was re-organized, for the three years service, at Indianapolis on the 20th of August, 1861, and mustered in on the 5th of September, 1861, with WILLIAM P. BENTON as Colonel. It marched from Indianapolis, by rail, on the 10th of September, and arrived at St. Louis, Missouri, on the day following, joining the Army then being formed by Gen. Fremont. In a few days after the Regiment marched toward the State Capital reaching Jefferson City on the 14th of September, where it remained in camp a week, during which time it was placed in the Brigade commanded by Col. Jeff C. Davis of the 22d Indiana Volunteers. On the 22d the march was resumed for Springfield. The Eighth made the march to that place in fourteen days, and returned to Otterville in seven days. On the 17th of December, the Regiment marched to Warrensburg, and assisted in the capture of thirteen hundred rebels. Returning to Otterville, it remained in camp until the 24th of January, 1862, when it marched for Springfield, joining the command of Gen. Curtis on the route. From this point the march was continued to Cross Timbers, Arkansas, and immediately after the great battle of Pea Ridge was fought on the 6th, 7th and 8th of March, in which the Eighth participated. It remained in camp at Cross Timbers for nearly a month, and then moved in the direction of Forsythe, Missouri, over the Ozark Mountains, and then proceeded down the valley of White River and across the country to Batesville, Arkansas, halting at Sulphur Rock for nearly two months. Leaving the latter place June 22d, it reached Helena, on the Mississippi River on the 13th of July. The command suffered severely on this arduous march by reason of the scarcity of provisions, there being but a scanty supply with the command and but little in the country; very often the daily rations consisted of four ears of corn with a small allowance of meat. During this march some skirmishing was had with the enemy in the cane-brakes of White River and an engagement fought at Cotton Plant. In August, while on an expedition from Helena a skirmish was had at Austin, Mississippi. On the 6th of October, the Eighth was placed in the command of Gen. Steele and proceeded, by steamer, to Sulphur Hill near St. Louis, Missouri, from which place it marched to Ironton on the 11th of October, and from thence marched and counter-marched through the south eastern portion of the State, until March 5th, 1863, when the Regiment embarked on a steamer at St. Genevieve to join Gen. Grant's Army then organizing at Milliken's Bend, Louisiana. Here it was assigned to Benton's Brigade, Carr's Division of the 13th Corps, McClernand

commanding. On the 29th of April, the Regiment crossed the Mississippi River and participated in the engagements at Port Gibson, on the 1st of May, losing in killed and wounded thirty-two; at Jackson on the 14th; at Champion Hills on the 16th; at Black River Bridge on the 17th; and from the 19th of May till the 4th of July, was engaged in the siege of Vicksburg. In the assault on the enemy's works on the 22d of June, the Eighth lost one hundred and seventeen in killed and wounded. On the 5th of July, it marched to Jackson, which, being evacuated by the rebels, the Eighth returned to Vicksburg on the 24th of July, where it remained till the 20th of August, when it embarked on a steamer for Carrollton, Louisiana. From this point a campaign was made through the Teche Country, under Gen. Banks. On the 12th of November the Regiment embarked from Berwick City for Texas, and on the 17th, took part in the attack and capture of a fort on Mustang Island, near Arkansas Pass. On the 27th, it was engaged in the attack and capture of Fort Esperanza, after which it marched to Indianola. Here, on the 1st of January, 1864, the Regiment re-enlisted, 417 out of 515 being re-mustered as Veterans. Prior to re-enlistment the Eighth sustained the following losses by death—killed in action forty-eight, died of wounds thirty-two, died of disease 137, total 217.

On the 22d of April the Regiment arrived at Indianapolis on Veteran furlough and remained in the State a month. Returning to New Orleans it embarked on the 27th of July for Morganza Bend, and the next day marched to Atchafalaya where it engaged the rebels and returned to Morganza Bend, from which place it embarked on steamer for Washington City, arriving there on the 12th of August. From thence it marched to Berryville, Virginia, where it was assigned to the 19th Corps, participating in the campaign of the Shenandoah Valley, under Gen. Sheridan. The Regiment was in the engagement at Opequan on the 19th of September and in the battles of Fisher's Hill on the 22d of September, and of Cedar Creek on the 19th of October. It left the Valley on the 6th of January, 1865, and arrived at Savannah, Georgia, by steamer from Baltimore, on the 16th of the same month. It remained on duty in Georgia until the 28th of August, 1865, when it was mustered out of service. On the 17th of September, the Eighth arrived at Indianapolis, in command of Lieut. Col. John R. Polk, with fourteen officers and 245 men, where it was finally discharged from service, after being publicly received in the Capitol grounds by Gov. Morton, on behalf of the State.

Eighth Regiment Infantry
(THREE YEARS' SERVICE)

Company G

PRIVATES

Simon D. Brady

Ninth Regiment Infantry

(THREE MONTHS' SERVICE)

The Ninth Regiment was organized and mustered into service, for three months, at Indianapolis, on the 25th of April, 1861, with ROBERT H. MILROY as Colonel. This Regiment was the first that left the State for Western Virginia, departing from Indianapolis on the 29th of May and arriving at Grafton on the 1st of June. From thence it marched toward Philippi, in the column commanded by Col. Kelly, and took part in the surprise of the rebel camp at that place on the morning of the 3d of June. Returning to Grafton, the Ninth was assigned to General Morris' Brigade and participated in all the marches and skirmishes of that command during its brief campaign, and in the engagements at Laurel Hill and Carrick's Ford. The Regiment returned home in the latter part of July, and was finally discharged at Indianapolis soon after.

Ninth Regiment Infantry

(THREE MONTHS' SERVICE)

Company E

Captain—WILLIAM P. SEGUR
First Lieutenant—HENRY A. WHITMAN
Second Lieutenant—WILLIAM S. STORY
First Sergeant—ROBERT H. HARRISON
Sergeants —JOHN SRINER
                BRUTUS A. BOURIE
                HENRY W. LAWTON
Corporals —DOUGLAS L. PHELPS
                JOHN W. TRUITT
                GEORGE H. ROBINSON
                GEORGE A. BASHFORD
Musicians—DAVID ALVERSON
                WILLIAM M. BENNETT

PRIVATES

Woodford C. Bennett
Lewis Bewley
James Boden
Isaac Barr
Frisbee T. Beck
Benjamin Cramer
Edward Criddle
John Cogan
Oscar B. Corwin
Isaac Carter
Warren Clossen
Thomas Corson
Dennis Doudican
Thomas F. Dean
Antoine Dushane
Joseph Elliott

John Finton
Samuel P. Freeman
Charles W. Fairfield
Samuel Farrier
Wash Fitsimmons
John B. Gearhart
David Gebford
John G. Greenwood
Thomas Hogarth
James Humbert
William B. Henderson
William H. Henry
Alfred Harris
Henry L. Hayward
Joseph Kickley
Morgan N. Kimberly

James S. Kimberly
Samuel Kelker
John Koons
Charles Lincoln
Frank Lavanway
Michael Mason
William M. McElvain
DeGroff N. McDonald
John S. Moore
John Neeb
Henry Notestine
John O'Connor
John R. Parker
John D. Rex
William R. Raffelt
George A. Reynerd

Henry Redeker
Edmond B. Stribley
Richard M. Stribley
Lorenzo Snider
Henry D. Shaw
Samuel Shoaff
Edward H. Smith
Frederick W. Steine
William B. Stevens
Martin L. Stewart
David Truby
Thomas Tansey
Andrew J. Tansey
Charles R. Weitzel
Henry Welch
Charles A. Zollinger

Eleventh Regiment Infantry

(THREE MONTHS' SERVICE)

The Eleventh Regiment was organized and mustered into service, for three months, at Indianapolis, on the 25th of April, 1861, with Lew Wallace as Colonel. On the 8th of May its camp was changed from Indianapolis to the immediate vicinity of Evansville, where it remained on duty blockading the Ohio River and preventing the shipping of contraband goods to the insurrectionary States. On the 7th of June, in obedience to the orders of Lieutenant General Scott, the Eleventh marched, by rail, to Cumberland, Maryland, arriving there on the 9th of June.

On the morning of the 10th of June the Regiment took the cars at Cumberland for New Creek Station, where it was disembarked and immediately marched to Romney, Virginia, twenty-three miles distant, arriving there at eight o'clock next morning. An attack was made upon the town, the only resistance being a few scattering shots from some stragglers, the main body having fled the place in the direction of Winchester on receiving intelligence an hour before of the advance of the Eleventh. The rebels were pursued some distance with no success, other than the capture of a small amount of arms, ammunition and provisions. Returning to Cumberland, the Regiment again went into camp.

On the 26th of June a body of mounted scouts, composed of thirteen picked men from the different companies, and commanded by Corporal David B. Hay, of Company A, was sent in the direction of Frankfort, on the Romney pike. Returning from the scouting expedition, they overtook forty-one mounted rebels and attacked them, killing eight and chasing the rest two miles. While crossing the Potomac River at Kelly's Island, with seventeen captured horses, they were attacked by seventy-five of the enemy, and fell back to a strong position, which they held till dark, when they returned to camp, with the loss of one man killed (J. C. Hollenback, of Company B), and two wounded (Corporal David B. Hay, of Company A, and E. P. Thomas, of Company K).

On the 8th of July the Eleventh marched, by the way of Hancock and Williamsport, to Martinsburg, Virginia, and from there to Bunker Hill, near Winchester, where it joined Gen. Patterson's command. Shortly after, the Regiment marched to Charlestown, and thence to Harper's Ferry, where the order for its return home reached it. On the 29th of July it reached Indianapolis, and was mustered out of service on the 2d of August.

Eleventh Regiment Infantry

(THREE YEARS' SERVICE)

The Eleventh Regiment was re-organized and mustered in, for the three years' service, on the 31st of August, 1861, with LEW WALLACE as Colonel, and left Indianapolis for St. Louis, on the 6th of September, arriving there on the 8th, and leaving the day following for Paducah, Kentucky. Here Lieut. Col. George F. McGinnis was promoted Colonel, in the place of Lew Wallace appointed Brigadier General. The Regiment remained at this post from September 11th till February 5th, 1862, during which time a march of 125 miles was made to Calloway's Landing, on the Tennessee River, and back again. On the 5th of February, it embarked on a steamer, which landed six miles from Fort Henry, on the opposite side of the river, from whence the Regiment marched, the next day, to Fort Heiman, where a slight skirmish occurred. On the 14th it marched to Fort Donelson, and on the 15th was engaged in the battle at that place, being in Col. Smith's brigade of Gen. Lew Wallace's division, and sustaining a loss of four killed and twenty-nine wounded. On the 17th the Eleventh returned to Fort Heiman, from whence it marched to Paris Landing, on the 6th of March, and there took steamer for Crump's Landing. From here it marched, on the 6th of April, to Shiloh Battlefield, and, on the day following, participated in the battle, fighting the enemy from half past five in the morning till half past four in the afternoon, losing eleven killed and fifty-two wounded. On the 19th of April it moved toward Corinth, and during the last of that month made two marches to Purdy and back again. Corinth being evacuated on the 30th of May, Wallace's Division was ordered to Memphis which place the Eleventh reached on the 20th of June, after a march of 120 miles across the country. In July it was sent by steamer to Helena, Arkansas, from which place, on the 4th of August, it marched to Clarendon returning on the 19th, after a march of 130 miles and the loss, by guerrillas, of one man killed, and two wounded. During the fall and winter the Eleventh engaged in expeditions from Helena to White River, to Tallahatchie River, to Duvall's Bluff and to Yazoo Pass. Colonel McGinnis being appointed Brigadier General in March, 1863, Lieut. Col. Dan Macauley was promoted Colonel. The Eleventh embarked from Helena on a steamer, on the 11th of April and reached Milliken's Bend on the 14th, where it joined Grant's Army, being in McGinnis' Brigade and Hovey's Division of McClernand's Corps, the 13th. Upon its arrival, the Regiment marched with its Corps to Carthage, and thence to Perkin's Plantation near Grand Gulf. Here the Army remained on transports to await the result of the attempt of the gunboats to silence the rebel batteries. The bombardment proving unsuccessful, the troops were disembarked and marched around to a point opposite Bruinsburg, and on the 30th of April were crossed over the river and marched to Port Gibson, where, on the 1st of May, an engagement was fought, the Eleventh capturing a battery and sustaining a loss of one man killed and twenty-four wounded. The next day the town was entered, and on the 3d of May the march was resumed. On the 16th the Regiment was engaged in the battle of Champion Hills, losing 167 in killed, wounded and missing. On the 19th it moved to Black River, and on the 21st marched to the vicinity of Vicksburg, where it remained in the trenches of our works until the 4th of July, when the surrender took place. The casualties to the Regiment during the siege were three killed and ten wounded. On the 5th of July it marched with an expedition to Jackson, with constant skirmishing on the route, the Regiment having nine men wounded. Returning to Vicksburg it remained in camp until August when it was transported to New Orleans, and, on the 13th of that month, was sent to Brashear City and through the Teche Country to Opelousas, near which place, on the 21st of October a heavy skirmish was had with the enemy. Returning from this expedition, the Regiment, on the 20th of November, marched, with Cameron's Brigade, to the banks of Lake Tasse, where a rebel camp was captured. On the 22d of December, it arrived at Algiers, and on the 19th of January, 1864, marched to Madisonville, where on the 1st of February, the Regiment re-enlisted as Veterans. Returning to New Orleans, it embarked, on the 4th of March, on a steamer for New York City, from whence it moved, by rail, to Indianapolis, reaching there on the 21st, when it was publicly received by the citizens and addressed by Governor Morton. Upon the expiration of its Veteran furlough, the Eleventh left Indianapolis, reaching New Orleans on the 8th of May, in the vicinity of which place it remained until July. On the 11th of that month it was assigned to the 2d Brigade, 2d Division of the 19th Army Corps, and on the 19th embarked on a steamer under sealed orders. Reaching Fortress Monroe on the 28th, the Eleventh proceeded to Washington, D. C., and from thence to Harper's Ferry, Virginia. Moving to Cedar Creek it skirmished with the enemy all day of the 13th of August, and on the 15th reached Winchester, from which place it made sundry marches, and, on the 22d had a skirmish near Halltown. On the 24th, in a reconnoisance, it lost two men killed and eight wounded, and on the 6th of September had a skirmish at Berryville. On the 19th it participated in the battle of Opequan, loosing eighty-one in killed and wounded. On the 20th it pursued the enemy to Fisher's Hill, and on the 22d was engaged in the battle at that place, skirmishing all night and following the enemy to Woodstock, losing two men killed and four wounded. On the 25th, it pursued the enemy to New Market, where they made a stand, but being flanked, were forced to retreat to Harrisonburgh, which place was reached by our forces on the 26th, skirmishing occurring all the way. Leaving this place on the 6th of October, the Regiment returned to Cedar Creek on the 10th, and on the 19th was engaged in the battle of Cedar Creek, losing fifty-two men, killed, wounded and missing. Upon the conclusion of Sheridan's campaign in the Shenandoah Valley, the Regiment marched to Baltimore, arriving there on the 7th of January, 1865, where it remained on duty until its muster out on the 26th of July, 1865. On the 3d of August it returned to Indianapolis, was publicly received by the Governor in behalf of the people of the State on the 4th, and in a few days after was finally discharged from service. During its three years' service the Eleventh marched 9,318 miles.

Eleventh Regiment Infantry

(THREE YEARS' SERVICE)

Company B

PRIVATES

Henry Crumley
James Cain

Jesse B. Carter
Charles Cotton

William Craigmill
Solomon Cramer

Company C

PRIVATES

Andrew Ennis
Robert H. Albertson
Patrick Clancy

James H. Forbus
William Hanna
John Johns
George Markle

Oliver P. Pence
John M. Price
William H. Rippetoe

Frederick Smith
William A. Watson
John S. Young

Company E

Corporal—HENRY STRONG

PRIVATES

George M. Beck
George W. Depew
James L. Hollopeter
Israel Hollopeter
Elijah Kent
Albert B. Knight

William Morthier
Charles M. Welch
Oscar F. Whitney
John Wilson
Jeremiah Andrews
Ephraim M. Hollopeter

Philip Gable
John Park
Jesse A. Brumley
Henry M. Bishop
Richard S. Highler
Richard H. Kaveny

John W. Lee
William E. Osborne
William H. Rollins
Benjamin Short
John Tippett
John M. Brown

Twelfth Regiment Infantry

(ONE YEAR'S SERVICE)

The Twelfth Regiment was organized from the surplus of companies that had reached Indianapolis in answer to the call for six Regiments of three months' troops, and was accepted for State service for one year, on the 11th of May, 1861, with JOHN M. WALLACE as Colonel. On the 11th of June the Regiment left Indianapolis for Evansville, where it occupied the camp lately vacated by the Eleventh Regiment. On the 18th of July, orders were received from the War Department for its transfer to the United States service for the remaining portion of its term of service, and on the 23d, the Regiment left Evansville for Baltimore, passing through Indianapolis, Columbus, Pittsburgh and Harrisburgh. Reaching Baltimore on the 27th, the Regiment went next day to Sandy Hook, Maryland, near Harper's Ferry, where it was assigned to Abercrombie's Brigade of Gen. Banks' Army of the Shenandoah. While here Col. Wallace resigned and Lieut. Col. William H. Link was promoted to the Colonelcy. The Twelfth remained in camp in Pleasant Valley near Maryland Heights, until the 16th of August, when it moved with the Army to Hyattstown, where it encamped sometime. Gen. Joe Johnston was reported to be on the opposite side of the Potomac, near Leesburgh with a large force, and this march was made with a view to prevent his crossing the river. The following month marches were made to Darnestown, Nolan's Ferry, Seneca Creek and Tuscarora Creek, and in October to Point of Rocks, Hyattstown, Urbana and Frederick. On the 11th, the Regiment left the latter place and marched through Boonsboro and Middletown to Williamsport, Maryland. On the 13th, the different companies were stationed at Williamsport, Dam No. 4, Dam No. 5, Sharpsburgh, and other points on the Maryland side of the Potomac, where they engaged in picket and outpost duty until March, 1862, during which time skirmishes and picket firing across the river were frequent. On the 11th of December, the rebels captured Capt. Reuben Williams and seven men, who had crossed over to the Virginia side from Dam No. 4, to see if the rebels were really over there. On the 1st of March, 1862, the Twelfth crossed the Potomac at Williamsport, and marched to Winchester, through Martinsburgh and Bunker Hill. On the 11th it had a skirmish with the enemy near Winchester, and on the following morning was the first Regiment to enter the town, which had been evacuated by the rebels the night before. On the 21st the Regiment moved to Berryville, and thence across the Shenandoah and over the Blue Ridge, through Snicker's Gap, to Aldie. Hearing of our victory at Winchester Heights on the 23d, it marched back again to the Shenandoah where it was met with orders to retrace its steps southward, toward Warrentown Junction, which place was reached on the 3d of April, via Aldie, Centreville, the Battlefield of Bull Run and Catlett's Station. The Regiment remained here until the 5th of May, when it marched to Washington, where on the 14th of that month it was mustered out of service, and immediately returned to Indiana.

Twelfth Regiment Infantry

(ONE YEAR'S SERVICE)

Lieutenant Colonel—WILLIAM H. LINK
Major—GEORGE HUMPHREYS
Adjutant—OSCAR M. HINKLE
Sergeant Major—FERDINAND F. BOLTZ

Company B

PRIVATES

Sylvester R. Larason

Company D

PRIVATES

Marion E. Griswold

Company F

Captain—GEORGE NELSON
First Lieutenant—OSCAR M. HINKLE
Second Lieutenant—JOHN M. GODOWN
First Sergeant—JAMES O'SHAUGNESSY
Sergeants—MARTIN L. MURPHY
    JAMES D. CAREY
    JOHN LYTER
    JAMES BINGHAM
Corporals—JOHN H. NEWLAND
    JOSEPH CRAWFORD
    HENRY H. YOUNG
    SCOTT SWANN
    GABRIEL SWIHART
Musician—ANDREW K. MCCURDY

PRIVATES

Leonard Aker	Hiram Forbing	William Kiser	Joshua Parker	Erman M. Smith
Martin Ames	John Fuller	James H. Kniss	Harvey Patterson	William H. Smith
Augustus C. Brown	Samuel Garrett	Andrew Koons	John W. Patrick	Robert J. Stewart
William Brown	William Hardwick	Clark A. Lewis	William Pio	Charles L. Thomas
James H. Browning	David Hurshberger	George A. Lewis	Levi Reynolds	Charles R. Thompson
John H. Cratcer	John Henning	John B. McGuire	John A. Rovenstine	Milton Thompson
Johnson M. DeHaven	Charles A. Holcomb	John H. McKee	Oliver Rogers	Louis Valentine
Joseph Depuy	James D. Humphrey	Alfred Mellin	Jacob A. Roof	William A. Wisrier
Joseph C. Dickey	William H. Hunting	Ambrose Middleton	Samuel Rowe	Frederick Teikenbrock
Jeremiah Fennessey	Henry B. Husselton	Caspar Miller	John W. Sherbondy	George Sanders
Cyrus Ferrington	Thomas Kennedy	Cyrus F. Mosier	Amos Sine	Robert Steele

Twelfth Regiment Infantry

(ONE YEAR'S SERVICE)

Company G

Captain—ARTHUR F. REED
Second Lieutenant—ELBERT D. BANDWIN
First Sergeant—ISAAC DEAN, JR.
Sergeants—AMOS RICHEY
JOSEPH H. AINSWORTH
FRANK H. AVELINE
ALBERT S. BRONSON
Corporals—FRANCIS R. WELDON
GEORGE W. EWING
ALFRED STONEY
WILLIAM H. HARRISON
SAMUEL D. SILVER
JAMES STROUSE
HIRAM A. SHINKLE
Musician —ELBRIDGE G. PAIGE
Wagoner —JOHN SEIPLE

PRIVATES

Charles B. Alford	John T. Cartwright	Samuel M. Karns	Robert G. Rogers	Frederick W. Shaffer
William A. Bell	Henry F. Drewes	Frederick G. J. Koehler	John A. Reaume	John Sleaster
Alfred W. Benskin	Annanias Davis	Jacob V. Kenagy	John M. Rame	Frank Savage
Andrew J. Barlow	John L. Duel	Henry F. Hellemyer	William Rinker	David W. Thomas
John T. Beaber	Upton L. Flenner	John H. Killinger	Darius Roberts	James T. Thomas
James A. Bounds	George C. Fisher	Anton Kayser	Philip W. Silver	Stillman P. Tasker
Thomas C. Beals	John Graham	William J. Koch	Jacob H. Seiple	Thaddeus Tanner
George M. Burwell	William Guynn	Isaac H. LaFevre	James A. Starbuck	William D. Wildman
Albert Benson	Mathias Henley	William Meyers	Conrad E. Snyder	Isaac B. Wilmington
Isaac M. Church	George Hare	Charles W. Mueller	James Shinn	Anton Zimmerman
John S. Campbell	Ferdinand C. King	Hiram McFee	Jacob V. Shurts	

Twelfth Regiment Infantry

(THREE YEARS' SERVICE)

Colonel—WILLIAM H. LINK
Adjutant—JARED D. BOND

Company B

Captain—ELBERT D. BALDWIN
First Lieutenant—FRANK H. AVELINE
Second Lieutenant—WILLIAM H. HARRISON
First Sergeant—ALFRED L. STONEY
Sergeants—CLAUDE HUGENARD
    CHARLES FISHER
    EUGENE BALDWIN
    GEORGE HARE
    FERDINAND KING
    ISAAC M. CHURCH
    STILLMAN B. TASKER
    ADDISON K. BELL
Wagoner—JEFFERSON CLARK

PRIVATES

Robert F. Akers	August Grumo	August Merrillett	Charles Evard	John Merrillett
George Case	John Grumo	Christian Oberly	Wesley Iba	John W. Ogden
Martin Connett	Charles Isbell	John Ryan	Casper Miller	Daniel Stuck
Frederick Freck	George F. Jones	Orrin Rima	Israel H. Hensey	Silas L. Slater
Henry Freck	Frederick Kayser	John Wisemental	John Kennedy	Louis Merrillett
	Frederick Myers	Julius P. Manuel	Jacob Kincade	

Company C

PRIVATES

John Cook

Company D

PRIVATES

George Eppie

Company E

PRIVATES

Thomas Hart

Company F

PRIVATES

John Huffman

Twelfth Regiment Infantry

(THREE YEARS' SERVICE—Continued)

Company G

PRIVATES

August Burgier   Henderson Lisle   John McGuire   Jerry C. McCloon   Charles D. Peak

Company H

PRIVATES

Charles O'Harra   John O'Brian   William O'Brian

Company I

PRIVATES

Franklin Geiger   Thomas Rose

Company K

Captain—GEORGE NELSON
First Lieutenant—JOHN M. GODOWN
Second Lieutenant—JAMES O'SHAUGNESSY
First Sergeant—JOHN B. MAGUIRE
Sergeants—JAMES C. PELTIER
         HORACE B. FRANKLIN
         JAMES A. McDOWELL
Coporals— LUCIUS T. BARBOUR
         JAMES O. BIRD
         FRANCIS H. MARTIN
         JACOB OVERLY
         STEVEN CHASE
Musician—WILLIAM R. RANNEY
Wagoner—DAVID A. SCOTT

PRIVATES

William Broome	George Meyer	Edward Taylor	Albert D. Scarlett	George P. Shafer
Christian Bischoff	Samuel Musser	Henry C. Burnett	Levi Spitler	James L. Scarlett
Isaiah Coleman	Perry N. Moore	William Collar	Henry Tracy	Christian Simmons
William Davis	Joseph Pompey	David P. Gilpin	Benjamin F. Bethell	John Sullivan
Thomas Griffin	Franklin Savage	Peter Hunter	Henry Blounker	James Allman
Augustus Hawn	Jacob Spence	John Linton	Ernest Hitzman	Thomas B. Scott
Conrad Hoffmyer	Albert Dyer	John Meyer	John Fridley	Charles Smith
George H. Johnston	Hiram Gibford	John Mook	Michael Hoffman	Richard Reed
John W. Jones	Oran Holmes	Henry Noll	Monroe Johnston	Henry D. Shaw
Samuel Kissinger	Elijah C. Stouder	John Rodgers	John W. Pio	

Thirteenth Regiment Infantry

(THREE YEARS' SERVICE)

The Thirteenth Regiment was originally accepted for State service, for one year, and was subsequently organized at Indianapolis for United States service, by volunteering from the companies of the State troops then in Camp Sullivan. It was one of the four Regiments that first entered service from Indiana for the term of three years, and was mustered in, at Indianapolis, on the 19th of June, 1861, with JERE. C. SULLIVAN as Colonel. On the 4th of July it left Indianapolis for the field and on the morning of the 10th joined Gen. McClellan's forces, at the foot of Rich Mountain, Western Virginia. On the next day it participated in the battle of Rich Mountain, under Gen. Rosecrans, losing 8 killed and 9 wounded. On the 13th it moved to Beverly, and from thence to Cheat Mountain Pass, where, under Gen. Jos. J. Reynolds, it took part in numerous skirmishes and, on the 12th and 13th of September, in the engagement which resulted in the defeat of Gen. Lee's forces on Cheat Mountain Summit and Elkwater. The Regiment marched with Gen. Reynold's Command in the reconnoisance in force at Greenbrier, on the 3d of October, and during the engagement supported Howe's Battery, 4th U. S. Artillery.

From the 29th of October till the 7th of November it was engaged in a scouting expedition through the country bordering the Holly and Kanawha Rivers. After this it marched to Allegheny, under Gen. Milroy, and on the 13th of December participated in the battle at that place. On the 18th the Regiment left Beverly and joined Gen. Lander's forces at Green Spring Run, where it remained till spring, during which time it took part in two expeditions of minor importance. On the 5th of March, 1862, it marched towards Martinsburgh, where Gen. Shields took command of the division. It then moved to Winchester, from whence it marched on a scout up the valley to Strausburgh. Returning to Winchester it participated in the battle of Winchester Heights on the 22d of March, losing six killed and thirty-three wounded. It then followed in the pursuit of Stonewall Jackson's Army, as far as New Market and Columbia Bridge. Col. Sullivan being appointed a Brigadier General on the 2d of May, Lieut. Col. Robert S. Foster was promoted Colonel. At Summerville on the 7th of May, while on a reconnoisance, the Regiment sustained a loss of four wounded and twenty-four prisoners. On the 13th it moved down the valley, crossed the Blue Ridge and reported to Gen. McDowell, who ordered the regiment to return to the valley to aid in driving the rebels out again. On reaching Port Republic it was found the rebels had gone in the direction of Staunton, when the Regiment was marched to Luray and from thence to Alexandria, where, on the 28th of June it embarked on a steamer and proceeded to Harrison's Landing, on the James River, arriving there on the 2d of July. Here it remained until the evacuation on the 15th of August, when it marched down the Peninsula to Fortress Monroe. On the 30th it went to Suffolk on the Nansemond River, in which locality it remained nine months, engaging in numerous operations in that region of country, the most important of which were reconnoisances to Black Water on the 3d of October, 17th of November and 15th of December; the battle of the Deserted Farm on the 30th of January, 1863; the defeat of Gen. Longstreet in his attempt to sieze Suffolk, from April 10th to May 3d, 1864; and the tearing up and bringing off of nearly forty miles of track from two Railroads, from the 13th to the 19th of May. In all of these operations the Regiment marched over four hundred miles and sustained a loss of two killed, nineteen wounded and seven prisoners. Col. Robert S. Foster being appointed Brigadier General on the 16th of June, Lieut. Col. Cyrus J. Dobbs was promoted Colonel. On the 27th the Regiment left Suffolk and joined Gen. Keyes at the White House on the Pamunkey River, from whence it

marched, on the 1st of July, on an expedition to destroy the railroads north of Richmond. Returning, it sailed from Portsmouth on the 28th, for Charleston Harbor, reaching Folley Island on the 3d of August. Here the Regiment was stationed for several months, participating in the operations on Morris Island during the siege of Forts Wagner and Gregg, and was the first Regiment to enter the Fort in the assault on Fort Wagner on the 7th of September. In December a portion of the Regiment re-enlisted as Veterans, at Folley Island, and reached Indianapolis, on Veteran furlough, on the 1st of January, 1864, where they were received by Gov. Morton in the Hall of the House of Representatives.

Leaving Folley Island on the 23d of February, the regiment joined Gen. Seymour at Jacksonville, Florida, where it remained until the 17th of April. It was then transferred, on transports, to Gloucester Point, Virginia, and assigned to the 2d Brigade, 3d Division of the 10th Army Corps, which ascended the James River in transports, and landed at Bermuda Hundred on the 5th of May. The Thirteenth participated in nearly all of the operations of Gen. Butler's army south of Richmond, and was conspicuous in the engagement at Wathal Junction on the 7th of May, Chester Station on the 10th, and a charge on the rebel rifle pits, near Foster's Farm, on the 20th; in all of which the loss was about two hundred. On the 26th it was withdrawn from the front and attached to the 18th Army Corps, 3d Division, 3d Brigade, and proceeded with it to the White House, and marching from thence joined the Army of the Potomac at New Castle on the 1st of June. Marching with this army to Cold Harbor, it was actively engaged on the 3d, in the battle at that place, and in all the operations in the vicinity of the Chickahominy, until the 12th, when it returned to the White House, and from thence to Bermuda Hundred. On the 15th it crossed the Appomattox River and was engaged in the assaults on the rebel works in front of Petersburg, returning to Bermuda Hundred on the 17th. The non-veterans left the regiment on the 19th, and reached Indianapolis on the 24th of June, when they were mustered out. On the 30th of July the regiment engaged in the charge on Petersburg, after the explosion of the mine, after which it remained in the trenches of our works until September. On the 15th of that month, it participated in the battle of Strawberry Plains and operations against Richmond, on the north side of the James River, engaging in the battle of Chapin's Bluff, and the assault on Fort Gilmore on the 19th, and the attack on the rebel fortifications in front of Richmond on the 10th of October. In November it was sent, with other troops, to New York City to preserve order during the election excitement, and on returning sailed with the first expedition to Fort Fisher, on the 3d of December, and returned to Chapin's Bluff on the 31st.

Upon the muster-out of the non-veterans, the veterans and recruits were by order of Maj. General Butler, on the 6th of December, 1864, re-organized into a battalion of five companies. This battalion was, subsequently, made a full regiment by the addition of five companies of drafted men. On the 3d of January, 1865, it sailed with the second expedition to, and engaged in the assault on Fort Fisher, on the 15th, and also participated in the capture of Fort Anderson, on the 19th of February, and the occupation, on the 22d, of Wilmington. After remaining here some weeks it marched to Raleigh, where it remained from the 14th of April till the 20th of July, when it was assigned to duty at Goldsboro. On the 5th of September it was mustered out and started for home on the 7th, arriving at Indianapolis on the 15th, with 29 officers and 550 enlisted men, where it was finally discharged.

Thirteenth Regiment Infantry
(THREE YEARS' SERVICE)

Company F

First Sergeant—BENARD CONRAN

PRIVATES

Joseph Christian	Patrick Kelly	William Cromer	Lewis Buchtold	Charles W. Truax
William D. Nettlehorn	James B. Humbert	Greenberry Cruse	Ferdinand Light	William Whitney
Andrew Laughlin	Francis Clauson			

Thirteenth Regiment Infantry
(Re-Organized)

Company A

Corporal—LEWIS BUCHTOLD

PRIVATES

Benjamin Alton	John Depew	Aaron Hiler	James Stafford	John B. Archer
Frederick Carr	Benjamin Hamilton	Nathan Johnson	Thomas Johnson	Samuel C. Winans

Company B
PRIVATES

Thomas Connor	Christopher Kridler	John S. Majors	Israel Shenner	Ezekiel T. Washburn
Greenberry Cruse	Laselle Long	Herman Opity	John H. Updike	William Russell
Henry John	Andrew J. Lounsberry	F. Scarborough	Henry L. White	James I. Stewart

Company C
PRIVATES

George W. Boyle	Joseph Dales	Archibald Richmond

Company D
PRIVATES

Michael Libely	George W. Riffel	William Stephaine	George Wilson	Jacob F. Hoag
Robert Marshall	David B. Rinehart	Annal Stroud	Jacob Huber	George C. Falk
John D. Rankins	George Rumbaugh	Solomon Summers	Allen Miller	Richard M. Johnson
Marion Rhoten	John Reed	Richard Troutmelt		

Company H

Corporals—HENRY MONASMITH
SYLVANUS S. CURRENT

PRIVATES

Thomas Arter	George Jacobs	Thomas Rabbitt	Jacob Shraff	John P. Fleener
Abram F. Collins	William Jones	John H. Short	Theodore Clark	Thomas B. Jones
James Hagan				

Company I
PRIVATES

Jacob Strouer

Company K
PRIVATES

Thomas T. Andrews	John Buchfink	Isaac Barr	Elam J. McKinzie	Dennis Ryan

Fifteenth Regiment Infantry

(THREE YEARS' SERVICE)

The Fifteenth Regiment was originally organized as one of the six regiments of State troops, at Lafayette, in May, 1861, and was re-organized and mustered into the United States Service, for three years, at the same place, on the 14th of June, 1861, with George D. Wagner as Colonel. Soon after, it moved to Indianapolis, which place it left on the 1st of July, for Western Virginia, stopping at Cincinnati until the 4th of July. Proceeding by rail to Clarksburg, it marched from thence to Rich Mountain, where it arrived on the 11th, while the battle was in progress, and next day formed part of the pursuing force, assisting in the capture of many prisoners. The Regiment was afterward stationed in Elkwater Valley, where it remained until November 19th, taking an active part in the operations of Gen. Reynolds that season, among which were the repulse of Gen. Lee and battle of Green Brier. The Fifteenth left Huttonsville on the 19th of November, and reported to Gen. Buell, at Louisville, the last of the same month. It took an active part in the campaign under Gen. Buell, arriving at Shiloh during the battle, in time to render excellent service—was constantly on duty during the siege of Corinth, and took part in the closing scenes of the battle of Perryville. In the pursuit of Bragg towards Cumberland Gap, the duty was arduous, forced marches and skirmishes being the daily routine for some time. In November, 1862, in connection with other troops, the Regiment marched to Nashville, where the Army of the Cumberland was re-organized, under Gen. Rosecrans. Col. Wagner being appointed a Brigadier General on the 29th of November, Lieut. Colonel Gustavus A. Wood was commissioned his successor. In the march toward Murfreesboro it participated, and in the battle of Stone River, on December 31st, 1862, and January 1st and 2d, 1863, it bore a conspicuous part, losing 197 officers and men killed and wounded, out of 440 engaged. After this the Regiment remained at Murfreesboro until June 24th, taking part in the various expeditions sent out from that place. It then marched to Tullahoma, where, as part of Crittenden's Corps, it aided in turning the rebel position on the left, compelling the evacuation of Tullahoma. The Regiment then remained in camp at Pelham, Tennessee, until August 17th, when the army advanced on Chattanooga, Gen. Wagner's brigade, of which the Fifteenth was a portion, being the first to enter Chattanooga. Here the Regiment performed post duty from September 9th until shortly before the battle of Mission Ridge, in which engagement it participated, suffering heavily. Its loss was 202, out of 334 engaged, being over sixty per cent. The day after the battle it marched, with other troops, to the relief of Gen. Burnside, at Knoxville, marching the whole distance—over one hundred miles—in six days; a great many of the men without shoes, and all on very short rations. The Regiment remained in the vicinity of Knoxville, on very severe duty, without baggage or tents, and with very little to eat, until February, 1864, when it was ordered to Chattanooga to do garrison duty. While there a portion of the Regiment re-enlisted on the 15th of February, 1864. It remained at that place, under Gen. Steadmen, until the 16th of June, 1864, when, in obedience to the orders of Gen. Thomas, it left for Indianapolis, to be mustered out of the service, its time having expired on the 14th of June. A detachment of veterans and recruits were left behind, and these were transferred to the 17th Regiment of Indiana Volunteers, (mounted infantry), in the month of June, 1864, and served with that organization until the 8th of August, 1865, when it was finally discharged.

Fifteenth Regiment Infantry

(THREE YEARS' SERVICE)

Company C

Captain—JOHN M. COMPARET
First Lieutenant—OLIVER H. RAY
Second Lieutenant—JOHN F. MCCARTHY
First Sergeant—JOHN F. MONROE
Sergeants — JONAS W. DORR
              JOHN B. MCALLISTER
              LEWIS A. FOSTER
              ANDREW J. MILLER
Corporals—MILTON P. WILSON
              JOHN STROUD
              JOHN P. JOHNSON
              WILLIAM DOUGALL
              ROYAL E. BARNEY
Musicians—HENRY WOODS
              HENRY R. WEASE
Wagoner—PHILIP HANDEY

PRIVATES

William Allison	Ira Miller	William W. Spencer	Joseph Wessell
George W. Anderson	Lewis H. German	John Stull	William A. Wise
George L. Banks	Lester Goodyear	John B. Underwood	Jacob Tucker
Joseph Burns	William D. Guthrie	Obadiah Vaughn	Thomas Bunce
Christian Benner	Samuel Kilgore	John M. Wilson	Joseph Castleman
Palmer H. Booth	Edward Marshall	Russell Wingo	Bruce Dollason
George Barns	John Moony	John H. Young	Jesse G. Godfrey
John M. Brewer	Joseph Q. Moxell	Noble Bouse	Henry Ladd
John Cagle	Asel J. Myers	David Boyle	William Livergood
William T. Campbell	Daniel B. Niehart	William Chatfield	Henry McDowell
Theodore Carter	Oliver Patterson	Thomas M. Gilbert	John A. Morgan
William Coffill	Oliver H. Perry	William Hakins	Frederick Myer
William N. Daffron	Amos E. Porter	Samuel J. Kuontz	Charles Parke
Thomas Duffie	Albert S. Radley	John D. Long	Pontius Solley
John Fitzgerald	Newsom Rank	Austin R. Miller	Lewis Stratton
Joseph Fitzallen	James L. Rich	George Miller	John Trayer
James C. Foster	Daniel Shadell	John F. Morris	Andrew C. Harris
Hubert Fullum	Carlos Sherman	Richard Murphy	Timothy Murphy
Franklin Gentry	David A. Spencer	Alfred M. Thompson	Daniel Nettleton

Seventeenth Regiment Infantry

(THREE YEARS' SERVICE)

The Seventeenth Regiment was organized at Camp Morton, Indianapolis, during May, 1861, and was mustered into the United States service on the 12th of June, 1861, for three years. On the 1st of July it left Indianapolis for Parkersburgh, Virginia, which place it reached on the 5th, after stopping three days at Cincinnati. Remaining in this vicinity until the 23rd, it took the cars and moved to Oakland, Maryland. Marching sixteen miles to the north branch of the Potomac, it was engaged until the 7th of August in constructing the fortifications known as Camp Pendleton. Proceeding by railroad from Oakland to Webster, and thence on foot up Tygart's Valley to Huttonsville; the Regiment reached Cheat Mountain Pass on the 12th, and afterward went into camp at Elkwater. While in this vicinity the Seventeenth participated in the operations of General Reynold's army, including the battle of Green Brier on the 3d of October, in which its loss was one killed. On the 19th of November it proceeded to Louisville, Kentucky, where it reported to General Buell on the 30th, and there lay in camp on Oakland Race Course until the 10th of December. Being assigned to General Nelson's division, the regiment marched to Camp Wickliffe, near New Haven, where it remained until February 10th, 1862, when it moved toward Green River. Crossing Green River it marched southward, arriving at Nashville on the 12th of March, and there remained until the march to the Tennessee River was begun. Colonel Hascall being appointed Brigadier General on the 25th of March, he was succeeded by Lieut. Colonel John T. Wilder. Leaving Nashville on the 29th of March, the regiment reached the field of Shiloh on the 8th of April. It then participated in the March to and siege of Corinth, and after its evacuation moved with Buell's army through Northern Alabama to McMinnville, Tennessee, where, on the 30th of August, it overtook Forrest and attacked and routed him. On the 3d of September the Seventeenth left McMinnville and marched via Murfreesboro, Nashville, Bowling Green, Elizabethtown and West Point, to Louisville, Kentucky, arriving there on the 25th of September, after marching 270 miles and having a skirmish with Bragg's rear guard on the 21st, near Munfordsville. Leaving Louisville on the 1st of October, it moved to Bardstown, where it remained in camp until the 18th, and then marched to Nashville, by the way of Lebanon, Columbia, Glasgow and Gallatin, reaching there on the 26th of November. Between this and the 1st of February, 1863, the regiment was engaged in numerous expeditions in different directions from Nashville, and then moved its camp to Murfreesboro. On the 12th of February orders were received for the regiment to mount itself, and the following month was occupied in foraging and pressing horses, until the regiment was fully mounted, after which it was kept constantly moving on scouting expeditions. On the 18th of May the men were armed with Spencer rifles, with which effective weapons each man became the equal of sixteen rebels. On the 24th of June it moved to Hoover's Gap, where the enemy was stronly posted. The rebel force of five regiments of infantry, three companies of sharpshooters and a battery, made several charges upon the Seventeenth, which were repulsed gallantly. The regiment held the rebels at bay until out of ammunition, when reinforcements from the other regiments of the brigade coming up, the enemy were driven from the field. The Seventeenth captured seventy-five prisoners and one hundred and twenty-five stands of arms, and sustained a loss of forty-eight killed and wounded. After this engagement it marched to Manchester, driving the enemy and capturing many prisoners. It then marched on a raid to Cowan, after which it scouted the country in various directions, and on the 21st of August skirmished with the enemy across the Tennessee River, near Chattanooga. After the evacuation of that place, the Seventeenth moved towards the North Chickamauga and Dalton, frequently skirmishing with the enemy. On the 11th of September it marched to near Ringgold, where it met Scott's brigade of rebel cavalry and two pieces of artillery, when a sharp fight ensued, resulting in the driving of the enemy to Tunnel Hill with severe loss. The regiment lost one killed and two wounded. Between this and the 18th frequent skirmishes occurred with the enemy, and on that day the division to which the seventeenth was attached

Seventeenth Regiment Infantry—Continued

was attacked in force, and compelled to fall back. The next day the regiment fought nearly all day in the battle of Chickamauga, breaking the enemy's lines every time they charged. On the 20th it repulsed a severe charge of the enemy, and then charged in return, driving the rebels and killing, wounding and capturing a great number; the regiment fought till 3 o'clock in the afternoon, when it was ordered back toward Chattanooga. On the 1st of October it started, as part of General Crook's command, in pursuit of General Wheeler, then in the Sequatchie Valley. On the night of the 3d the regiment attacked Crew's rebel brigade at Thompson's Cove and routed them, capturing a number of arms and the battle flag of the Second Kentucky Cavalry, presented to them by the ladies of Elizabethtown, Kentucky; the regiment lost but one wounded. The next day it marched to McMinnville, where it skirmished with the enemy, and drove him out of and beyond the town, losing two killed and four wounded. On the 7th of October, when beyond Shelbyville, the regiment struck the enemy and attacked him, driving him from the field and into Farmington, where he made a stand; here the Seventeenth charged the rebels, capturing three of Wheeler's guns, a great number of small arms and three hundred prisoners; the regiment lost forty-eight killed and wounded, including three commissioned officers. Crossing the Tennessee River at Lamb's Ferry on the 9th, further pursuit was abandoned, and the regiment moved to Huntsville, Alabama, from whence it started, on the 13th, in pursuit of the enemy under Forrest, Roddy, Wharton and others. On the 27th it went into winter quarters at Maysville, from whence, on the 18th of November, in pursuance of the orders of General Thomas, two hundred and fifty of the best mounted men marched to near Chattanooga, and crossed the Tennessee on Sherman's pontoon on the night of the 23d. Moving in the direction of Cleveland, they went round by Tyner's Station, whilst the battle was raging at Mission Ridge, to within seven miles of Ringgold, and destroyed rebel wagon trains and stores. They returned to Cleveland on the 26th, after destroying, altogether, seventy-seven wagons. Being attacked the next day by Kelly's brigade, they were forced to destroy the foundry at Cleveland and fall back to near Chattanooga, losing one man killed. On the 30th they marched toward Knoxville, running through the rebel lines to get into the town. Leaving there on the 5th of December, they crossed the Chilhowee Mountain into North Carolina, and then into Tennessee, camping at Charleston on the 14th of December. The majority of the regiment, then dismounted and in camp at Pulaski, having re-enlisted on the 4th of January, 1864, left the next day for Nashville, where they were joined on the 18th by the part of the regiment at Charleston. Two hundred and eighty-six having been re-mustered as veterans, the regiment left Nashville on the 22d of January for Indianapolis, on veteran furlough.

Arriving there on the 25th, it was publicly received in the Capitol Grounds, and was addressed by Governor Morton, Colonel Wilder and others. While in Indiana the veterans were allowed to purchase horses, and being remounted, left Indianapolis by rail on the 2d of April, and on arriving at Louisville went into camp until the 18th, when it proceeded to march to Nashville, reaching there on the 25th, after riding one hundred and eighty-six miles. Leaving there next day, the regiment reached Sherman's army, then on the march to Atlanta, on the 10th of May. From this time until the 31st of October it was actively and constantly engaged in the cavalry and scouting operations incident to the march upon and capture of Atlanta, and the pursuit of Hood's retreating army northward. It participated in the numerous skirmishes, the raids to cut the enemy's communications, and was conspicuously engaged at Pumpkin Vine Church, Big Shanty, Belle Plain Road, Kenesaw Mountain, Marietta, Chattahoochie River (being the first troops to cross this stream), Stone Mountain, Flat Rock, New Hope Church, Rome, Coosaville, Leesburgh and Goshen. On the 1st of November, 1863, after turning over its horses to Kilpatrick's cavalry, the regiment left Rome, Georgia, for Louisville, Kentucky, where, on the 24th, it was re-mounted. Moving from Louisville on the 28th of December, it reached Nashville on the 8th of January, 1865, from whence it marched to Gravelly Springs, Alabama, arriving there on the 25th. Here it remained until the 12th of March, when it marched with General Wilson's cavalry command into the interior of Alabama. On the 1st of April the commands of Roddy and Forrest were overtaken and attacked at Ebenezer Church, on Bogue's Creek, twenty-nine miles from Selma; the Seventeenth participated and charged the rebels gallantly, capturing one hundred prisoners and one gun, and losing eight killed, eleven wounded and five missing. On the 2d it participated in the engagement at Selma, and in the taking of the rebel works surrounding the town; the Seventeenth first drove the rebels into their forts and then out of them, and afterward drove them from the interior works and their position behind the railroad embankment into the town, taking all the forts from number eighteen to the river on the west side of the town. Four pieces of artillery, and about three hundred prisoners were captured. Out of 421 officers and men engaged, the Seventeenth lost 12 killed and 80 wounded. After the battle the regiment moved to Montgomery, and from thence to Columbus, Georgia, from which point it marched to Macon, near which place it engaged the enemy on the 20th of April, and drove him into the city, saving two important bridges which the rebels were in the act of firing. By a ruse the enemy were led to believe that our force was but the advance of two divisions of cavalry, and the city was surrendered, and with it Generals Howell Cobb, Mackall, Mercer and Gustavus W. Smith, three thousand prisoners, including officers of all grades, five stands of colors, sixty pieces of artillery and three thousand small arms. The Seventeenth had in the action during the day 451 officers and men, of whom one was killed and two wounded. Camping near the city for a month, it moved into Macon on the 22d of May, where it did post duty until the 8th of August, 1865, when it was mustered out of service. Leaving Macon soon after, the regiment arrived at Indianapolis on the 16th of August with 675 men and 25 officers, and was the day following publicly received in the Capitol Grounds and addressed by Lieutenant-Governor Conrad Baker, General Vail, General White, General Wilder and others; in a few days afterwards it was finally discharged from service. During its term of service, the Seventeenth Regiment marched over four thousand miles, and captured over five thousand prisoners, more than six thousand stand of arms, seventy pieces of artillery, eleven stand of colors and more than three thousand horses and mules. All this was done with a loss of three officers and sixty-six men killed, and thirteen officers and one hundred and seventy-six men wounded—a total of killed and wounded of two hundred and fifty-eight.

Seventeenth Regiment Infantry

(THREE YEARS' SERVICE)

Company A
PRIVATES

William G. Coppill   Rufus Hollingsworth   Henry Herrick   James C. Gibson   Lewis A. Foster
Benjamin Kirkham

Company C
PRIVATES

William A. Ashbury   George W. Burns   Frederick Donahoe   John Moony   Fred Seidensticker
John Amy   Thomas Duffie   Andrew C. Harris   Timothy Murphy   Milton O. Williams

Company F
PRIVATES

Franklin Ayres   David T. May   John Stull   William H. Thompson   Silas Wolverton
Benjamin F. Atkins

Company K
PRIVATES

William Allison   George W. Connerly   Russel Wingo   Ira Miller   James C. Foster
John Baldwin   William Youngman   Amos E. Porter   Vincent A. Dent   John Keiler
Harvey Clampitt   Michael Wahl   John B. McAllister

Eighteenth Regiment Infantry

(THREE YEARS' SERVICE)

The Eighteenth Regiment was organized and mustered into service at Indianapolis, on the 16th of August, 1861, with Thomas Pattison as Colonel, and left the State for St. Louis on the 17th of August. From that place it proceeded into the interior of Missouri, and participated in Fremont's march to Springfield, and in the return march to Otterville, under General Hunter, after which it moved with Pope's army to the Black Water, and there took part in the capture of a large number of prisoners. In February, 1862, the regiment marched with General Curtis's forces to Cross Hollows, and thence to the battlefield of Pea Ridge, where, in the engagement near Leetown on the 6th of March, the brigade to which it was attached saved from capture another brigade, and the Eighteenth Regiment recaptured the guns of the Peoria Artillery. On the next day, in the battle near Elkhorn Tavern, the regiment participated in the advance, which resulted in turning the enemy's left, compelling him to abandon the field. On the 6th of April it marched for Helena, Arkansas, reaching that place on the 13th of July, taking part in the engagement at Cotton Plant, while on the march. Embarking from Helena on transports, on the 11th of October, the regiment reached Sulphur Springs, Missouri, a few days after, and remained on duty in Southeast Missouri during the winter. In the spring of 1863 the Eighteenth was transferred to Grant's army, and, as part of the division commanded by General Carr, participated in the flanking of the enemy's position at Grand Gulf, and in the battle at Port Gibson on the 1st of May, (capturing a stand of colors and some artillery,) and in the engagements at Champion Hills, on the 15th, and Black River Bridge on the 17th of May. From the 19th of May until the capitulation, it was engaged in our works in the rear of Vicksburg. During the assault it was the first regiment to plant its colors on the enemy's works, where they were kept for eight hours. Leaving Vicksburg, the regiment moved to New Orleans, and during the fall participated in a campaign up the Teche River, and in the operations in that part of Louisiana. On the 12th of November it embarked for Texas, where, on the 17th, it was engaged in the capture of a fort on Mustang Island, and also in the successful attack on Fort Esparanza on the 27th of November. On the 1st of January, 1864, the regiment re-enlisted at Indianola and started home on veteran furlough; it was stopped at Baton Rouge, and formed part of a column that defeated a rebel force organizing for an attack on the garrison at that place. Reaching Indianapolis on the 4th of June, it remained in the State until the 16th of July, when it proceeded to Virginia, joining General Butler's forces at Bermuda Hundred, where it had several severe skirmishes with the enemy near Deep Bottom. On the 5th of August it was transferred to Washington, D. C., and assigned to the Second Division of the Nineteenth Army Corps, and marching to Berryville, Virginia, via Snicker's Gap, joined Sheridan's army in the Valley on the 19th of August. In the campaign that followed, the regiment participated in the battle of Opequan on the 19th of September, losing 54 killed and wounded; in the pursuit and defeat of Early at Fisher's Hill on the 22d of September, losing 7 killed and wounded, and in the battle of Cedar Creek on the 19th of October, losing 51 killed and wounded, and 35 prisoners. On the 6th of January, 1865, it left for Savannah, Georgia, reaching there on transports, on the 16th, where it was occupied for three months in building fortifications. On the 3d of May it was detached from General Grover's division and sent to Augusta, Georgia, and was the first to raise the stars and stripes on the U. S. Arsenal, and over the city. Returning to Savannah on the 7th of June, it was subsequently transported to the southern portion of the State, where it remained until ordered to be mustered out. On the 28th of August, 1865, it was mustered out and left for Indianapolis, arriving there on the 17th of September, and on the day following was publicly welcomed by the citizens in the Capitol Grounds, where addresses were made by Governor Morton, Gen. H. D. Washburn (its former Colonel) and others. In a few days after it was finally discharged from service.

Eighteenth Regiment Infantry

(THREE YEARS' SERVICE)

Company D
PRIVATES

Henry Sheperd

George Lundroff

William Kilen

George Hickman

William Zinn

Green Gutock

Twenty-Second Regiment Infantry

(THREE YEARS' SERVICE)

The Twenty-Second Regiment was organized at Madison on the 15th of July, 1861, and mustered in for three years at Indianapolis, on the 15th of August, 1861, with Jeff. C. Davis (then a captain of the regular army), as Colonel. On the 17th of August it moved to St. Louis, where it joined the army of Gen. Fremont, and was soon after sent up the Missouri River to the relief of Col. Mulligan at Lexington. While on the route near Glasgow, on the 19th of September, its Major, Gordon Tanner, received a severe gun-shot wound, from which he afterwards died at Jefferson City. Before reaching Lexington news reached the regiment of the surrender of Mulligan's forces, when the expedition was abandoned. The Twenty-Second then marched with Fremont's army to Springfield, and back again to Otterville, from whence it moved in December, with other troops, and participated in the capture of about 1,300 prisoners at Blackwater. Col. Davis was appointed a Brigadier General on the 18th of December, 1861, and, being attached to his division, the Twenty-Second, under command of Lieut. Col. Hendricks, marched on the 24th of January, 1862, with Gen. Curtis's expedition against Price at Springfield, which resulted in the retreat of the latter from that place, and, eventually, in the great battle of Pea Ridge, on the 6th and 7th of March. In this battle the Twenty-Second bore a conspicuous part, losing 9 killed and 32 wounded, including Lieut. Col. John A. Hendricks, who fell mortally wounded on the first day's engagement.

The regiment then crossed the State of Arkansas to Batesville, and thence, on the 10th of May, to Cape Girardeau on the Mississippi, where it embarked on transports and joined the besieging army at Corinth, Mississippi, two days previous to the evacuation of that place. It then joined in the pursuit, under Pope, going as far as Booneville, and afterwards was stationed at different points in Northern Mississippi until the 17th of August, when it joined Buell's army, and marched with it through Tennessee and Kentucky to Louisville, reaching that city on the 27th of September. Leaving there on the 1st of October, it marched in pursuit of Bragg's army, and on the 8th had a bloody engagement with the enemy at Perryville, losing fifty per cent. of the men engaged. Fifty-six men were killed in this battle, and among the number was Lieut. Col. S. I. Kieth. On the 13th the regiment had a severe skirmish near Lancaster, and marched as far as Crab Orchard in the pursuit. Moving into Tennessee the Twenty-Second reached Nashville on the 28th of November, in which vicinity it remained until the forward movement was commenced by Rosecrans in December. On the march to Murfreesboro it had a skirmish with the enemy at Nolensville on the 26th of December, losing four wounded. On the 31st of December, 1862, and 1st and 2d of January, 1863, the regiment was actively engaged in the battle of Stone River, losing 12 killed, 36 wounded and 30 missing. After the battle the Twenty-Second encamped near Murfreesboro until the march toward Chattanooga was commenced, during which, on the 24th of June, it skirmished with the enemy at Liberty Gap. The Twenty-Second was not engaged in the battle of Chickamauga, having been left to guard the right at Valley Head, and only reached the battlefield on the evening of the 20th of September. It participated in the grand charge up Mission Ridge on the 25th of November, after which it moved into East Tennessee. While encamped at Blain's Cross Roads, on the 23d of December, a sufficient number of men re-enlisted to retain a veteran organization. In February, 1864, the veterans visited Indiana, and were cordially received at Indianapolis on the 13th, and welcomed home in an address by Governor Morton, and by speeches from others.

In the campaign of 1864 the Twenty-Second bore a distinguished part, marching with Sherman's army from Chattanooga in May, and engaging in all of the following named battles and skirmishes: Skirmish at Tunnel Hill, May 7th; skirmish at Rocky Face Ridge, May 9th; battle of Resacca, May 15th; battle of Rome, May 17th; battle of Dallas, May 27th; skirmish at Big Shanty, June 14th; skirmish in front of Kenesaw Mountain, June 19th; skirmish at Chattahoochie River, July 7th; battle of Peach Tree Creek, July 19th; battles in front of Atlanta, July 28th, and August 7th; skirmish at Red Oak Station, August 20th; battle of Jonesboro, September 1st, and the skirmishing during the siege of Savannah, from the 16th to the 21st of December. In the forward movement through South and North Carolina, it was engaged in the battle of Averysboro, on the 16th of March, 1865, and in the last engagement of Sherman's army at Bentonville, on the 19th of March, 1865. After the surrender of Johnston's army, the regiment moved with its corps—the Fourteenth—through Virginia to Washington, D. C., where, early in the month of June, 1865, it was mustered out of service, and returning to Indiana, was publicly received by the citizens of Indianapolis on the 16th of June, and addressed by Gov. Morton, Gen. Hovey and others, after which it was finally discharged the service.

Twenty-Second Regiment Infantry

(THREE YEARS' SERVICE)

Company C
PRIVATES

Calvin A. Anderson
Philip A. Bittinger
Thomas J. Bristoe

M. V. B. Childers
Silas Corson
David S. Hamilton

William Henry
Andrew J. Mills
William J. Myers

John B. Richards
Adam Rowe
John Ryan

Edward W. Shadel
Armistead Wildman

Company H
PRIVATES

William O. Bryant
Francis Buchta
George Cromer
John J. Carter
Cyrus Cole

George W. Collins
Thomas J. Crum
Isaac E. Dailey
Ira Fry
James V. Grider

George Hynes
George Jossee
Zachariah Jenkins
John Link
George Miller

Charles Pico
William H. Petega
William Whaley
John Amos
Levi H. Baldwin

John Clark
Dallas F. Hardy
Thomas Miller
Allen Talley
William Talley

Twenty-Sixth Regiment Infantry

(THREE YEARS' SERVICE)

The Twenty-Sixth Regiment was mustered into service, for three years, at Indianapolis, on the 31st of August, 1861, with William M. Wheatley as Colonel. On the 7th of September it left Indianapolis for the field, and on arriving at St. Louis was sent to the interior of the State, and participated in the Fremont campaign to Springfield. Returning to Sedalia, it was placed on duty guarding the Pacific Railroad, and was kept on this duty until July, 1862. From that time until the 1st of May, 1863, it was engaged in active field duty, moving with the army into Southern Missouri, and thence into Arkansas. During this campaign it participated in the battles of Newtonia, Missouri, Prairie Grove and Van Buren, Arkansas. At the battle of Prairie Grove, on the 7th of December, 1862, the regiment was conspicuously engaged, and suffered severely in killed and wounded. After the engagement at Van Buren, the Twenty-Sixth did guard duty until the 1st of June, 1863, when it was ordered to join Gen. Grant's army in the rear of Vicksburg, and was actively engaged in the trenches until the surrender on the 4th of July. It then went up the Yazoo River and retook Yazoo City. After the surrender of Port Hudson, the regiment was transferred to that place, and was subsequently stationed at Carrolton, Louisiana. On the 29th of September, the regiment engaged the enemy at Camp Sterling, near Morganza, and was defeated, losing nearly one-half of its officers and men, mostly by capture. The prisoners were taken to Tyler, Texas, where they were held for many months.

During the month of October the regiment proceeded to Texas with Gen. Herron's expedition, landing at Brazos Santiago, and then moved to Brownsville, on the Mexican frontier, where, on the 1st of February, 1864, it was re-enlisted. Arriving in Indiana in April, it remained there a month on veteran furlough, returning to the field in Louisiana on the 1st of June. On reaching Donaldsonville it was assigned to the garrison of Fort Butler, where it remained until the spring of 1865. On the 18th of February, 1865, in pursuance of the orders of Gen. Canby, the retained recruits of the Sixtieth Regiment, whose term of service did not expire with that of the organization, were transferred to the Twenty-Sixth, the new organization retaining the designation of the Twenty-Sixth Regiment.

When the campaign opened against Mobile, in the latter part of March, 1865, the Twenty-Sixth, as part of Gen. A. J. Smith's 16th Corps, was transferred to that vicinity, and was actively engaged for several days, participating in the seige and in the assault on Spanish Fort. Upon the occupation of the city, it was assigned to duty there, but was subsequently marched via Montgomery and Selma, Alabama, to Meriden, Mississippi. At the latter place it did post duty for some time, and was then transferred to Macon, Mississippi, where it still remains at the close of this sketch, (October, 1865,) in command of Col. John G. Clark, the veterans and retained recruits numbering 375 men.

In September, 1865, a detachment of non-veterans and recruits, whose term of service had expired, arrived at Indianapolis in charge of Major Alden H. Jumper for final discharge. These were present at a public reception given them and other troops in the Capitol grounds, on the 18th of September, and were addressed by Governor Morton and others.

Twenty-Sixth Regiment Infantry

(THREE YEARS' SERVICE)

Company D

PRIVATES

Samuel A. Weaver
Garrett T. John
Benjamin F. Newby

Twenty-Ninth Regiment Infantry

(THREE YEARS' SERVICE)

The Twenty-Ninth Regiment was organized at Laporte, and mustered into service for three years, on the 27th of August, 1861, with John F. Miller as Colonel. On the 9th of October it joined General Rousseau's command at Camp Nevin, Kentucky, and moved with the army to the vicinity of Mumfordsville, remaining there until the movement upon Bowling Green was commenced in February, 1862. Reaching Nashville in March, it moved with McCook's Division to the Tennessee River, and participated in the battle of Shiloh on the 7th of April. In this engagement the regiment was under fire for more than five hours, suffering severely in killed and wounded.

In the seige of Corinth it took an active part, and upon the evacuation moved with Buell's army through Northern Alabama and Tennessee into Kentucky, and followed in the pursuit of Bragg through the latter State, returning to Nashville in December. Marching with Rosecrans' army towards Murfreesboro, it participated in the battle of Stone River on the 31st of December, 1862, and the 1st and 2d of January, 1863, losing many men and officers. After the occupation of Murfreesboro, the regiment remained at that place until May, when it moved forward with Rosecrans' army to Tullahoma, and, afterwards, to Chattanooga. In addition to the engagements before mentioned, the Twenty-Ninth, after joining Rosecrans' army, participated in the skirmishes had with the enemy at Lavergne, Triune and Liberty Gap.

In the great battle of Chickamauga the regiment was engaged both days, and sustained heavy losses. After this battle the regiment was stationed at Bridgeport, Alabama, where the regiment re-enlisted as a veteran organization, on the 1st of January, 1864, and the same month proceeded to Indianapolis on veteran furlough.

On returning to the field, the regiment was stationed at Chattanooga, where it remained until December, when it moved to Decatur, Alabama, and was engaged in a skirmish at that place on the 27th of December, 1864. Returning to Chattanooga, it remained at that place until May, 1865, when it moved to Dalton, Georgia, where it participated in a skirmish with the enemy. Subsequently the Twenty-Ninth marched to Marietta, Georgia, where it was stationed at the closing of this sketch (October, 1865), doing post duty.

On the 5th of January, 1864, Col. Miller (who, since the month of February, 1862, had been serving as Post and Brigade Commander at Nashville and elsewhere) was promoted Brigadier General, whereupon Lieut. Col. David M. Dunn was commissioned Colonel.

Twenty-Ninth Regiment Infantry

(THREE YEARS' SERVICE)

Company G

PRIVATES

Freeborn J. Fletters
Joseph Conway

William V. Scarlett
John W. Eaton

Thomas H. Smead

Company H

PRIVATES

Robert H. Campbell
William Ream

Robert Keown
David M. Leard

Daniel Lahmar
William H. Reavis

Noah Bowman
Andrew J. Buckhart

Company I

PRIVATES

Robert Ames
John Beiderman
Joseph P. Bishop
William H. Dawson

George H. Lee
John M. Loomis
Oliver Loomis
Levi Lewis

Sylvester Lovell
Frederick Miller
George Reprogal
William S. Reprogal

Peter Rothman
Francis Smith
Allen Bodine
Joel Wall

Company K

PRIVATES

Frederick Stickley
Theodore Titus
Jacob E. Tolbert

Thirtieth Regiment Infantry

(THREE YEARS' SERVICE)

The Thirtieth Regiment was organized at Fort Wayne, and mustered into service on the 24th of September, 1861, with Sion S. Bass as Colonel. Moving to Indianapolis, it proceeded thence to Camp Nevin, Kentucky, reporting to Gen. Rousseau on the 9th of October. Joining the brigade of Gen. McCook, soon after, it moved with Buell's army to Munfordsville and Bowling Green, and in March, 1862, marched to Nashville. From this point it moved to the battlefield of Shiloh, and participated in the engagement there on the 7th of April. The regiment lost its commanding officer, Colonel Bass, who fell severely wounded, and died at Paducah in a few days afterward. Lieut. Col. Joseph B. Dodge succeeded Col. Bass as Colonel. Besides the loss of its Colonel, the regiment suffered severely in killed and wounded.

Marching with the army to Corinth, it participated in the siege of that place, and then moved with Buell's command through Northern Alabama and Tennessee to Kentucky. In the fall of 1862, it engaged in the pursuit of Bragg beyond Crab Orchard, Kentucky, and then moved to Nashville, where it rested until the forward movement of Rosecrans' army commenced.

Proceeding with that army to the vicinity of Murfreesboro, it took part in the three days' battle at Stone River, on the last day of 1862 and the two first days of 1863, losing heavily. In the campaign that followed the regiment was actively engaged, and after the occupation of Chattanooga, marched out with the army and participated in the battle of Chickamauga, where it again suffered severely. After this battle it moved to Whiteside and Tyner's Station, Tennessee, where a small portion of the regiment re-enlisted in December. Marching to Blue Springs, Tennessee, these were re-mustered as veterans in January, 1864, and soon after proceeded to Indiana on veteran furlough. The regiment remained at Blue Springs until April, and then moved forward with Thomas' army in the campaign against Atlanta, participating in all the battles and skirmishes that transpired up to the occupation of that city. After the muster out of the non-veterans, while the regiment was at Atlanta, the veterans and recruits were consolidated into a Residuary Battalion of seven companies, on the 3d of December, 1864, by order of Gen. Thomas J. Wood. The battalion was then placed in command of Lieut. Col. Henry W. Lawton, and moved northward with the 4th Corps to Nashville, and there participated in the battle fought against Hood's forces, on the 15th of December. Subsequently it moved in the pursuit of the enemy to Huntsville, Alabama, and then proceeded with the 4th Corps into East Tennessee. Returning to Nashville, the battalion remained there until June, 1865, when it was transferred to Texas with the 4th Corps. On the 12th of July the company of the Residuary Battalion of the Thirty-Sixth Regiment, commanded by Captain John P. Swisher, was transferred to the Residuary Battalion of the Thirtieth Regiment, and made Company "H" thereof, in pursuance of the orders of Gen. Sheridan.

The battalion, since its arrival in Texas, has made many long marches, but has not been otherwise engaged, and at the closing of this sketch (October, 1865) was still on duty in that State as a part of Gen. Sheridan's army of occupation.

Thirtieth Regiment Infantry

(THREE YEARS' SERVICE)

Colonel—Sion S. Bass
Major—Orrin D. Hurd
Adjutant—Edward P. Edsall
Quartermaster—Peter P. Bailey
Assistant Surgeon—Samuel A. Freeman
Sergeant-Major—Nellis Borden
Quartermaster-Sergeant—Marcus D. Kirk
Commissary-Sergeant—William Ferguson

Company A

Captain—George W. Fitsimmons
First Lieutenant—Henry W. Lawton
Second Lieutenant—Edwin R. Stribley
First Sergeant—Isaac Carter
Sergeants—John Cogan
 Henry Campbell
 Wall Stribley
 John Sterling
Corporals—Thomas Lee
 Thomas J. Kennedy
 Thomas Coleman
 Nathan Tilbury
 James Durbrow
 Charles Lincoln
 David A. Robinson
 J. O. Farrell
Musicians—William D. Maier
 Ezra Alderman
Wagoner—John D. Thompson

PRIVATES

Ransom Allen
Joseph Badiac
John Brick
Michael Cronon
Alexander Coomer
Oliver Fickle
Simon Gilbert
Evan R. Hildebrand
Joseph Johnson
Lewis Jones
Charles W. Ludwick
Reuben Myres
Thomas H. Notestine
Charles Perry
Charles Stribley
Tamma Stine
Philip Schrum
Samuel Shaw
Joseph Vaugier
Cyrus W. Bennett

Henry Corl
William Frederickson
James L. Gandy
Philip Hines
George H. Hannon
Samuel Keefer
William Ludwick
John Millenbaugh
Aaron Matthews
Eli Olds
David Ross
Gustavus Raup
Emuel Rupe
Jacob Stemeler
Martin Strouss
John Troutner
Alexander J. Wilson
Hiram Allen
James Evar
Julius Grojohn

John Grimes
John P. Haynes
Edward Holcomb
Thomas Hollister
John Hardendorf
James Lockwood
Nathan Mason
Jacob McKee
A. Prindle
Edward Randall
Ralph Southern
Arnold Stiltz
Thomas B. Toomey
Ephraim Wright
Hiram Watson
Jacob M. Young
William Allen
Charles Bourjoice
John C. Burt
William Dunlap

John P. Esslestine
George A. Hany
Francis Hutchison
J. Hartsock
E. Julian
Isaac Klinger
John Leatherman
Jacob Lepper
Alexander McGready
Harrison Prindle
J. Ploumer
H. W. Rider
Robert Southern
Jesse A. Schouse
Ebenezer Taylor
David Touney
P. Trumbull
D. Trumbull
Christian Winkler
Lawrence White

Company D

Captain—JOSEPH W. WHITAKER
First Lieutenant—CHARLES A. ZOLLINGER
Second Lieutenant—DOUGLAS L. PHELPS
First Sergeant—GEORGE W. BENTLEY
Sergeants — JOHN M. BOSEKER
     GEORGE W. BELL
     THOMAS MEAD
Corporals — JAMES HARPER
     ROBERT BELL
     HARRISON R. GODDARD
     JESSE ADAMS
     PETER F. DICKENSON
     HENRY KELLEY
     ALLEN GODDARD
     WALTON BRADFORD
Musicians—ZACHARIAH MILLER
     JOHN SHULTZ
Wagoner—THOMAS C. HYDE

PRIVATE

Thomas Brooks	Perrington Small	Horace Wright	Robert Buckmaster
Peter Baltzell	James E. Sowder	John Wells	William Brown
Alfred Balser	Robert W. Swann	Morris Zollinger	David Copp
Alfred R. Brown	Simon Vandoler	C. S. Bridgement	John A. Johnson
Frederick Barnbrook	George W. Wilbur	James Buckfield	Andrew Klendius
Abram Cockafair	Sylvanus Watson	Edward D. Bingham	Martin Keesler
James Dawkins	Henry Wyant	William Fulton	James M. Kerns
John Eden	John Zoler	Adam Fredline	Andrew J. Luke
John Harper	Lewis L. Bowers	Tobias Fike	William Perkins
John P. Herr	John Brooks	Jacob Grosh	John T. Pollock
John Hatfield	Peter Chamberlain	Byron Holmes	William Shields
John L. Harrod	William M. Cutler	Daniel Humbecker	Jervis Tilbury
George W. Louthen	William T. Cress	John Hutchinson	Marquis Tilbury
Marquis Marquart	Robert Cartle	Marquis Hill	William Thayer
Isaac Marquart	Henry G. Dawkins	William Hatfield	Jonas H. Thorp
Lewis Matthews	Daniel Donovan	James H. Jameson	James Wright
Daniel Michael	Cyrus Fike	James Johnson	Edward Wright
Henry Miller	Hiram Hutchinson	Dennis Keefe	William Webb
John W. Meeks	Aca. C. Mason	James J. Mitchell	David Kinnison
James M. Nesbitt	James Nelson	Elias Miller	Joseph Devese
Mathias F. Nesbitt	William Perrin	John W. Nesbitt	Thomas Devese
Simon P. Pierson	Joseph Peters	John B. Ritter	Robert M. Sriver
George W. Pembroke	Benjamin F. Ritter	Jeremiah Scoles	John Smith
Henry Richard	John Smalts	William Strong	Myron Skinner
Charles Roy	William Shurman	Homer Strough	William Schlandroff
John Rulo	Asa Turner	Van. B. Turner	George Triterpo
James Richard	Martin Todd	Charles S. Wilbur	

Thirtieth Regiment Infantry—Continued

Company E

Captain—JOSEPH H. SILVER
First Lieutenant—JOSEPH PRICE
Second Lieutenant—ISAIAH C. McELFATRICK
Sergeants — THOMAS HOGARTH
                CHARLES M. JONES
                EDWARD HOLMES
                WILLIAM W. WHEELER
Corporals — JACOB FORBING
                CHRISTIAN BOSEKER
                THOMAS HUMPHREY
                ROBERT S. MURPHY
                HAMILTON FULTON
                ALBERT KNAPP
                ANDREW CUNNINGHAM
                PETER EDSALL
Musician — BENJAMIN BLYLER
Wagoner — ELI CRAMER

PRIVATES

Joseph Bryant	Homer Robinson	Samuel Kellogg	Henry Bush
James M. Boyd	Charles Roberts	Simon Malone	William Berford
Nicholas Duing	James Ryan	Charles Murray	William Bloomfield
Charles H. Broughton	Duane D. Scott	Elmor C. Nelson	William Cooper
John Collier	Amos Staily	James Orin	George Custer
Jacob Frazier	Jacob Farvinger	John O'Dair	Joseph H. Gardner
Charles V. Fair	George E. Gardner	John H. Rhoads	Alfred Harris
Milton Fulton	Nicholas Huberty	Edward Strack	Samuel Harshberger
William H. Fass	James Hoffman	Josiah Smeadley	George Johnson
James Henderson	William Isbull	John A. Stoby	Joseph Kelley
Frank Haraman	Marion Isbull	James Swain	Almond P. Lampkin
Frank Iten	Wesley P. Johnson	Noah Wilson	Peter McAlly
John Inks	James S. Kimberly	John Whittern	William Papenaugh
Joel Lipes	Martin Keesler	Robert Wybourn	Charles Ringwalt
George E. Murphy	Edward Kirkham	Robert Burk	Nicholas Sanguinot
William O'Dair			

Thirtieth Regiment Infantry—Continued

Company K

Corporal—JOSEPH W. COPE

Thirtieth Regiment Infantry

(RE-ORGANIZED)

Lieutenant Colonel—HENRY W. LAWTON
Quartermaster—THOMAS J. NOTESINE
Commissary Sergeant—WILLIAM W. WHEELER

Company A

Captain—DENNIS J. KENNEDY
First Lieutenant—EVAN R. HILDEBRAND
Second Lieutenant—REUBEN R. MYERS
Sergeant—CHARLES W. LUDWICK
Corporals—OLIVER FICKLE
        MICHAEL CRONAN
        PHILIP SCHRUMM
        SAMUEL SHAW
        RANSOM ALLEN
        LEWIS JONES
        CHARLES STRIBLEY
        CHARLES PERRY

PRIVATES

John Ake	Nathan L. Barber	John Kirtz	William Shroeder
Joseph Badiac	Charles Crary	Charles Lincoln	Patrick Murphy
John Brick	Samuel Hooser	George W. C. Moore	Michael Mason
Nathan W. Beabers	Michael Hallsberry	William McMahon	John McKee
Thomas J. Burgess	Joseph Johnson	William H. Patterson	

Company C

PRIVATES

Robert S. Bailey
Nathan B. Moore

Thirtieth Regiment Infantry (Re-organized)—Continued

Company E

Captain—George W. Bently
Sergeants—John L. Harrod
          James M. Nesbit
Corporals—David S. Henderson
         Simon P. Pearson
         Charles Roy

PRIVATES

William Brown
David Capp
Daniel Hilkey
Samuel Hill

Charles W. Hancock
Martin Keisler
James M. Kerns
William Perkins

William Shields
William Thayer
Jarvis Tilbury
Marquis Tilbury

James Wright
Edmund Wright
William W. Webb

Thirtieth Regiment Infantry (Re-organized)—Continued

Company F

Captain—THOMAS HOGARTH
First Lieutenant—WILLIAM W. WHEELER
First Sergeant—ALBERT KNAPP
Corporals—WILLIAM ITEN
ELIJAH F. JUDKINS

PRIVATES

Joseph Bryant
James M. Boyd
William Bailey
Nicholas Duing
William McCullogh
Claudius D. Royce
Heman Toby
Charles R. Asher
Lindsey Boatman
Samuel Bodle
David Cooper
Henry C. Collins
Helper Croomer
Walter F. Cox

James H. Cox
James Dodson
David Emrich
Samuel Fariss
Jacob Fryar
George W. France
George D. Frazier
Allen Huff
John M. Hendricks
Nicholas Kronchie
James F. Lanks
Edward A. Lane
Harrison Long
Enis Messimore

Amos W. Moore
Peter Muncy, Jr.
Joel McAllister
Henry Mayer
Jonas Nihart
Jefferson T. Nolen
Sidney S. Porter
John Pursinger
William Ricketts
David Reed
John M. Reynolds
William Stutler
James W. Stultz
Andrew Shanks

Joseph Smith
Lawrence Shaffer
Daniel Sternogle
Eli Tribbit
George M. Tipton
David Taylor
Andrew Wolf
Levi Wolf
Henry Kent
Michael Wilkins
John Winborough
Joseph Ward
Andrew Wallace
Amos P. Carr

Thirty-Second Regiment Infantry

(FIRST GERMAN)

The Thirty-Second (or First German) Regiment was organized at Indianapolis, through the exertions of August Willich, (a distinguished officer of the German Revolution of 1848,) who was mustered in with the regiment as its Colonel on the 24th of August, 1861. In the latter part of September it proceeded to Madison, Indiana, and from thence to Louisville, Kentucky. Early in October it marched to New Haven, Kentucky, where it remained in camp a short time and then moved to Camp Nevin, where it remained until the 9th of December. As part of Gen. R. W. Johnson's brigade of McCook's division, the regiment moved forward to Munfordsville, and there encamped. The duty of picketing the south side of Green river and protecting the working parties engaged in repairing the railroad bridge, was assigned to the Thirty-Second. While engaged in this duty on the 17th of December, four companies were attacked near Rowlett's Station by Gen. Hindman, with a force of eleven hundred infantry, four pieces of artillery and a battalion of Texan rangers, under Col. Terry. One company advanced and drove back the attacking party until the infantry supports were discovered, when it fell back slowly, the enemy's lines advancing upon it. Another company to the left was attacked at the same time, but more feebly. In the meantime the two other companies hastened up, and the remainder of the regiment crossed to the south side of the river on a bridge constructed the day before by the pontoniers of the Thirty-Second. Lieut. Col. Von Treba assuming the command, advanced this portion of the regiment on the run to the scene of conflict, and soon joined the other companies. Forming the regiment in line of battle, he advanced it steadily and drove the enemy back. The cavalry then charged first the skirmish line and next the protecting companies, and again on the right wing. At this juncture the regiment formed a hollow square, upon which the Rangers threw themselves, to be driven back severely punished, losing their leader. An infantry charge was then made against the invincible square, which was also repulsed. After this the whole force of the enemy retired, leaving the regiment in possession of the field. The enemy's loss was thirty-three killed and fifty wounded, while that of the regiment was ten killed, twenty-two wounded and eight missing. For its gallantry on this occasion the regiment was highly complimented in special orders by Gen. Buell and Gov. Morton, and the name "Rowlett's Station," directed to be placed on the regimental colors.

In February, 1862, the regiment moved forward to Bowling Green, and thence to Nashville, where it rested a brief period, and then marched to the field of Shiloh, where it participated in the battle on the 7th of April. In this engagement its loss was six killed, ninety-three wounded and four missing. In the siege of Corinth which followed, the regiment was engaged for many days, and had eight wounded. The Thirty-Second, after the evacuation of Corinth moved eastward with Buell's army as far as Stevenson, Alabama, and then proceeded to Nashville, Tennessee. On the 17th of July, Col. Willich was appointed a Brigadier General, and soon after Lieut. Col. Henry Von Trebra was commissioned Colonel. In September the regiment marched with Buell's army in its retreat to Louisville, and took part in the pursuit of Bragg through Kentucky. Returning to Nashville in November, it went into camp for over a month, and then proceeded with the army toward Murfreesboro. On the 21st of December, 1862, and 1st and 2d of January, 1863, it was engaged in the battle of Stone River, losing twelve killed, forty wounded and one hundred and fifteen missing. After this engagement the Thirty-Second remained at Murfreesboro until June, when it moved forward with Rosecrans' army toward Chattanooga, engaging on the march, in a severe skirmish at Liberty Gap, on the 24th of June. On the 19th and 20th of September it participated in the battle of Chicamauga, losing twenty-one killed, seventy-eight wounded and seventeen missing. After the battle it fell back to Chattanooga, where it remained until the battle of Mission Ridge was fought, on the 25th of November, in which it bore an honorable part.

The Thirty-Second then marched to the relief of Burnside at Knoxville, and remained in East Tennessee until just before the commencement of the Atlanta campaign. It then joined Sherman's army and marched with it to Atlanta, engaging in the following battles and skirmishes: At Resacca, May 15th; Allatoona Hills and Dallas, May 27th; Peach Tree Creek, June 19th; Paid Springs, June 22d; before Atlanta, June 21st, and many other minor skirmishes on the route. The non-veterans, immediately after the capture of Atlanta, proceeded to Indianapolis, where they were mustered out on the 7th of September, 1864. On the 6th of October, 1864, in pursuance of the orders of Gen. Thomas, the remaining recruits were organized into a residuary battalion of four companies, and placed in command of Lieut. Col. Hans Blume. Upon the return of the 4th Corps to Tennessee the battalion was left at Chattanooga, where it remained on duty until early in June, 1865. It was then transferred to New Orleans, joining the 4th Corps at that place, and soon after moved with Sheridan's Army of Observation into Texas, where it was still on duty (at Salado Creek) at the close of this sketch—October, 1865.

Thirty-Second Regiment Infantry

(FIRST GERMAN)

Surgeon—John M. Josse
Principal Musician—John Orff
Musicians—Valentine Schilling
Lewis Nonngasser
August Friese
Elias Schilling

Company A

Sergeant—Frederick Woehler

PRIVATES

Frederick Braun
Peter Colling
Ottman Ehinger
George Hessenaur
John Hilt
Richard Kelix
Jacob Labinsky

Henry Welke
Louis Schermeyer
William Bullerman
John Nill
Charles Christianson
Loren Haufnagle
George Ritzman

Company C

Musician—Theodore Wittich

PRIVATES

Stephen G. Brewster
John Blair
Elbert Bronson
Thomas Davidson

Thirty-Third Regiment Infantry

The Thirty-Third Regiment was organized and mustered into service, for three years, at Indianapolis, on the 16th of September, 1861, with John Coburn as Colonel. On the 28th of September it proceeded to Louisville, and reported to Gen. Robert Anderson, who ordered it to Camp Dick Robinson. Marching by way of Lexington, the regiment arrived there on the 2d of October, and reported to Gen. Thomas. On the 13th of October it marched to Crab Orchard, and from thence to Camp Wildcat, to reinforce Col. Garrard's regiment, and, on the 21st, engaged the enemy at Wildcat, defeating Zollicoffer's forces. After this, it marched to London, Kentucky, and thence back to Crab Orchard, reaching the latter place on the 15th of November, and remaining there until the 3d of January, 1862. Moving to Lexington, it garrisoned that place till April 11, 1862, when it proceeded to Cumberland Ford, joining Gen. George W. Morgan's forces at that place. The regiment then engaged in the skirmishes and marches by which Cumberland Gap was taken on the 18th of June, and, subsequently, participated in the marches and skirmishes in East Tennessee, until the Gap was evacuated, on the 18th of September. It then marched as escort to the ammunition convoy to Manchester, Kentucky, and thence, with the army of Greenupsburg, Kentucky, enduring many hardships, and arriving there on the 3d of October. Moving to Oak Hill, Ohio, it proceeded, on transports, to Covington, Kentucky, where the regiment was refitted and sent to Lexington. From there it moved to Danville and remained in camp till the latter part of January, 1863, when it marched with the army of Kentucky to Louisville, and from thence by transports to Nashville, reaching the latter place on the 9th of February.

From Nashville the Thirty-Third marched to Brentwood and thence to Franklin. On the 4th of March it marched toward Columbia, and fought Van Dorn's forces, and on the 5th again engaged the enemy at Thompson's Station. In the last named engagement about four hundred of the regiment were captured, and about one hundred killed and wounded. The prisoners were paroled and exchanged in about two months, and returned to the field. The other portion of the regiment remained at Franklin, and engaged in the fights at that place. About the first of July the regiment moved with Rosecrans' army toward Tullahoma, and was in the advance on Shelbyville. From thence it moved to Guy's Gap and Murfreesboro, remaining there till the 5th of September. During September and October the regiment was stationed at Manchester, Estill Springs, Cowan, Decherd, and Tracey City. From the latter place it moved to Christiana, Tennessee, on the 5th of November, and while there the regiment reenlisted as a veteran organization in January and February, 1864. On the 25th of February, four hundred and fifty veterans returned home on veteran furlough, and on the return of these to Tennessee, the whole regiment joined Sherman's army, and marched from Chatanooga to Buzzard's Roost on the 1st of May, with the 20th Corps.

In the Atlanta campaign that followed, the Thirty-Third was almost constantly engaged in marching and fighting, participating in the following engagements: at Resacca, on the 15th of May; at Cassville, May 19; at New Hope Church, May 25; at Golgotha Church, June 15; at Culp's Farm and Kenesaw, June 22; at Marietta, July 3d; at Peach Tree Creek, July 20; and in front of Atlanta in July and August. It marched to Turner's Ferry, on the Chattahoochie, on the 26th of August, and fought there on the 28th. On the 2d of September it advanced on Atlanta, driving out a brigade of rebel cavalry, when the city was surrendered, by Mayor Calhoun, to Col. Coburn, of the Thirty-Third, in command of the troops. The regiment lost, in this campaign, more than three hundred killed and wounded, and many of the best men in it. After the surrender, the regiment remained in camp, at Atlanta, until the 15th of November, when it marched with the left wing (Slocum's) of Sherman's army in the memorable "march to the sea."

The following narrative of the diurnal marchings of the Thirty-Third has been furnished by an officer of the Regiment, and, as it gives some information, in detail, not heretofore published concerning the march of the left wing of Sherman's army, it is thought proper to embody it in this sketch:—

Left Atlanta November 15th. Marched all night, and on the evening of the 16th encamped twenty-two miles from the city.

November 17th. Crossed Yellow Stone River and encamped about ten miles from Social Circle.

November 18th. Marched through Social Circle, on the Atlanta and Augusta Railroad, destroying the track, and encamped five miles south of the town.

November 19th. Marched along the railroad, through Rutlege, (tearing up the track,) to Madison, at which place the railroad buildings and market house were burned.

November 20th. Marched to Eatonton, during a hard rain and on very muddy roads.

November 21st. Marched fourteen miles and camped within eight miles of Milledgeville—still raining.

November 22d. Laid by until evening, waiting for trains to pass, then crossed Little River and marched all night, reaching Milledgeville at five o'clock A. M. on the 23d.

November 23d. Rested at Milledgeville and destroyed arsenal and magazine.

November 24th. Crossed the Oconee River and marched twelve miles.

November 25th. Marched twelve miles, crossing Buffalo River and swamp.

November 26th. Marched eighteen miles and camped at Sandersville, skirmishing with Wheeler's troops all day.

November 27th. Marched fifteen miles to Davisboro, destroying the railroad.

November 28th. Reached the Ogeechee River and swamp, and remained there until the night of the 30th, guarding the Pontoon bridge. Crossed the river and swamp that evening, and marched all night, passing through Louisville and encamping about five miles beyond.

December 1st. Marched fifteen miles on the Millen road.

December 2d and 3d. Marched twelve miles on each day, and on the 4th marched five miles, through swamps.

December 5th. Marched fifteen miles, and encamped ten miles from the Savannah River, and sixty miles from Savannah.

December 6th. Marched six miles, the roads bad and blockaded.

December 7th, 8th and 9th. Continued skirmishing, and roads blockaded.

December 10th. Struck the Charleston Railroad ten miles from Savannah, destroyed it and marched to within one mile of the rebel works surrounding Savannah, when the Regiment went into position and fortified. Remained here until the morning of the 21st, when the rebels evacuated the city and our army moved in. The health of the command during the march was excellent, only four or five men requiring hospital treatment, and no deaths occuring. Three men were lost by capture, but none by battle or skirmish. In this march the whole 20th Corps marched together to Savannah.

The Regiment remained in camp at Savannah until the 2d of January, 1865, when it crossed the Savannah River into South Carolina and went into camp about nine miles from Savannah, where it remained until the 17th. It then moved to Perrysburg, and remained there until February 1st, when it marched fifteen miles. On the 2d it passed through Robertsville and marched twenty-four miles, encamping near Lawtonville, and on the 3d passed through Lawtonville and marched twelve miles.

On the 4th it marched ten miles, with occasional skirmishing and roads blockaded, and on the 5th marched fourteen miles to Buford's Bridge, on the Salkahatchie—the roads bad and barricaded.

On the 6th it crossed the river and swamp, and on the 8th struck the Charleston and Augusta Railroad at Graham's Station, sixteen miles west of Branchville. Two days were spent in destroying this road east as far as Williston.

From there the regiment moved in the direction of Columbia, crossing the South and North Edisto rivers, and the Saluda and Catawba rivers north-west of Columbia. It then marched to Winsboro, on the railroad from Columbia to Yorkville, destroying this road and crossing the Wateree river. From there it moved, through Liberty Hill and Chesterfield Court House, to Cheraw, at which place it crossed the Great Pedee river and moved on to Fayetteville, North Carolina, which place was reached on the 11th of March. Resting here two days the army crossed Cape Fear river, and moved on in the direction of Goldsboro. On the 16th the regiment was engaged in the battle of Averysboro, two men receiving slight wounds. It also participated in the battle of Bentonville, suffering no loss. On the 23d it reached Goldsboro, where the command remained until the 10th of April, when it marched to Raleigh, which place was occupied by our troops on the 13th.

On the 1st of May the Thirty-Third started from Raleigh homeward bound, reaching Richmond, Va., on the 10th. Resting here two days, the march was resumed and Washington City reached on the 21st. It remained here until the latter part of June, when the command was ordered to Louisville, Kentucky, where it was mustered out on the 21st day of July, 1865. While at Washington a part of the Twenty-Seventh (previously consolidated with the Seventieth,) Seventieth and Eighty-Fifth regiments, were assigned to the Thirty-Third, and were mustered out with it, at Louisville, the numbers on the rolls, being about fifteen hundred men. The regiment was at all times during its term of service, one of the most powerful regiments in the army, being kept well recruited and well together.

The regiment was commanded by Colonel Coburn during the most of the first year's service, (who after that time, was in command of a Brigade,) and then by Lieut. Col. Henderson, till the Atlanta campaign, when it was commanded by Major Miller till after the surrender of Atlanta. When these Field Officers were mustered out of the service, Colonel Burton commanded it until the end of the war.

Thirty-Third Regiment Infantry

Company I

PRIVATES

John A. Burt
Romulus Cloud
George Meseler
Philip Struck
William H. Teague
Nicholas Wycoff

Thirty-Fourth Regiment Infantry

The Thirty-Fourth Regiment was organized at Anderson on the 16th of September, 1861, with Asbury Steele as Colonel, and started for the field on the 10th of October, going by way of Indianapolis to Jeffersonville, where it went into camp and remained until the 15th of November. It was then ordered to New Haven, Kentucky, where it remained until the 14th of December, and then marched to Camp Wickliffe, Kentucky, remaining there until February 7, 1862, and then moved to Green river. On the 14th it was ordered back to the Ohio river, going by way of Elizabethtown, and striking the river twenty miles below Louisville. Here the regiment embarked on transports, with Gen. Nelson's division, and started down the river on the 17th, arriving at Cairo on the 20th, where it was detached from the division and sent to New Madrid, Missouri, arriving there on the 3d of March. The regiment was engaged in the siege of that place until the evacuation on the 14th of March, and then marched to St. Merriweather's landing, fourteen miles below, drawing with it two thirty-two pounder siege guns, which they placed in position on the night of the 15th. On the next morning it was attacked by seven rebel gunboats, and after a spirited engagement of two hours, the enemy was obliged to withdraw, with the loss of one boat, which was disabled. This battery cut off the rebel retreat from Island No. 10, and was the means of the subsequent capture of the whole garrison. Returning to New Madrid on the 7th of April, it remained there as a garrison until June 14, during which time it assisted in the capture of Fort Pillow.

Embarking for Memphis, it reached that city on the 15th of June, and on the 26th it took transports for the mouth of White river, where it joined Col. Fitch's command, and proceeded up White river as far as Aberdeen, Arkansas. Here the command disembarked on the 8th of July, and on the night of the 9th the regiment engaged the enemy ten miles from Aberdeen, and drove him back to Duvall's Bluff. It then marched to Clarendon, and re-embarking, started for Helena, where it arrived on the 14th. At this post it remained during the fall and winter of 1862, making frequent expeditions against the enemy, one of the most important of which was the clearing of Yazoo pass, in which operation the regiment was engaged for two weeks in removing the heavy timber which the rebels had felled into the stream, to obstruct navigation. During this expedition the regiment had four men wounded, in a skirmish.

The regiment was then assigned to Hovey's division, and on the 10th of April started on the Vicksburg campaign, and was engaged during that month in constructing bridges to facilitate the marching of the army from Milliken's Bend to a point below Vicksburg. Crossing the Mississippi at Bruinsburg, on the 30th of April, it marched all night and engaged the enemy at daylight on the 1st of May at Port Gibson, making a charge during the battle and capturing two field pieces and forty-nine prisoners. The regiment lost forty-nine killed and wounded. On the 16th it participated in the battle of Champion Hills, and, while advancing in line of battle, captured the Forty-Sixth Alabama regiment, its colors, field officers and one hundred and twenty-seven men. The Thirty-Fourth lost seventy-nine men killed and wounded. Among the latter was Lieut. Col. Swain, who died from his wounds on the 17th of June, 1863. Moving forward with the army, it participated in the siege of Vicksburg until its final surrender, losing, in all, thirteen men in killed and wounded. It then marched to Jackson, and was engaged nine days in besieging that place, losing eight men killed and wounded.

Returning to Vicksburg it embarked for New Orleans on the 4th of August, remained there until the 12th of September, and then moved to Brashear City. While in this section it took part in Banks' expedition up the Teche as far as Opelousas. On the return march it engaged the enemy at Carrion Crow Bayou, on the 3d of November, after which it proceeded to New Iberia, where it remained until the 19th of December. While here four hundred and sixty of the regiment re-enlisted on the 15th of December, 1863. On the 23d of December it embarked on steamship for Pass Cavallo, Texas, reaching there January 8th, 1864, where it remained until the 21st of February. Returning to New Orleans it remained there until the 20th of March, when it left for Indianapolis on Veteran furlough, reaching there on the 1st of April.

Returning to the field it was placed on duty at New Orleans until the 18th of December, 1864, when it embarked for Brazos Santiago, Texas. This regiment fought the last battle of the war, on the 13th of May, 1865, at Palmetto Ranche, adjoining the old battle-field of Palo Alto. Two hundred and fifty of the regiment fought five hundred of the enemy mounted, with a battery of six field pieces, driving them a distance of three miles in the space of three hours. By this time the rebels got their battery in position, and pouring a destructive fire into their ranks, compelled the main body of the regiment to fall back, leaving Companies "B" and "E" behind as skirmishers to cover the movement. These companies being unsupported, were furiously attacked, and finally surrounded and forced to surrender. The loss to the regiment was eighty-two in killed, wounded and prisoners. After this engagement the regiment fell back to Brazos Island, from whence it moved to Brownsville, where it remained until the 16th of June, when it marched to Ringold Barracks, two hundred and sixty miles up the Rio Grande, and were the first Union troops to re-occupy that place. Remaining there till the 24th of July, 1865, it returned to Brownsville, where it was stationed at the closing of this sketch (October, 1865).

Thirty-Fourth Regiment Infantry

Company E

PRIVATES

Edward Courtney
Henry Hartey
Jacob W. Roberts
Harvey Wood

Company G

Corporal—JAMES H. LARIMORE

PRIVATES

John Austin
James E. Gatewood
Henry Griffith

Company H

PRIVATES

Columbus Howdyshel

Thirty-Fifth Regiment Infantry

(FIRST IRISH)

The Thirty-Fifth (or First Irish) Regiment was organized at Indianapolis, and mustered in on the 11th of December, 1861, with John C. Walker as Colonel. On the 13th it left for Kentucky, where it remained in a camp of instruction at Bardstown for six weeks, and then moved with Buell's army to Bowling Green, and thence to Nashville. On the 22d of May, 1862, the organized portion of the Sixty-First (Second Irish) Regiment and the unassigned recruits for the same were ordered to proceed to Tennessee, in charge of Col. Bernard F. Mullen, of the Sixty-First, and there join the Thirty-Fifth, with which regiment they were to be consolidated. These transferred men joined the Thirty-Fifth at Nashville, where the consolidation was perfected, Col. Mullen becoming Lieut. Colonel, and subsequently Colonel of the regiment. From Nashville the Thirty-Fifth moved into the interior of Tennessee as far as McMinnville, from which place it marched, during September, 1862, with Buell's army to Louisville, as part of Stanley Matthew's Brigade. Van Cleve's Division of Crittenden's Corps.

From Louisville the regiment marched in the pursuit of Bragg through Kentucky, participating in the battle of Perryville, October 8th, and in the skirmishes of the march. Returning to Nashville, it remained inactive until December, when it proceeded on a foraging expedition, during which it had a severe skirmish with the enemy, on the 9th of December, at Dobbin's Ford, near Lavergne, losing five killed and thirty-five wounded. After this it marched with Rosecrans' army toward Murfreesboro, where it participated in the battle of Stone River, on the 31st of December, 1862, and 1st and 2d of January, 1863. In this engagement the regiment fought on the extreme left, and sustained a loss of one-third of the number engaged, having 29 killed, 72 wounded and 33 missing—making a total loss of 134. The Thirty-Fifth remained in the vicinity of Murfreesboro until the march upon Chattanooga was commenced, in which it took part. In the engagement at Chicamauga on the 19th and 20th of September, it participated, sustaining heavy losses.

While encamped at Shell Mound, Tennessee, the regiment reenlisted as a veteran organization, on the 16th of December, 1863, and soon after started for home on veteran furlough, reaching Indianapolis on the 2d of January, 1864. Returning to Tennessee in February, it went into camp at Blue Springs, Tennessee, until the Atlanta campaign opened. On the 3d of May, as part of the 2d Brigade of the 1st Division of the 4th Corps, it moved from camp and participated in all the marches, battles, skirmishes and scouts of that historical campaign. At Kenesaw Mountain, on the night of the 20th of June,

while the regiment was in the front line, it was fiercely and unexpectedly attacked and thrown into mementary con. fusion. The regiment rallied, and for half an hour fought a desperate hand to hand conflict with the enemy, the men using their muskets as clubs, and bayoneting the enemy whenever opportunity offered, and finally, with the aid of a portion of another regiment of the brigade, drove the enemy back. The Thirty-Fifth lost in this affair 11 killed (in cluding its commanding officer, Major Dufficey,) and 54 wounded. On the 4th of July, when near Marietta, the regiment, while on duty as part of the skirmish line, advanced and captured the enemy's rifle pits and twenty-eight srisoners. This was accomplished, notwithstanding the regiments on its right and left were repulsed, leaving the Thirty-Fifth exposed to a severe flank fire. Its losses were four killed and seven wounded.

After the passage of the Chattahoochie river the regiment, being very much decimated, was ordered to guard the supply train of the corps, and continued on this duty until the 31st of August, when it rejoined its command and marched with the army around Atlanta, participating in the battle of Jonesboro. On the 9th of September the regiment entered Atlanta, where it remained until the enemy commenced his retrograde movement in the rear of Sherman's army, when it marched with the 4th Corps in pursuit. At Franklin, Tennessee, the regiment having received 400 drafted men and substitutes, was placed in the front line, on the 30th of November, and gallantly repulsed a charge which the enemy made upon the works. In the two days' fight at Nashville it took a conspicuous part, but fortunately lost but few men. After the rout and complete demoralization of the enemy, the regiment participated in the pursuit as far as Duck river, when it was detached and assigned to the charge of the pontoon train.

In the movements of the 4th Corps to Huntsville and Knoxville, the regiment took part, returning to Nashville in the spring of 1865. In June it was transferred with the 4th Corps to Texas, where it remained on duty with Sheridan's army until the month of September, when it was mustered out of service and returned home. Reaching Indianapolis on the 20th of October, it was present at a public reception given to returned troops in the Capital grounds, on the 21st, at which addresses were made by Governor Morton and others.

The losses to the regiment from the commencement of the Atlanta campaign up to and including the battle of Nashville, are officially reported as follows: Killed, one officer and 20 men; wounded, two officers and 116 men—total killed and wounded, 139.

Thirty-Fifth Regiment Infantry

(FIRST IRISH)

Company B

PRIVATES

Henry Downing
Henry Merring
William Pope
George Rentz
Adam Stoup

Company C

Corporal—PATRICK MORRISON

PRIVATES

Abraham Coleman
Andrew Kenney
John W. McCarty

Michael O'Leary
Patrick Smith
Patrick Boyle

George Doan
Conrad Lower
Benjamin Lester

Joseph Heidinrich
Harvey A. Jones
Martin Mills

Thirty-Eighth Regiment Infantry

The Thirty-Eighth Regiment was organized and mustered into service, for three years, at New Albany, on the 18th of September, 1861, and on the 21st of the same month started for Elizabethtown, Kentucky. The fall and winter was passed in camp at Camp Nevin, on Nolin's Fork of Barren river, and at Camp Wood on Green river, near Munfordsville. In February, 1862, it moved with Buell's army in its campaign against Bowling Green and Nashville, reaching the latter place on the 6th of March. On the 25th it moved to Franklin, and from thence to Columbia, and thence to Shelbyville, remaining there until the 11th of May. During its stay in this vicinity, it made frequent and rapid marches to intercept Morgan's cavalry. On the 13th of May the Regiment had a skirmish with the enemy near Rogersville. On the 29th of May it moved toward Chattanooga and arrived opposite that place on the 7th of June, after which it returned to Shelbyville and then moved to Stevenson. It then moved to Decherd, where it remained from the 17th of August until Bragg crossed the Tennessee river, when the regiment fell back to Nashville, and from there marched, with Buell's army, to Louisville.

The regiment engaged in the campaign through Kentucky, and took part in the battle of Perryville, losing twenty-seven killed, one hundred and twenty-three wounded and seven prisoners. Returning from this campaign, the regiment reached Bowling Green on the 2d of November, where it was placed in the First Division of the Fourteenth Army Corps. Early in the following month it moved to Nashville, and from there to the vicinity of Murfreesboro, where, on the 31st of December, 1862, and 1st and 2d of January, 1863, it participated in the battle of Stone River, losing fourteen killed and eighty-six wounded. After the battle the regiment went into camp at Murfreesboro and remained there until the campaign against Chattanooga was commenced. During its stay there it marched out to Hoover's Gap and took part in a severe skirmish, losing one killed and fifteen wounded.

Moving with its corps to Chattanooga, it was engaged on the 19th and 20th of September in the battle of Chicamauga, losing nine killed, fifty-nine wounded and forty-two missing—making a total loss of one hundred and ten. Returning to Chattanooga the regiment remained inactive until the 23d and 25th of November, when it took part in the engagements at Lookout Mountain and Mission Ridge. The following winter was passed at Rossville, Georgia, and Chattanooga. While at the former place the regiment re-enlisted on the 28th of December, 1863, and, on the 3d of January, 1864, started home on Veteran furlough, reaching Indianapolis on the 9th, with three hundred and sixty men and officers.

On the 26th of February the regiment returned to Chattanooga, and moved to Tyner's Station in March and Graysville, Georgia, in April. On the 7th of May it marched with Sherman's army in the campaign against Atlanta, engaging in all the skirmishes and battles, including the engagement at Jonesboro, in which the Thirty-Eighth carried the rebel works in a charge. In this charge, the color-bearer being killed, as he planted the colors inside the works, First Lieutenant Joseph W. Redding seized the colors and carried them throughout the day. In the Atlanta campaign the regiment lost one hundred and three killed, wounded and missing.

On the 4th of October it marched in pursuit of Hood's retreating army as far as Gaylesville, Alabama, and then returned to Atlanta, from whence it marched, in November, with the Army of Georgia in its campaign through Georgia. After the occupation of Savannah, the regiment remained there until the 5th of February, when it again moved, passing through the Carolinas to Goldsboro, taking part in all the battles and skirmishes worthy of note during the campaign, among which was the battle of Bentonville. From Goldsboro it proceeded to Raleigh, and, after Johnson's surrender, marched, via Richmond and Alexandria, to Washington—a distance of one hundred and ninety-two miles—making the entire distance in six days, an average of thirty-two miles a day. From Washington the regiment was transferred to Louisville, Kentucky, and after remaining at that place for some time was, on the 15th of July, 1865, mustered out of service. Leaving for home, it reached Indianapolis on the 18th of July, with about six hundred men and officers, and on the same day was present at a public reception given to over three thousand returned soldiers in the Capitol grounds, and was addressed by Gov. Morton and others. In a few days after the regiment was finally discharged from service.

Thirty-Eighth Regiment Infantry

Company B

PRIVATES

Scott Arney
James Bartley
Otho W. Baher
Abram B. Cook

William W. Cutler
Cyrus Davis
Edwin Horn
August Lott

Joseph H. Nesbitt
John H. Sneider
George W. Shores
Thomas Stafford

Percival Spencer
Horace Wright
Benjamin F. Williams
George Williams

Company C

PRIVATES

George W. Bromer
Richmond Bricker
Leroy M. Burdick
John S. Burgess
Adah Coolman

Frederick Carter
John R. Dishong
George W. Gill
Samuel Keever

William Kramer
Charles Maxfield
Allen Porter
Charles Sweet

Joseph Shafer
George W. Wait
Warren W. Wait
George W. Walker

Company E

PRIVATES

James Eaton

Company H

PRIVATES

George H. Butler
William Carter
William Delvin
Henry Ever
Henry W. Frank

Oregon Haines
William Henry
Jacob Racine
William Zengefus
Charles Zengefus

Company K

PRIVATES

Henry C. Anderson
Mortimer Broughton
Forbus H. Broughton

Alonzo Kelley
Volney C. Leonard
William McDonald

James A. McDonald
John A. Pitty
Charles W. Weibkie

Jacob Hausman
Asbury McIntyre
Garrett Rawlings

Fortieth Regiment Infantry

The Fortieth Regiment was organized at Lafayette on the 30th of December, 1861, and at once proceeded to Kentucky, going into a camp of instruction near Bardstown. In February, 1862, it moved with Buell's army to Bowling Green and Nashville, and from thence it marched into Northern Alabama. When Bragg crossed the Tennessee river and marched northward, the Fortieth was stationed in Southern Tennessee, near the line of the Chattanooga railroad, and when Buell's army marched into Kentucky the regiment moved to Nashville, and marched with the army to Louisville. From thence it moved through Kentucky in pursuit of Bragg, and returned to Nashville in November, where it was assigned to the 6th Division of the 14th Army Corps. In December it marched toward Murfreesboro, and participated in the engagement at Stone River on the 31st of December, 1862, and 1st and 2d of January, 1863, losing nine killed, sixty-three wounded and thirteen missing—making a total of eighty-five. After this battle the regiment remained in the vicinity of Murfreesboro for some time, and, when the army was reorganized, it was assigned to the Second Brigade of the First Division of the Twenty-First Army Corps, commanded by Maj. Gen. Crittenden.

The regiment participated in the march to Chattanooga and in the battle of Chicamauga on the 19th and 20th of September. Returning to Chattanooga, it was engaged in the battles of Lookout Mountain and Mission Ridge in November, and then marched into East Tennessee, where it remained during the winter. In January, 1864, the regiment re-enlisted as a Veteran organization at Blain's Cross Roads, Tennessee, and soon after visited Indiana on Veteran furlough.

When the Atlanta campaign opened the Fortieth was at Cleveland, Tennessee, from whence, on the 8th of May, it moved as a part of the Second Brigade, Second Division of the Fourth Army Corps, commanded by Maj. Gen. O. O. Howard. In all the marches, movements, engagements and skirmishes of the campaign, the regiment took an active part. In the battles at Dallas, Kensaw Mountain, Chattahoochie River and Peach Tree Creek it bore a conspicuous part. In the latter engagement it engaged the enemy while in position in the portion of our lines most furiously attacked, at the time Hood made his desperate attempt to break through Sherman's lines. After the occupation of Atlanta the Fourth Corps, to which the Fortieth was attached, was sent back to Chattanooga to observe the movements of the rebel army under Gen. Hood.

On reaching Chattanooga the Fortieth was placed on duty there until November, when it moved toward Nashville, and on the 15th of December it participated in the battle at that place. After the rout of Hood's army it joined in the pursuit, going as far as Huntsville, Alabama. Returning to Nashville, the regiment remained there during the spring of 1865, and in June marched to Johnsonville, and there it took transports for New Orleans, joining the Fourth Corps at that place.

From New Orleans it was transferred with the 4th Corps to Texas, where it became part of Sheridan's Army of Occupation. At the closing of this sketch (November, 1865,) the Fortieth was still in service, and stationed at Port Lavaca, Texas.

Fortieth Regiment Infantry

Company A

PRIVATES

John W. Bowers

Forty-Second Regiment Infantry

The Forty-Second Regiment was organized at Evansville on the 9th of October, 1861, with JAMES G. JONES as Colonel. Soon after it marched to Henderson and thence to Calhoun and Owensboro, Kentucky, from which place it went to Nashville, Tennessee, where it arrived on the 25th of February. It then moved into the interior of the State and then to Huntsville, Alabama, and from thence retraced its steps to Nashville. Moving from there with Rousseau's division of Buell's army to Louisville, it took part in the pursuit of Bragg through Kentucky, participating in the battle of Perryville on the 8th of October, losing one hundred and sixty-six in killed, wounded and missing.

Returning to Nashville the regiment marched with Rosecrans' army toward Murfreesboro, and then took part in the battle of Stone River on the 31st of December, 1862, and 1st and 2d of January, 1863, losing seventeen killed and eighty-seven wounded. After this engagement the Forty-Second went into camp near Murfreesboro, where it remained until the 24th of June, and then marched with the first brigade of Gen'l Negley's division to Chattanooga. On the 19th and 20th of September the regiment was engaged in the battle of Chicamauga, losing eight killed, fifty-three wounded and thirty-two missing, making a total of ninety-three. Subsequently it participated in the storming of Lookout Mountain and the battle of Mission Ridge in November, losing forty-three in killed and wounded.

On the 1st of January, 1864, the regiment re-enlisted as a Veteran organization at Chattanooga, and soon after returned to Indiana, on veteran furlough, reaching Indianapolis on the 28th of January, where it was publicly received and addressed by Governor Morton and others. On its return to the field in March it joined Sherman's army near Chattanooga, and on the 7th of May it marched from Ringold on the campaign against Atlanta, participating in all the principal battles of that campaign, losing one hundred and three officers and men, killed and wounded. During this campaign, while in Six Mile Range near Alatoona, the regiment was on picket duty seven days and nights within fifty yards of the rebel skirmish line, without being relieved. After the capture of Atlanta, the Forty-Second marched to Kingston, Rome, Resacca and, through Snake Creek Gap, to the Chatuga Valley, and from thence to Gaylesville, Alabama, in pursuit of Hood's army, and then back again to Rome and Atlanta.

In November it moved with Sherman's army from Atlanta to Savannah, participating in the skirmishing on the route and the siege of Savannah. From Savannah it moved through the Carolinas to Goldsboro, North Carolina, taking part in the battles of Averysboro and Bentonville, losing ten men and officers killed and wounded. After the close of active operations the regiment marched to Washington via Richmond, leaving Goldsboro, on the 10th of April, 1865. From Washington it proceeded to Louisville, Kentucky, where, on the 21st of July, 1865, it was mustered out, and left for Indianapolis, reaching that place on the following day. On the 25th of July it was present at a public reception given to several regiments of returned soldiers, in the Capitol grounds, on which occasion Major Gen'l Sherman was present. Addresses were made by Governor Morton and Gen'l Sherman. In a few days after the regiment was finally discharged from service.

During its term of service the Forty-Second lost in killed, wounded and missing six hundred and twenty-nine, of which number eighty-six were killed on the field, four hundred and forty-three were wounded and one hundred taken prisoners. Its strength at the time of its muster-out was eight hundred and forty-six, officers and men.

The regiment has participated in battles and skirmishes as follows: Wartrace, Perryville, Stone River, Elk River, Chicamauga, Lookout Mountain, Mission Ridge, Ringold, Rocky Face Ridge, Resacca, Alatoona Mountains, Kenesaw, Chattahoochie River, Peach Tree Creek, Atlanta, Janesboro, Savannah, Charleston, Black River and Bentonville.

Forty-Second Regiment Infantry

Company E

PRIVATES

Joseph Ballsler
Joseph Brislogh
Patrick Conan
William L. Cavanaugh
James D. Durer
John Ghegghwil
James Harris·

Charles Hunter
Marshall Jones
Rawling B. Richards
Jacob Swigert
William Tasker
John W. Waters
Samuel A. Wilson

Forty-Fourth Regiment Infantry

(THREE YEARS' SERVICE)

The Companies composing the Forty-Fourth Regiment were raised in the Tenth Congressional District and rendezvoused at Fort Wayne, where the organization of the regiment was completed on the 24th of October, 1861, with HUGH B. REED as Colonel. In December it was transported to Indianapolis and from thence to Henderson, Kentucky. Reporting to Gen'l Thomas L. Crittenden, it was assigned to Gen'l Cruft's brigade, and went into Camp at Calhoun, on Green River. Here it remained until February, 1862, when it was transferred to Fort Henry and from thence to Fort Donelson, where it participated in the siege and battle at that place, suffering considerable loss in killed and wounded.

After the capitulation the regiment marched to Fort Henry, and from thence it was transported on steamers to Pittsburg Landing. In was engaged on both days at the battle of Shiloh, losing thirty-three killed and one hundred and seventy-seven wounded, making a total of two hundred and ten. After this it marched on Corinth, taking part in several skirmishes before Corinth, and upon the evacuation of that place, joined in the pursuit of the enemy, going as far as Boonville. Returning from this expedition it moved with Buell's army into Northern Alabama and Southern Tennessee, and when Bragg marched his army northward, it moved across the Cumberland Mountains to Nashville and thence to Louisville, Kentucky, reaching there on the 26th of September. In the campaign through Kentucky it was actively engaged, participating in the battle of Perryville and going as far as Wildcat in the pursuit of Bragg.

Returning to the vicinity of Nashville, it participated in a skirmish on Russell Hill, at Silver Springs. About the 1st of December it went into camp near Nashville. From the 20th of August to the 1st of December the regiment had marched over seven hundred and twenty-five miles, being an average march of ten miles a day, and the whole performed without tents or shelter of any kind.

The Forty-Fourth moved with the army of the Cumberland toward Murfreesboro, where it participated in the battle of Stone River on the 31st of December, 1862, and the 1st and 2d of January, 1863, sustaining losses as follows: Eight killed, fifty-two wounded and twenty-five missing, making a total loss of eighty-five.

After remaining in camp near Murfreesboro for some months, it moved with Van Cleve's division of Rosecran's army across the Cumberland Mountains to Chattanooga, going by way of McMinnville, Dunlap, Jasper, Bridgeport, Shell Mound, and Whiteside. It participated in the engagement at Chicamauga on the 19th and 20th of September, and on the 22d, in connection with the Thirty-Ninth Indiana, fought the enemy again at Mission Ridge. In these engagements the regiment lost three killed, fifty-nine wounded and twenty missing, making a total of eighty-two. About the middle of October it was assigned to provost duty at Chattanooga, and while here the regiment re-enlisted in January, 1864, and returned to Indiana, on veteran furlough, reaching Indianapolis on the 26th of January. Returning to the field the regiment was again placed on provost duty at Chattanooga, on which duty it continued until the 14th of September, 1865, when it was mustered out of service. It then returned home, reaching Indianapolis on the 17th of September, in command of Colonel Curtiss, with thirty officers and six hundred and seventy men. Of these one hundred and ninety-three were original enlisted men, of whom thirty-three returned as commissioned officers, eighty-nine as non-commissioned officers, and seventy-one as privates. The regiment, during its term of service, lost three hundred and fifty in killed and wounded, and by death from disease fifty-eight. In July, 1865, three hundred and sixty remaining recruits of the Sixty-Eighth and Seventy-Second Indiana were transferred to the Forty-Fourth and these continued in service with the latter regiment until its muster out.

Just before its final discharge the Forty-Fourth was present at a public reception given to returned troops in the Capitol grounds at Indianapolis, on which occasion it was addressed by Governor Morton, Generals Grose and Washburn and others.

Forty-Fourth Regiment Infantry

(THREE YEARS' SERVICE)

Colonel—HUGH B. REED   Adjutant—CHARLES CASE   Quartermaster—WILLIAM BAYLESS   Chaplain—G. C. BEEKS

Company A

PRIVATES

Nelson A. Sowers
Adam Clark

Elias Cransshorn
Anderson Henderson

William H. Kesterson
George Kesterson
Jacob Malott

Francis P. McCutcheon
Daniel Sinks

David J. Wilborn
William Wilborn

Company B

PRIVATES

Thomas Hanoher
Joseph Mosier

Henry Barnes
John Easton

Henry Slack
Asa Bills

William Tiffany
Thornton Van Buskirk

William Williams
Michael Bankhart

Company C

Second Lieutenant—PHILIP GRUND
First Sergeant—CALEB CARMEN
Sergeant—SEDGWICK LIVINGSTON
Sergeant—JOHN H. STRONG

Sergeant—WILLIAM RILEY
Corporal—JOSEPH KINMAN
Corporal—E. B. SLOCUM

Corporal—JACOB KRESS
Corporal—THADDEUS HELM
Musician—ROYAL DEAN
Wagoner—WILLIAM HENDERSON

PRIVATES

Joseph Bay
George S. Decay
James Eldrige
John Elzy
Christian Earman
Henry Fry
Amos French
Jackson Hyser
Alexander Humbert
William N. Logan
Leander McGinnis
Marion McGinnis
Joseph Merica
Isaiah McDowell
William Nodding
Alexander Runel
Emri Sites
Milton Sites
Owen L. Shaw
Samuel Sweet
Joseph Smith
James Taylor
Alonzo Woodworth
William Weaver
James Shaw
James Berry
John Crawford

Charles Devine
John Engle
James M. Flutter
Michael Harrison
John Keefer
Jacob Luly
George Meyers
Willard Story
Christian Smith
A. William Crawford
L. B. Carr
Hugh Dennis
John C. Dee
Jacob Fogwell
William Hyser
William P. Henderson
John Higgs
William Higgs
Charles Johnston
William McDermitt
James McDonald
Joseph Nicodemus
George Perrin
A. L. Robonson
Thomas Russel
Peter Stahl
Jacob Smith

Jacob Stalkofe
Joseph Sedgwick
William Woodford
Henry Wilkinson
William Waterhouse
Peter T. Bulger
Thompson P. Burch
Stephen Bounger
Joseph Bates
Ransom H. Bell
George W. Countryman
Thomas Comer
James M. Clark
John Cavanaugh
William Colter
Sylvester Dinkens
John W. Dodge
William Engle
John Engle
George Earl
William Goder
Raphael Gull
Adam Huffmyer
Robert Hamilton
Joseph Humbert
George W. Higgs

James N. Halstead
Joseph W. Hersh
Wesley A. Logan
Noah S. Long
George A. Lewis
William Lyon
Harman L. Moyer
Eli Meiser
Joseph Manor
Corbin Murray
James L. Miller
Alexander Ormiston
August Perot
Joseph Parisot
Francis Provert
James S. Potts
John R. Phelps
Otto Reese
John Slocum
John W. Smith
John Swanson
Henry Schreiver
Frederick Uhls
George W. Valentine
Martin H. Wright
George W. Belcher
William Blesh

Miles W. Beckett
Joseph Belch
George H. Fairhurst
Wiley C. Hooper
Gottlieb Ketsel
Peter Kutch
Mordecai M. Kiger
Presely Lemon
Thomas Montgomery
Walter W. McGeehe
Hardin Metcalf
Thomas Patterson
Edmond Polk
Jonathan Postleweight
John Shoaff
William H. Snellbaker
Caleb Thayer
Henry Tishendorf
Gottlieb Tishendorf
Charles Tegmire
Samuel Wetsel
Christian Winkleman
Wallace Walker
Wilson W. Young
John W. Kress
Joseph Daniel
Nicholi Gobert

Company D

Captain—FRANKLIN K. COSGROVE
First Lieutenant—CHARLES H. WAYNE
Sergeant—DAVID K. STOFER
Sergeant—GEORGE SHELL

Sergeant—LAFAYETTE PERKINS
Corporal—GEORGE W. SQUIER
Corporal—PHILEMON MILLINGTON
Corporal—THOMAS N. STANLEY
Corporal—SANFORD WORDEN

Corporal—JOHN C. CASEBEER
Corporal—BURKE D. SHAFFER
Musician—JOSEPH H. ECKLES
Wagoner—JOSHUA LONSBERRY

PRIVATES

A. Anderson
Joseph Conway
Alfred Daugherty
Emanuel Deitrick
Horace Gustin
William H. Johnson
William M. Johnson
Henry Markle

Joseph Shook
Cyrenius Saunders
Henry Wentworth
Ezra Worden
David Worden
Nathan Rex
Alfred Wilson
Thomas Blackburn

William H. Casebeer
Ebenezer Conway
Samuel Hagerman
James Hannon
Jerome A. Kenyon
Charles Morse
Lewis E. Shook
Platt J. Squiers
Ira Worden

Philip Baker
John H. Bartholomew
Thomas Clements
Emanuel Deitrick
Andrew Dunhour
William Farmer
Horace Gustin
Oliver Gustin

Charles T. Hickman
William H. Hannon
Norman Luce
James McBratney
Lucius C. Palmer
John H. Wentworth
John W. Gustin
Samuel Hartel

Company G

PRIVATES

Henry O'Grady   Aruna Bradley

Company K

Sergeant—GEORGE W. GORDEN

PRIVATES

William F. Hinkle   Robert Douglas   Charles M. Thomas

Forty-Fifth Regiment

(THIRD CAVALRY)

The Third Cavalry. Forty-Fifth Regiment, was organized as follows:

Six Companies that had been originally organized for the First Cavalry (Twenty-Eighth Regiment), at Madison on the 22d of August, 1861, and sent to the Army of the Potomac, under the command of Lieut.-Colonel SCOTT CARTER, were, on the 22d of October, 1861, by General Orders of the Adjutant General of the State, united with four Companies that had been accepted in September and October, 1861, and sent to Kentucky, the ten companies bearing the designation of the Third Cavalry (Forty-Fifth Regiment). In December, 1862, two new companies were organized and added to the organization. The companies with the Army of the Potomac were designated as companies "A," "B," "C," "D," "E" and "F." Of this right wing of the regiment Colonel Scott Carter was the commanding officer. The companies serving in Kentucky were designated as companies "G," "H," "I" and "K." The two companies organized in December, 1862, were designated as companies "L" and "M."

THE RIGHT WING.

The right wing of the Third Cavalry joined Hooker's division of the Army of the Potomac at its camp near Budd's Ferry, south of Washington, on the Maryland side of of the Potomac. In December, 1861, a detachment composed of Companies "A," "B" and "F," proceeded into St. Mary's county, Maryland, for the purpose of breaking up the contraband travel and trade between Baltimore and Virginia. This detachment was kept on this duty for four months. Company "E" was also detached for similar duty, during the same period, along the river in the vicinity of Maryland Point and Port Tobacco. When Hooker's division embarked for the Peninsula the Third Cavalry was left behind, and did duty in lower Maryland until early in May, 1862, when it moved to the vicinity of Washington, remaining there until the 25th of May. It then marched rapidly to Thoroughfare Gap, reaching there next day, and joined the command of Gen. Geary, with which it continued for three weeks. After this it joined Gen. Shield's force at Luray, in time to participate in the movement back to Front Royal. From there it moved to Bristow Station, where it remained until the 7th of July, when it was ordered to report to Gen. King at Falmouth.

The battalion remained at Falmouth until its evacuation on the last of August, during which time it was engaged in scouting the country south of Fredericksburg, and had several skirmishes with the enemy's cavalry. In one of these expeditions, it went to Anderson Turnout, on the Virginia Central railroad, within about twenty miles of Richmond, and, after a brief engagement, dispersed a squadron of rebel cavalry and captured several prisoners. After the evacuation of Fredericksburg, the battalion proceeded to Washington and then northward, taking part in the Maryland campaign, as part of Gen. Pleasanton's command, and engaging in a number of cavalry skirmishes, commencing with Poolesville and ending with Martinsburg, and, also, in the battles of South Mountain and Antietam.

Late in the month of October the Army of the Potomac began an advance movement, crossing the river at Berlin and moving along the eastern base of the Blue Ridge to Warrenton. Pleasanton's cavalry division formed the advance of the army, and on the 1st of November encountered the enemy's cavalry at Philamont, on the 2d at Union, on the 3d at Upperville, and on the 4th at Barber's Cross Roads. The enemy contested the ground with much stubborness, but were compelled to give way before our cavalry. In all these engagements the battalion bore an active part. It moved with the army about the middle of November from Warrenton to Falmouth, and was present at the battle of Fredericksburg in December, 1862, but was not brought into action. On the 29th of April, 1863, it crossed the Rappahannock with a brigade of Pleasanton's division of Averill's column of Stoneman's raiding expedition, and proceeded to Rapidan Ford, where a skirmish was had with rebel cavalry without accomplishing any result. In obedience to orders from Gen. Hooker, the command returned, entering our lines on the day succeeding the battle of Chancellorsville, and before the army had re-crossed the river.

When Lee commenced his second invasion of Maryland, the cavalry corps of Pleasanton took up its line of march for the purpose of heading Lee's cavalry, then preparing to start on a raid at Culpepper Court House. Marching with Gen. Buford's division, the battalion was engaged in a severe cavalry battle on the south side of the Rappahannock, near Beverly Ford. A few days subsequent to the battle of Beverly Ford there was a re-organization of the cavalry corps, in which the battalion of the Third Cavalry was assigned to Gen. John Buford's division, and remained attached to his command until his death. On the 21st of June it participated in the cavalry battle at Upperville, between the cavalry corps of the Army of the Potomac and Stuart's rebel cavalry, in which it met a rebel brigade at close quarters, and aided in driving it back with heavy loss. A few days afterward it crossed the

Forty-Fifth Regiment—Continued

Potomac and marched to Gettysburg, entering that place on the morning of the 30th of June, and encamping a mile from the town on the Chambersburg pike. The next morning the enemy advanced in force, and for two hours, until the arrival of the First Corps, Buford's division of cavalry held the enemy in check. So soon as the infantry came up the cavalry were withdrawn from the immediate front, but still remained on the field.

About the close of the first day's fighting, and whilst our troops were falling back through the town, hard pressed by the enemy, the battalion, with the Eighth New York Cavalry, was sent forward to check the heavy flanking force of rebel infantry, until our troops could get into position on the hills behind the town. The movement, though a hazardous one, was successful. After this the battalion was not actively engaged until Lee's army began its retreat, when the battalion moved with the cavalry force in pursuit, engaging the enemy at Williamsport, Boonsboro, Beaver Creek, Funkstown, Falling Waters, Chester Gap, Brandy Station, and on the Rappahannock—the last named fight being on the 4th of August.

The battalion remained in the vicinity of Culpepper Court House during the Winter of 1863, engaged in performing picket and outpost duty, and taking part in several reconnoisances. On the 27th of February, 1864, it was detailed, under command of Major Patton, to take part in Gen. Kilpatrick's Richmond raid, and did not rejoin the army until the 15th of March. About the middle of April Col. Chapman's brigade, to which the battalion belonged, was transferred from the 1st cavalry division of the Army of the Potomac to the 3d cavalry division, then commanded by Gen. J. H. Wilson, to which division it remained attached until ordered home to be mustered out of service. It marched at midnight on the night of the 3d of May from camp near Stephensburgh, and crossed the Rapidan at Germania Ford at daybreak on the morning of the 4th, driving off the enemy's pickets. It participated in the cavalry engagement at Craig's Meeting House on the 5th, and at Spottsylvania C. H. on the 8th. On the morning of the 9th of May Gen. Sheridan started with his entire cavalry corps upon his great raid upon Richmond, passing to the rear of Lee's army and cutting off communication between him and that city. The battalion formed a part af this force, participating in the important engagements of Yellow Tavern on the 11th, and Meadow Bridge on the 12th. The cavalry column proceeded from the front of Richmond to Haxall's Landing on the Potomac, and communicated with the force then operating under Gen. Butler in front of Bermuda Hundred. After a halt of three days, the command being supplied with rations and forage,

marched to White House. It then repaired the railroad bridge, upon which the command was crossed over the Pamunkey river, and rejoined the army near Chesterfield, on the 25th of May. It participated in the engagement of Wilson's division with the rebel cavalry at Hanover C. H. on the 30th and 31st of May, and at Salem Church on the 3d of June.

On the night of Sunday, June 12th, the army of the Potomac, leaving its position at Cold Harbor, began the movement across the Chickahominy and James Rivers. The battalion of the 3d Cavalry at the advance of Wilson's Division, being dismounted, forced a passage over the Chickahominy, at "Long Bridge, in the face of great natural obstructions, driving off the enemy's pickets. Pontoon bridges were speedily laid and the passage of one column of the army secured. The Division was then moved rapidly to the right in order to cover the movement of the army toward the James, supported by a Division of the 5th Corps, and engaged the enemy on the 13th at White Oak Swamp and Riddle's Shop. In the latter part of June it took part in Wilson's raid upon the Southside and Danville railroads, participating in the engagement at Nottoway Court House, Roanoke Station and Stony Creek.

On the 21st of July, 1864, Colonel George H. Chapman, who had the immediate command of the battalion, or of the brigade to which it was attached, was promoted Brigadier General. In August the non-veterans were mustered out, leaving in the battalion but one hundred and eighty-nine veterans and recruits. These were organized into two companies "A" and "B" and sent to the Shenandoah valley. Joining General Sheridan's army it participated in the battle of Opequan Creek on the 19th of September, and, also, in the battle of Cedar Creek on the 19th of October. In the latter engagement it captured two pieces of artillery and four stand of colors. On the opening of the campaign of 1865, it accompanied Sheridan on his raid down the James River Canal and again joined the army of the Potomac at Petersburg, participating in the battle of Five Forks and Sailor's Creek. At the latter place it captured five stand of colors. It was, also, engaged at the battle of Appomattox Court House, capturing two pieces of artillery. At the close of the war it was transferred to Louisville, Kentucky, where it remained until ordered to proceed to Indianapolis for muster-out. Arriving at Indianapolis the two companies were mustered out of service on the 7th of August, 1865.

This battalion participated in over seventy battles, cavalry engagements and stated skirmishes, always bearing itself in a gallant manner, and winning an honorable name throughout the army with which it served.

Forty-Fifth Regiment—Continued

Up to July, 1864, the casualties in the battalion were as follows, to wit:

Officers and enlisted men killed in action, or who died of wounds received, - - - - - - - - 41

Died in hospital of disease, - - - - - - 40

Wounded in action, - - - - - - - - 232

Taken prisoners, or missing in action - - - - 107

Deserted, - - - - - - - - - - - 7

Officers discharged on account of disability from disease or wounds, - - - - - - - - 10

Enlisted men discharged for like causes, - - - 168

Total, - - - - - - - - - - 605

No reports have been furnished of the casualties subsequent to July, 1864.

LEFT WING.

Companies "G," "H," "I," and "K," constituting the left wing of the Third Cavalry, were organized at Madison and transferred to Kentucky in October, 1861. For over a year, the companies were separated and did duty with different commands. On reaching Kentucky the companies went into camp at Camp Wickliffe where they remained until the movement toward Nashville commenced, in which the companies joined. After the battle of Shiloh they marched to Corinth and thence into Northern Alabama and Southern Tennessee. The companies marched with different Divisions of the army in the Buell and Bragg campaign, returning to Nashville in November and going into camp near Edgefield Junction.

Companies "L" and "M" were organized in December, 1862, and remained at Indianapolis for near a year. When they moved they marched with General Wilcox's command of six months' troops and joined the Left Wing in East Tennessee.

The battalion marched with Rosecrans' army toward Murfreesboro, and was engaged in the campaigns of the winter of 1862 and those of the spring, summer and fall of 1863, terminating with the battle of Mission Ridge. It then moved into East Tennessee under command of Lieut. Colonel Robert Klein, where it was actively engaged in scouting and skirmishing until the campaign against Atlanta commenced. Joining Sherman's army it moved with it to Atlanta, engaging in all the cavalry operations of that campaign. In the march through Georgia the battalion accompanied Sherman's Cavalry and while at Savannah, in pursuance of the orders of General Sherman, the remaining veterans and recruits were transferred to and consolidated with the Eighth Indiana Cavalry, the consolidation bearing the name of the Eighth Cavalry. After the consolidation the detachment participated in all of the marches, engagements and skirmishes of the Eighth Cavalry, and continued to serve with that organization until its muster out at Lexington, North Carolina, on the 20th of July, 1865, and then returned home with that regiment and was finally discharged with it at Indianapolis.

Forty-Fifth Regiment

(THIRD CAVALRY)

Major—Charles Case

Forty-Seventh Regiment Infantry

(THREE YEARS' SERVICE)

The Forty-Seventh Regiment was organized at Anderson, on the 10th of October, 1862, with JAMES R. SLACK as Colonel, the regiment being composed of companies raised in the Eleventh Congressional District. On the 13th of December it left Indianapolis for Kentucky and reached Bardstown on the 21st, where it was assigned to General Wood's brigade of Buell's army. From thence it moved to Camp Wickliffe, arriving there on the 31st of December, and remained there until the 14th of February, 1862, when it marched to West Point, at the mouth of Salt River, and there took transports for Commerce, Missouri. Arriving there on the 24th of February, it was assigned to Gen. Pope's army, and marched at once to New Madrid, and there engaged the enemy, being the first regiment to enter Fort Thompson. Moving to Riddle's Point it participated in the engagement at that place between the shore batteries and rebel gunboats. From thence it moved to Tiptonville, Tennessee, where it remained for nearly two months.

After the capture of Fort Pillow the regiment was transported to Memphis, reaching that place on the 30th of June, and remaining there during the following month, Colonel Slack being in command of the post. On the 11th of August it had a skirmish with the enemy at Brown's plantation, Mississippi, losing a few men in killed and wounded. Moving to Helena, Arkansas, the regiment remained there until March, 1863, when it took part in Gen. Quinby's expedition to Yazoo Pass. Returning from this expedition it joined Grant's army and moved with it to the rear of Vicksburg, engaging in the battles and skirmishes of that campaign. In the battle of Champion Hills on the 16th of May, it lost one hundred and forty-three in killed and wounded. Going into the trenches near the enemy's works at Vicksburg, it remained in them until the surrender on the 4th of July, being almost constantly engaged in the siege. After this it marched to Jackson with Sherman's expedition, and took part in the engagement at that place.

Returning to Vicksburg it took transports for New Orleans in August, from whence it moved to Berwick Bay. While in this portion of Louisiana the Forty-Seventh participated in Bank's expedition through the Teche country, engaging the enemy at Grand Coteau. It then moved to New Iberia, and while there in December, 1863, the regiment re-enlisted and left Algiers on the 9th of February, 1864, for home on veteran furlough, reaching Indianapolis on the 18th, with four hundred and sixteen veterans. On the 19th it was present at a public reception given to the veterans of the Twenty-First and Forty-Seventh regiments at Metropolitan Hall in that city; on which occasion addresses were made by Gov. Morton, Col. Slack and others.

Upon its return to the field the regiment moved with Banks' army up Red river in the spring of 1864, engaging in the marches, battles and retreats of that unfortunate campaign. On the 28th of July it engaged the enemy at Atchafalaya Bayou, Louisiana, losing several wounded. The regiment was then stationed at Morganza, at which post it remained on duty for some time. On the 31st of December, 1864, Col. James R. Slack was commissioned a Brigadier General, whereupon John A. McLaughlin was promoted Colonel of the regiment. In February, 1865, it was transported to Dauphin Island, Alabama, near Mobile, and in Canby's campaign against that city the Forty-Seventh took an active part. After the fall of Mobile it moved to Shreveport, Louisiana, with Gen. Herron to receive the surrender of Gen. Price and the army of the Trans-Mississippi Department. At this place the regiment remained until the 23d of October, 1865, when it was mustered out of service. Reaching Indianapolis with five hundred and thirty men and thirty-two officers, it was present on the 1st of November at a reception given to the regiment in the Capitol grounds, and was addressed by Gov. Morton, Gen. Slack, and Cols. Milton S. Robinson and John A. McLaughlin. The next day the regiment was finally discharged.

Forty-Seventh Regiment Infantry

(THREE YEARS' SERVICE)

Company C

PRIVATES

James Cronan   Joshua Dury   Aaron Baker

Company E

Sergeant—SHERMAN L. BALLARD   Sergeant—HENRY W. ZENTS

PRIVATES

Joseph Evans   Daniel Hatfield
Hiram Richards   Samuel N. Lockwood
John Rine   Joseph Pointsett
Samuel W. Stirk   Wilmer T. Stirk
James T. M. Davis   Thomas W. Zents
William H. Bowman

Company G

PRIVATES

Samuel Anderson   Joseph Foltz

Company H

Corporal—DAVID LARIMORE

Forty-Eighth Regiment Infantry

The Forty-Eighth Regiment was organized at Goshen on the 6th of December, 1861, with Norman Eddy as Colonel, and left for Fort Donelson via Cairo, on the 1st of February, 1862, where it arrived the day after the surrender. It then moved to Paducah, where it remained until May, when it moved up the Tennessee river and engaged in the siege of Corinth. After the evacuation of Corinth it was assigned to the First Brigade, Second Division of the Army of the Mississippi, and took part in the marches and counter-marches in pursuit of Gen. Price. On the 19th of September it participated in the battle of Iuka, losing one hundred and sixteen men in killed and wounded out of four hundred and twenty engaged. On the 3d and 4th of October, it was engaged in the second battle at Corinth, (under Rosecrans,) and lost twenty-six killed and wounded. The regiment next moved down the Mississippi Central railroad as far as Oxford, Mississippi, and on its return marched to Memphis, where, in January, 1863, it was assigned to the First Brigade, Seventh Division of the Seventeenth Army Corps. After remaining here two months it was transported down the Mississippi, and joining the army of Gen. Grant, marched with it to the rear of Vicksburg. During this campaign the regiment participated in the skirmish of Forty Hills, on the 3d of May; the battle of Raymond, on the 13th of May; the battle of Jackson, on the 14th of May, and the engagement at Champion Hills, on the 16th of May, losing in the latter battle thirty-three killed and wounded. It was actively engaged in the trenches during the long siege of the rebel works at Vicksburg, and took part in the assault on the 22d of May, losing thirty-eight in killed and wounded.

After the surrender of Vicksburg it remained in that vicinity until August, and then moved up the river to Memphis, and from thence marched across the country to Chattanooga, and while in that vicinity engaged the enemy at Tunnel Hill. From the latter place it marched back to Huntsville, Alabama, and while stationed there, in January, 1864, the regiment re-enlisted as a veteran organization, and returned home on veteran furlough, reaching Indianapolis on the 6th of February, with three hundred and sixty-nine veterans, and on the 8th were publicly received in welcoming speeches by Governor Morton and others. After the expiration of its furlough it proceeded to Huntsville, Alabama, where it remained until June.

The Forty-Eighth then moved to Cartersville, Georgia, and was kept on duty in that vicinity, looking after guerrillas and protecting Gen. Sherman's railroad communications during the campaign against Atlanta. It was continued on this duty until Hood's invasion, when it joined Sherman's army, and marched with the First Brigade, Third Division of the Fifteenth Army Corps in its campaign from Atlanta to Savannah. From Savannah it first moved to Beaufort, and then on the campaign through the Carolinas, going through Columbia, Cheraw, Fayetteville and Goldsboro to Raleigh.

From Raleigh it moved northward, after the surrender of Johnson's army, making the distance from Raleigh to Petersburg, one hundred and sixty-five miles, in six days. From Petersburg it marched to Washington, and soon after its arrival there was transferred to Louisville, Kentucky, where it was mustered out of service on the 15th of July, 1865. Returning to Indianapolis it was present at a public reception given to a large number of returned troops, in the Capitol grounds, on the 18th of July, on which occasion addresses were made by Governor Morton, General Hovey and others.

While at Washington about two hundred and fifty men were transferred to the Forty-Eighth from the Twelfth, Eighty-Third, Ninety-Seventh and Ninety-Ninth regiments, being retained recruits whose organizations had been mustered out. These transferred men served with the Forty-Eighth until its final muster-out and were discharged with it. During its term of service the regiment lost in battle two hundred and thirteen men, in killed and wounded.

Forty-Eighth Regiment Infantry

Company D

PRIVATES

Thomas B. Crawford   Chester Schie

Fifty-Fifth Regiment Infantry

(THREE MONTHS' SERVICE)

The Fifty-Fifth Regiment was organized at Indianapolis, under special orders, and mustered into service for three months, on the 16th of June, 1862, with John R. Mahan as Lieut. Colonel, who continued to command it until its final discharge. It was assigned to the duty of guarding the Fort Donelson prisoners at Camp Morton, where it remained until August and then proceeded to Kentucky, with other troops sent there to resist the invasion of General Kirby Smith. The Regiment remained on duty in Central Kentucky until the expiration of its term of service when it returned to Indianapolis, where it was mustered out.

Fifty-Fifth Regiment Infantry

(THREE MONTHS' SERVICE)

Company E

Captain—CHARLES EMERY
First Lieutenant—BRUTUS A. BOURIE
Second Lieutenant—WILLIAM L. THOMPSON
Sergeants—CYRUS T. MOSIER
　　　　　CHARLES E. THOMAS
　　　　　WILLIAM BROWN
　　　　　FRANCIS A. STAPELFORD
Corporals—JEROME EVANS
　　　　　GEORGE W. HERRICK
　　　　　HENRY H. ROBINSON
　　　　　WILLIAM S. THOMAS
　　　　　WILLIAM TODD
　　　　　LEVI PEA
　　　　　JOHN T. ORBISON
　　　　　KING KISTLER
Musicians—JAMES LEROY
　　　　　ABRAHAM TALBOT

George W. Argo	John H. Felter	Ivory Kimball	George Roach
Albert Alton	Samuel Gill	John T. Lines	Marion D. Roberts
William Bickell	Andrew Granstaff	Frances F. McClelland	John Slocum
Edward Beans	Charles W. Griswold	Byron W. McLain	Thomas Shue
William Beach	Miles Griswold	William B. McMakin	William Smitley
Benjamin Brown	Nelson J. Gillman	Simon P. Nichols	Benjamin Sharp
James Borden	Benjamin Hardman	Owen Owens	Andrew J. Steward
Benjamin Barnes	Jacob Harst	Daniel Opleger	John P. Thomas
John Barnes	John Nanenstine	Luther M. Oliphant	Liverton D. Thomas
George Behrens	Amos Hartman	William G. Osborn	Thomas L. Traul
Joshua C. Cooper	John Haynes	Joseph T. Pool	Llyod Upton
Frank Curtien	Oregon Haynes	Lemuel J. Platter	John W. Vance
Samuel Cully	Perry Haynes	Christopher Platter	Joseph T. Vorhis
John W. Demorest	Enoch Hollopeter	August Pettyjohn	Adam Wolf
Isaac L. Depew	Samuel Jewel	Andrew Pea	George W. Wait
Washington Dale	Samuel Kile	Austin M. Puett	Elbridge G. Wheelock
Algernon L. Ferris	Ambrose Kintz	John Rowland	William B. Ward
John L. Fitch	Frederick King	William Radcliffe	Michael Wann
Daniel France			

Fifty-Ninth Regiment Infantry

(THREE YEARS' SERVICE)

Governor Morton authorized the raising of the Fifty-Ninth Regiment in October, 1861, and commissioned JESSE I. ALEXANDER, of Gosport, Colonel. At that time there was being recruited a regiment in each Congressional District, and as Col. Alexander's instructions were " not to interfere with the filling up of other regiments," recruiting for the Fifty-Ninth progressed but slowly. But the Colonel, with energy and perseverance, succeeded in getting the organization completed and mustered into the service on the 11th of February, 1862. On the 13th of February the regiment was ordered to New Albany, where it was armed with Enfield Rifles. On the 18th it left on transports for Cairo, arriving there on the 20th, and on the following day it embarked for Commerce, Missouri, reaching there on the 22d, and was the first regiment to report to General Pope for duty with the "Army of the Mississippi."

On the 25th of February it moved to Benton, where it was first brigaded with the 34th, 43d, 46th and 47th Indiana regiments—Colonel Slack commanding—and afterwards transferred to Colonel Worthington's brigade. On the 1st of March the regiment marched in the direction of New Madrid, arriving there on the 3d, and participating in siege of that place, and upon the evacuation was one of the first regiments that entered the town and took possession of Fort Thompson. Crossing the Mississippi on the 7th of April, it marched down to Tiptonville, assisting in the capture of over five thousand prisoners. Returning to New Madrid on the 10th of April, it embarked on transports on the 12th, and proceeded, with the fleet, to Fort Pillow, from which expedition it returned on the 17th. It then proceeded from New Madrid to Cairo, and thence to Hamburg, Tennessee, where it disembarked on the 22d of April, and went into camp. At this place Gen. N. B. Buford was assigned to the command of the Brigade to which the Fifty-Ninth was attached, and during the month of May the Forty-Eighth Indiana was placed in the same Brigade, and from that time until the final muster-out of both organizations, the two regiments remained together.

From the 24th of April until the 29th of May, the regiment was engaged in most of the skirmishes and reconnoisances, and in the building of forts, etc., during the march to and siege of Corinth, and after the evacuation marched with the pursuing column that followed the enemy to Boonville, returning to the vicinity of Corinth on the 12th of June. On the 13th it moved its camp to Clear Creek, where it remained until the 6th of August. While at this place it marched on an expedition to Ripley and back, being absent twelve days. Moving from Clear Creek to Jacinto, it remained there until the 7th of September, when it proceeded to Rienzi, at which place it received two hundred and fifty recruits from Indiana. On the 1st of October it went to Corinth, and was there engaged, on the 3d and 4th of October, in the battle of Corinth. After defeating the enemy, it joined in the pursuit of Price to the Hatchie, and then returned to Corinth, arriving there on the 10th of October.

On the 2d of November, the regiment marched with General Quimby's division to Grand Junction, and thence to Davis' Mills and Moscow. On the 29th of November it again broke camp and proceeded, by the way of Cold Water, Holly Springs, and Oxford, to Yocana river, where it remained a few days, and then returned to Oxford, from whence it moved to Lumpkins' Mill. On the 26th of December it started to Memphis, with the escort of the Commissary train, arriving there on the 28th, and on the 31st started back with the train, going through Collierville to Lafayette, and arriving there on the 1st of January, 1863. Returning to Memphis on the 3d, it went into camp about three miles east of the city, where it remained until the 1st of March, doing guard duty. It then proceeded down the Mississippi, on transports, to Helena, Arkansas, stopping a few days at Woolfolk's Landing. On the 12th of March it embarked with the Yazoo River expedition, arriving at the encampment, near Fort Pemberton, on the 25th of March. Re-embarking on the 6th of April, the regiment returned to Helena on the 10th, from which place it proceeded, on the 13th of April, to Milliken's Bend, arriving there on the 15th of April.

On the 24th of April it commenced, with other troops, the march for Vicksburg, going down the west side of the Mississippi to Grand Gulf, arriving there on the 1st of May, and at once crossing over to the east side, near Bayou Piere, from whence it marched to the battle ground of Port Gibson, reaching there just as the battle closed. Marching with Grant's army, in the First Brigade of the Seventh Division of the Seventeenth Army Corps, it was engaged at Forty Hills, Raymond and Champion Hills. At Jackson its skirmishers, under Captain John E. Simpson, were the first to enter the city, and it had the gratification of seeing its tattered flag waving from the dome of the Capitol, in that city. At the Big Black river it formed the rear-guard for the Seventeenth Corps, and was the last regiment to cross, destroying the bridges behind it. It then moved up and took its position, in line of battle, in front of the rebel fortifications at Vicksburg. In the assault on the enemy's works on the 22d of May the regiment participated, suffering heavy losses. In this assault Lieut. Tripp was killed, and Capt. Buck, Lieuts. Riley and Maxwell wounded. Of the enlisted men one hundred and twenty-six were killed and wounded. During the siege of Vicksburg, the Fifty-Ninth formed part of Gen. Blair's command, and with it went up the Yazoo river to Satarlia, returning to its old position in the trenches on the 4th of June, where it remained until the surrender. On the 4th of July it marched into Vicksburg and on the same day Gen. McPherson issued a congratulatory order in which he complimented in the highest terms of praise the soldiers of the Seventeenth Corps. On the 5th of August, Gen. Sanborn, who had long commanded the brigade and division to which the Fifty-Ninth was attached, issued his farewell order to the soldiers of the First Brigade, announcing his intention to leave the military service, and recounting their deeds on the battle-

Fifty-Ninth Regiment Infantry—Continued

field from Corinth to Vicksburg, and complimenting them for the glorious record they had made.

The regiment remained at Vicksburg until the 13th of September, when it embarked on transports and proceeded up the river to Helena, where it remained until the 28th of September, and then embarked for Memphis. Remaining there until the 5th of October, it proceeded by rail to Corinth, and from thence moved to Glendale, where it remained until the 17th of October, when the remainder of the division arrived from Memphis. On the 19th of October, it commenced the march for Chattanooga, arriving there in time to take part in the victory of Mission Ridge. On the 17th of December it began its return march, reaching Bridgeport, Alabama, on the 18th, where it went into camp. While there the regiment was transferred to the Fifteenth Army Corps and assigned to the Third Division thereof. Starting for Huntsville on the 23d of December, it reached there on the 26th and went into camp. While there the regiment re-enlisted as a Veteran organization on the 1st of January, 1864, for which the Fifty-Ninth was complimented by Brig. Gen'l John E. Smith, in orders, on the 3d of February. It left for home on the 3d of March in company with the Forty-Eighth, reaching Indianapolis on the 8th, where, on the 10th, the two regiments partook of an excellent dinner prepared by the ladies of the city, and in the afternoon had a public reception in the State House Grounds, where they were warmly greeted by Governor Morton and others.

Returning to the field by the way of New Albany, Louisville and Nashville, the Fifty-Ninth arrived at Huntsville on the 3d of April, and went into camp, remaining there until the 22d of June. Starting for Kingston, Georgia, and reaching there on the 1st of July, it joined Sherman's army, then on its march to Atlanta. On the 13th of July it moved to Etowah river, and guarded the bridge over that stream until the 26th of August, when it was ordered to report to General Steadman, at Chattanooga. On arriving there, on the 27th, it marched into East Tennessee after Wheeler's Cavalry, returning to Chattanooga after an absence of four days. Moving from thence to Tullahoma, it reported to Gen. Milroy, and remained on duty there until the 21st of September. Returning to Chattanooga, it marched with a wagon train as far as Cartersville, Georgia, arriving there on the 28th of September, after which it took up its old position on Etowah river.

On the 12th of November it moved towards Atlanta, and on the 15th it commenced the grand "march to the sea," following the fortunes of General Sherman through Georgia to Savannah. General Smith, on the 25th of December, issued a highly complimentary order, in which he stated that General Sherman had complimented the Division for its soldierly bearing, and made special mention of the Fifty-Ninth for its good marching. From Savannah the regiment marched through the Carolinas to Raleigh, and from thence to Washington City, where it participated in the grand review. From Washington it was transferred to Louisville, Kentucky, where, on the 17th of July, 1865, it was mustered out of service. Arriving at Indianapolis, it was present at a public reception in the Capitol grounds on the 18th of July, on which occasion the regiment was addressed by Governor Morton and others. In a few days afterward it was finally discharged from service. The regiment, during its term of service, received in recruits, drafted men, etc., seven hundred and seventy-seven, and lost, in killed, wounded and missing, and by disease, seven hundred and ninety-three men. It has traveled by rail, three thousand seven hundred and fifty-six miles, by water four thousand six hundred and eighteen miles, and by land five thousand three hundred and five miles; making in all, thirteen thousand six hundred and seventy-nine miles.

Company A
PRIVATES

Lorenzo D. Casteel	George Dick	William Kegg	William S. Watkins

Company E
PRIVATES

John Hortz	Henry Knarl	Henry Sumner	Andrew Theime
John G. Kinney	Robert Lock	David Smith	George Wiechselfelder

Company F
PRIVATES

Joseph Barrett	Thomas E. Kendall	George P. Shafer	John Sunn
Thomas Flannigan	William Nycum	William M. Stewart	

Company K
PRIVATES

David B. Anderson	George Gullard	Henry Lahnord	Neil McNair	Frederick Sherer
John Bielsar	Michael Hoffman	Allen H. Moore	William McNair	George M. Vandeventer
Martin Flutter	Thomas Hart	William Meyer	John W. Pio	William Warntz
	Monroe Johnson		William J. Stephenson	

Sixty-Fifth Regiment Infantry

The Sixty-Fifth Regiment was organized under the call of July, 1862, at Princeton, and was mustered in at Evansville, (with the exception of Company "K,") on the 18th and 20th of August, 1862, with JOHN W. FOSTER as Colonel. The nine companies were at once moved to Henderson, Kentucky, where it went into camp to protect the place from guerrillas. On the 27th of August, the regiment embarked on transports, and went up Green river to Ashbysburg, landing at 9 o'clock in the night. Marching all night, it attacked Adam Johnson's rebel regiment the next morning, and after a severe skirmish, and some loss to the enemy, the regiment took possession of the town of Madisonville. Company "K" was mustered in on the 10th of September, and joined the regiment in the field. After the engagement at Madisonville, the companies were distributed in different counties in that portion of Kentucky west of the Nashville railroad, and there remained on duty until the 18th of August, 1863, when they all reported at Glasgow. Here the regiment joined Col. Graham's brigade of cavalry, the regiment having been mounted in April, 1863, by order of Gen. Burnside. The companies, while on the local duty above mentioned, engaged the enemy as follows: Company "D" in a skirmish near Vanderburg, on the 12th of September, 1862, losing one killed and six wounded, and on the 13th it had another skirmish, in which three were wounded. Company "E" had a skirmish at Dixon, on the 29th of July, 1863, losing one man wounded.

The regiment was moved to the field in East Tennessee, arriving at Knoxville on the 1st of September, the brigade to which it was attached being the first Union troops to arrive at that point. During this march Colonel Foster assumed the command of the brigade. Several companies of the regiment were sent out on a raiding expedition, returning to Knoxville after an absence of two days. On the 5th of September the regiment marched up the valley, and taking possession of a captured train of cars, moved up the valley one hundred and ten miles above Knoxville, capturing on the way another train and two locomotives, besides other property. Returning from this expedition on the night of the 6th, it moved the next day with its brigade up the same valley, and on the 20th engaged the enemy near Zollicoffer. On the 22d a severe fight was had with the enemy at Blountsville, in which the regiment lost fifteen in killed and wounded. The Sixty-Fifth was engaged in another fight at Rheatown, on the 11th of October, in which Company "A" had one man wounded. On the 14th of October the regiment fought the enemy at Blountsville without loss, and on the 15th at Bristol, losing one man captured.

On the 17th of November the regiment moved with the division across to Tazewell, and on the 1st of December it had a severe fight at Walker's Ford, Tennessee, assisted by the Fifth Indiana Cavalry, in which both regiments fought all day against great odds, the Sixty-Fifth losing two killed, eight wounded and two missing. Company "K" at this time was at Mulberry Gap, numbering forty-five men, from whence it expelled a whole rebel regiment by a night attack. After Longstreet's retreat the regiment and all the cavalry had a battle with Longstreet's infantry at Bean Station, on the 14th of December, in which the regiment lost two killed, ten wounded and five missing. On the following day it fought at Powder Spring Gap, losing ten wounded and four missing, and on the same day again engaged the enemy at Skaggs' Mills, losing one killed and two captured. On the 17th of January, 1864, the regiment had a fight at Dandridge in which one man was mortally wounded.

On the 21st of April, 1864, the regiment was dismounted and assigned to the Second Brigade, Third Division, Twenty-Third Army Corps, and on the 30th of April it joined Sherman's army, then about moving on its Atlanta campaign. It was in the battle of Resacca on the 14th of May, and in all the skirmishes and battles of this campaign, up to the capture of Atlanta, sustaining a loss of eleven killed, twenty-three wounded and five prisoners; total, thirty-nine. The regiment participated in the march in pursuit of Hood into Alabama and Tennessee, engaging the enemy at Columbia, Tennessee, and at Franklin on the 30th of November, '64. In the battle of Nashville, on the 15th and 16th of December, it bore a conspicuous part. After this it moved to the Tennessee river in pursuit of Hood's retreating army.

In January, 1865, the regiment was transferred to Alexandria, Virginia, and from thence sailed to the vicinity of Fort Fisher, near Wilmington, North Carolina, and after landing bore the brunt of the attack on Fort Anderson, on the 18th of February, 1865, and did the skirmishing for the troops at Town Creek on the 20th. The regiment was not afterwards engaged, but moved to Greensboro, with the Twenty-Third Corps, after the surrender of Johnson's army, where on the 22d of June, '65, it was mustered out of service, and proceeded to Indiana, and was finally discharged at Indianapolis, soon afterwards.

The regiment, during its term of service, has lost as follows: Killed, twenty-six; wounded, eighty-six; captured, sixty-one; total, one hundred and seventy-three.

Sixty-Fifth Regiment Infantry

Company A

PRIVATES

Philip Green

Seventy-Third Regiment Infantry

The Seventy-Third Regiment was organized and mustered into service on the 16th of August, 1862, at South Bend, with GILBERT HATHAWAY as Colonel. The regiment was recruited entirely from the Ninth Congressional district, and entered the service one thousand and ten strong, in less than three weeks from the date recruiting commenced. It was ordered at once to Lexington, by way of Louisville, Kentucky. The defeat of the Union forces at Richmond, Kentucky, on the 30th of August, necessitated the evacuation of Lexington and the regiment made a long and weary march to Louisville, distant ninety miles. On the 1st of October the Seventy-Third was assigned to the Twentieth Brigade (Harker's) of the Sixth Division (Wood's) of Buell's army, and commenced the pursuit of Bragg. On the 8th of October it was deployed in line in reserve and witnessed the battle of Chaplin Hills, losing one man killed. It then pursued Bragg as far as Wild Cat, with slight skirmishing. Returning, it marched to Glasgow, Kentucky, and from thence to Gallatin, Tennessee, where on the 7th of November, it surprised the enemy, driving him out of the place, capturing nineteen prisoners.

On the 26th of November the regiment marched into Nashville, having previously encamped for several days at Silver Springs and engaged in an expedition to Lebanon. While foraging, on the 1st and 25th of December, it skirmished with the enemy, and on the 26th of December marched with the army, under Gen. Rosecrans, to engage the enemy. Pressing him back with skirmishing the army reached Stone River on the 29th, and on the evening of that day the Seventy-Third, with the Fifty-First Indiana, was the first of the whole army to cross Stone River, under the fire of the enemy. The Twentieth Brigade encountering Breckenridge's whole division was compelled to re-cross, which was effected after dark without serious loss. On the 30th the day was passed in artillery firing and sharp skirmishing. On the 31st most terrific fighting occurred. The right wing of our army was driven back two miles, and the Twentieth Brigade was double-quicked a mile and a half to reinforce it, and taking position on the extreme right of the whole army, immediately engaged two rebel brigades. The Seventy-Third fought for twenty minutes at very close range, losing more than one-third of the number engaged; and then, charging, drove the force in its front from the field, and in turn was compelled to fall back a short distance by a rebel brigade on its flank. But the enemy's advance was checked and the right wing and army saved by the desperate fighting made at this point. Gen. Rosecrans complimented the regiment, in person, immediately after the battle and recognized these facts. More or less fighting, with some loss to the regiment, occurred on the 1st and 2d of January, 1863. During these operations the regiment was at the front and under fire for six days, and on the 3d of January, being completely exhausted, it was placed in reserve. The enemy retreated the same

day. During this battle the regiment occupied, at different times, the following important positions: the extreme right of the whole army, the extreme left and the centre. Every member of the color guard, except the color bearer, was either killed or wounded. The regiment lost twenty-two killed, forty-six wounded and thirty-six missing.

On the 10th of April, the regiment was assigned to Col. A. D. Streight's "Independent Provisional Brigade," organized and mounted for the purpose of penetrating into the enemy's country and cutting his communications. Embarking at Nashville on steamers it moved down the Cumberland and up the Tennessee river, disembarking at Eastport, Mississippi. The brigade was mounted by impressments from the country and moved by land to Tuscumbia, Alabama, in company with Gen. Dodge's Division of the Sixteenth Army Corps. On the 28th of April, the "Independent Provisional Briagde" left Tuscumbia on its perilous expedition. Gen. Dodge's division was to have co-operated by a movement eastward, but failed of success. On the morning of the 30th of April, at Day's Gap, Alabama, the Provisional Brigade, numbering fifteen hundred, was attacked by four thousand cavalry, under Generals Forrest and Roddy. The Seventy-Third occupied the left flank of the line formed and gallantly repulsed a fierce charge made by the enemy, some of whom charged within twenty feet of its colors. The whole brigade then charged the enemy's line and drove him from the field, capturing two fine pieces of artillery. The brigade at once pushed southward to execute its mission, but the enemy, having collected his scattered cavalry, overtook and attacked the brigade late in the afternoon, at Crooked Creek, Alabama. A spirited engagement was kept up until night closed the battle, with a loss to the Seventy-Third during the day of twenty-three killed and wounded. The enemy, however, was repulsed with a heavy loss.

On the 2d of May the brigade was again attacked at Blount's Farm, Alabama. The Seventy-Third bore the brunt of this fight, and here the gallant Colonel Gilbert Hathaway fell mortally wounded while at the head of and cheering on his men. On the 3d of May, Colonel Streight, being nearly out of ammunition and exhausted by five days' incessant traveling and skirmishing, and surrounded by superior forces, surrendered his brigade to the enemy, at Cedar Bluffs, Alabama, on most honorable conditions, which, after surrender, were basely violated by the enemy. The men were soon forwarded north and exchanged. The officers were kept in close confinement nearly two years, with the exception of a few who were specially exchanged or escaped.

The men of the regiment were kept in parole camp for several months and then sent to Tennessee, where, on the 28th of March, 1864, Major Wade, being released from rebel prison, assumed the command of the regiment. During the spring of 1864 the regiment was engaged in

Seventy-Third Regiment Infantry—Continued

guarding the Nashville and Chattanooga Railroad, and during the summer it was placed on duty picketing the Tennessee river from Draper's Ferry to Limestone Point, with headquarters at Triana. While performing this duty many encounters occurred between parties of the enemy and detachments from the regiment, in nearly all of which success attended the union arms. For its bravery and efficiency in this line of duty, the regiment was several times complimented by Gen. Granger. During this time and until April, 1865, the regiment was attached to the First Brigade, Fourth Division, Twentieth Army Corps.

In the latter part of September, 1864, the regiment, after having been engaged in defending Prospect, Tennessee, during Wheeler's raid, was ordered to Decatur, Alabama, and from there to Athens, Alabama, which place Forrest had captured a few days before with a garrison of six hundred. The enemy abandoning the place, Lieut. Col. Wade was ordered to hold it, and at once went to work to put it in condition for defense, constructing a bomb-proof in the fort, etc. At three o'clock in the afternoon of the 1st of October the pickets of the Seventy-Third were driven in by the enemy, who numbered four thousand cavalry and four pieces of artillery, under command of General Buford. The garrison numbered five hundred men and two pieces of artillery. Skirmishing continued during the rest of the day. At six o'clock next morning the enemy opened with a fierce artillery fire, which was kept up without intermission for two hours. The rebel firing was extremely accurate. Our artillery spiritedly replied, inflicting much loss on the enemy, while the bomb-proof affording ample protection to our forces, no loss was sustained by the garrison. At eight o'clock A. M., General Buford sent in a flag of truce and demanded the surrender of the place, which was promptly refused. So soon as the flag of truce disappeared the fire upon the enemy was resumed. The enemy, repulsed at every point, retired in haste.

On the 26th of October Gen. Hood appeared before and invested Decatur, Alabama, with an army of thirty-five thousand men. The Seventy-Third had previously been ordered to that place to assist in its defense. The Union garrison numbered five thousand and so stubborn was the resistance they made to the large army investing the place, that after four days' fighting, Hood raised the siege and withdrew his army, saying that "it would cost more to take the place than it was worth." In the engagement the Seventy-Third bore an honorable part, losing one killed and six wounded.

Part of the winter of 1864 was passed in Stevenson, Alabama, and in January, 1865, it was moved to Huntsville and then placed on duty along the line of the Mobile and Charleston Railroad, with headquarters at Larkinsville, Alabama. While upon this line, skirmishing with the enemy was of almost daily occurrence. On the 16th of February a detachment of twenty men repulsed an attacking party of rebel cavalry, killing and wounding five and taking one wounded prisoner. On the 30th of April, fifteen men from company "D" attacked thirty rebel cavalry, killing two and wounding two, without loss to themselves. Other skirmishes occurred in which the regiment lost four killed and two wounded. The regiment remained on this duty until the summer of 1865, when it proceeded to Nashville, where on the 1st of July, 1865, it was mustered out of service. Returning home the Seventy-Third was publicly received in the State House grove at Indianapolis and addressed by Governor Morton and Gen. Hovey.

The remaining recruits were transferred to the Twenty-Ninth Indiana, with which regiment they still continue to serve, it being stationed at Marietta, Georgia, at the close of this sketch—November, 1865.

Company F

SERGEANT—Horace Gamble

Seventy-Fourth Regiment Infantry

(THREE YEARS' SERVICE)

The Seventy-Fourth Regiment was raised in the Tenth Congressional District and was partially organized at Fort Wayne. Proceeding to Indianapolis eight companies were mustered into service at that place, on the 21st of August, 1862, and at once moved to Louisville, Kentucky, under command of Col. CHARLES W. CHAPMAN. The command was then sent to Bowling Green where it remained until the 5th of September and then returned to Louisville. On the 1st of October it marched from that place with the Second Brigade of the First Division (Schoepf's) of the Army of the Ohio, in pursuit of Bragg, and participated in that campaign. It reached Gallatin, Tennessee, on the 10th of November, and afterwards moved to Castillian Springs, Tennessee, where, on the 4th of December, Companies "C" and "K" joined the regiment, making the organization complete.

These two companies were left at Indianapolis to fill up their ranks and complete their organization. On the 27th of August they moved to Louisville and from thence started to Bowling Green to join the regiment, but were stopped at Munfordsville on the 30th, to assist in the defense of that place. On the 13th of September they were sent down the Railroad to Cave City, but returned the same day on account of the advance of Bragg's army. At four o'clock, A. M., on the 14th, they were sent out as skirmishers to meet Bragg's advance, which they fought for one hour and a half, and then were ordered back to the main works. They afterwards took part in the engagement at that place until surrendered, after a gallant defense, against greatly superior numbers, on the 17th of September. They were paroled and sent to Bowling Green and thence to Brandenburg and New Albany. On the 17th of November they were exchanged and joined the regiment as before stated.

On the 7th of December the regiment aided in driving Morgan's rebel forces across the Cumberland river at Hartsville, and on the 25th of December marched northward from Gallatin after Morgan's command. Overtaking it on the 30th of December, its brigade drove them across the Rolling Fork of Salt River. Upon the re-organization of the Army of the Cumberland the regiment was assigned to the Second Brigade, Third Division of the Fourteenth Corps. On the 13th of January, 1863, it moved from Gallatin to Nashville, and next day to Lavergne, where it remained until the 3d of June, when it moved to Triune. From this place it marched on the campaign against Tullahoma on the 23d of June, which place was entered on the 6th of July, after skirmishing with the enemy at Hoover's Gap on the 26th of June. On the 11th of August, the regiment moved from Tullahoma and participated in the campaign against Chattanooga. On the 1st of September it crossed the Tennessee river, and on the 12th skirmished with the enemy at Dug Gap, Georgia. The Seventy-Fourth was one of the first regiments engaged at Chicamauga on the 19th of Sep-

tember, and, with the Tenth Indiana, was the last to leave the field. In this battle it fought in Croxton's Brigade, Brannan's Division of Thomas' Corps, losing twenty killed, one hundred and twenty-nine wounded and eleven missing; total one hundred and sixty.

On the 22d of September the Seventy-Fourth reached Chattanooga, and was constantly skirmishing in front of that place during its siege. It was in the charge at Mission Ridge on the 25th of November, losing two killed, and sixteen wounded; total eighteen. After this victory it followed the enemy as far as Ringold, Georgia, and returned to Chattanooga on the 27th. Upon the reorganization of the army under Gen. Thomas, the regiment was attached to the Eighth Brigade, Third Division of the Fourteenth Army Corps, and it remained in the same organization until mustered out of service. It participated in the reconnoisance of its corps to Buzzard's Roost on the 22d of February, 1864. Returning to Ringold on the 26th of February it remained there until the 10th of May, when it marched with Sherman's army on its Atlanta campaign. In this campaign it was engaged almost constantly in skirmishing until the 1st of September, participating in the fight at Dallas, Kenesaw and Lost Mountain, Chattahoochie River, near Peach Tree Creek and many other places around Atlanta. Lieut. Col. Myron Baker, commanding the regiment, was killed in front of Atlanta on the 5th of August, and prior to September 1st, the regiment lost on this campaign forty-six men and officers. On that day the brigade to which it was attached carried the enemy's works at Jonesboro, Georgia, capturing four pieces of artillery and over seven hundred men. The regiment, in this engagement, lost thirteen killed and forty wounded; total fifty-three. Many of the wounded afterwards died.

The regiment was with the corps in its pursuit of Hood's army northward from Atlanta from the 3d to the 25th of October. On the 15th of November it marched with the Army of Georgia and made the campaign through Milledgeville to Savannah, which place it reached on the 22d of December. While on this march the regiment had a skirmish with Wheeler's cavalry at Rocky Creek Church, on the 2d of December, driving the enemy easily. On the 20th of January, 1865, it moved from Savannah and crossed the Savannah river at Sister's Ferry on the 5th of February. It marched through South Carolina and North Carolina to Fayetteville, and thence to Goldsboro and Raleigh, where it arrived on the 13th of April. On the 30th it started for Washington, encamping near Richmond on the 7th of May, and arriving at Washington on the 19th of May, where it was mustered out of service on the 9th of June, 1865. On the 16th it reached Indianapolis and was publicly received by Governor Morton and addressed by him at a reception given to returned regiments in the Capitol grounds.

Seventy-Fourth Regiment Infantry

(THREE YEARS' SERVICE)

Company C

Captain—CARL C. KINGSBURY
First Lieutenant—JOEL F. KINNEY
Second Lieutenant—ANNANIAS DAVIS
First Sergeant—WILLIAM H. ANDERSON
Sergeants—JOHN D. OLDS
      FRISBEE T. BECK
      ELI G. ANDERSON
      WILLIAM DARKER
Corporals—ADAM LEWIS
      GEORGE A. CRAW
      JOHN PETTIJOHN
      JEREMIAH A. SHORBE
      RICHARD W. DICKENSON
      JAMES K. BRADLEY
      WILLIAM H. BRY
      ELI LAYMAN
Musicians—CYRUS H. BARNES
      JAMES RAY
Wagoner—JAMES T. BROWN

PRIVATES

John W. Bowers
John H. Brown
Jonah Carson
William Fogwell
John Fitzgerald
William Gillend
John W. Hilton
George H. Kall
John Kridler
Isaiah Magner
Joseph Makins
Joseph Hyton
Lorenzo Nickerson
Joshua Nickerson
Benjamin W. Powell
Joseph Rulo
Joseph B. Reed
Daniel Van Tassel
Emanuel Wyers
Martin Wagner
Jacob Wyres
Stephen Walton
Samuel A. Bauserman

Michael Barrone
Alexander F. Brown
Enoch B. Barnhard
Nicholas Dolan
George T. Edwards
John B. Geahart
John Hallien
John W. Hathaway
Adam Hass
Benjamin Linnscott
Robert M. McCune
John B. Magner
Jacob W. Miller
Jacob Maize
John Magner
William H. Moses
John W. McMillen
Thomas Quicksell
Alfred Roach
Adam Row
John B. Richards
John Swank

Thomas Tansey
Andrew Van Horn
George Van Buskirk
James Watson
Jacob W. Barnhard
Samuel Duffen
Samuel Flutter
Oliver J. Gronour
Robert J. Goble
George Linnscott
William C. Lewis
Edward Leasure
Eli Magner
Jacob W. Miller
Nelson H. Orn
William Park
John H. Simpson
Samuel Simonette
Daniel Williams
John Walton
Calvin A. Anderson
Jonathan C. Chasteen

Clark F. Crebelius
George J. James
Andrew J. Mills
John Peacock
James Runnion
Charles F. Redman
David Shinn
Silas Corson
Thomas J. Curtis
Joseph H. Dearborn
Benjamin Fennimore
David S. Hamilton
Nicholas Hockbon
Andrew J. Mills
Richard Mills
Edward W. Shadell
Thomas W. Smith
William J. Sibert
Francis M. Byfield
Thomas Corson
George Jossee
Nathan Sanders

Seventy-Fifth Regiment Infantry

(THREE YEARS' SERVICE)

The Companies composing the Seventy-Fifth Regiment were raised in the Eleventh Congressional District, the camp of rendezvous being at Wabash. On the 19th of August, 1862, the regiment was mustered into service, with JOHN U. PETIT as Colonel, and moved to Louisville, Kentucky, on the 21st, one thousand and thirty-six strong. From thence it proceeded to Lebanon, and upon the advance of Bragg's army returned to Louisville. In the campaign that followed it took an active part, marching to Frankfort, Scottsville, and Gallatin, and then back to Cave City in pursuit of Morgan's forces. Most of the winter of 1862 was passed in camp near Gallatin, and in January, 1863, the regiment moved to Murfreesboro, where it remained until June 24th, serving in Gen. Reynold's Division and engaging in scouting and other arduous duty. During this time it served in the Second Brigade, Third Division, Fourteenth Army Corps, which was known as the "Indiana Brigade," being composed of the Seventy-Fifth, Eighty-Seventh and One Hundred and First Indiana regiments.

On the 24th of June the Seventy-Fifth started towards Tullahoma, and on the march engaged in the battle at Hoover's Gap. It was the first regiment to enter the rebel works at Tullahoma, about the 1st of July. Marching with Rosecrans' army towards Chattanooga it crossed the Tennessee and, on the 19th and 20th of September, participated in the battle of Chicamauga, losing seventeen killed and one hundred and seven wounded; total one hundred and twenty-four. After this engagement the regiment returned to Chattanooga where it remained some months, engaging in the battle of Mission Ridge on the 25th of November and losing five killed and seventeen wounded; total twenty-two. The winter of 1863 was passed in the vicinity of Chattanooga, and early in the spring of 1864 the regiment moved to Ringold, Georgia, preparatory to engaging in the Atlanta campaign.

On the 27th of April, 1864, all the troops composing Sherman's Army were ordered to concentrate at Chattanooga. On the 7th of May Thomas occupied Laurel Hill. On the 12th the whole army, except Howard's Corps, moved through Snake Creek Gap on Resacca. On the 15th the battle of Resacca was fought and the same night the rebel army retreated across the Oostanaula. Near Adairsville the rear of the rebel army was encountered, and a sharp fight ensued. On the 28th the enemy made an assault at Dallas, but met with a bloody repulse. On the 27th of June an assault was made upon the enemy's position on Kenesaw, without success. On the 2d of July Kenesaw was abandoned by the enemy. On the 4th, Thomas demonstrated so strongly on the enemy's communications as to cause him to fall back to the Chattahoochie river, and cross the river on the 9th. On the 20th the enemy sallied from his works in force and fought the battle of Peach Tree Creek. On the 22d a general battle was fought in front of Atlanta, the rebels being defeated. On the 28th the enemy made another assault upon our besieging lines, but were driven back in confusion. The siege of Atlanta vigorously progressed, with constant skirmishing. On the 25th of August the bulk of Sherman's army moved by a circuit around Atlanta, struck its southern communications near Fairburn, destroying the West Point Railway and Macon Railroad. This caused the enemy to evacuate Atlanta on the 2d of September. On the 4th the army moved slowly back to Atlanta, and rested in clean, healthy camps. Thus, after four months' campaign, ended one of the greatest achievements of the war.

During the Atlanta campaign the regiment marched and fought with the Second Brigade, Third Division, Fourteenth Army Corps, engaging in the battles at Dalton, Resacca, Dallas, Kenesaw Mountain, Peach Tree Creek, and Jonesboro. After the occupation of Atlanta, the reigment rested for a brief period.

On the 1st of October Hood's army marched to strike Sherman's rear. On the 4th the regiment moved from Atlanta in pursuit, and marched with its corps to Pine Mountain, arriving in that place in time to threaten the rear of French's rebel division, then investing the garrison at Allatoona. The enemy retreated to Dallas, and thence marched for Resacca and Dalton. The regiment marched in pursuit as far as Gaylesville, when it halted for a time in the rich valley of the Chattooga. Then returning to Atlanta it started from that city on the 16th of November with Sherman's army in its famous "march to the sea," reaching Savannah in December. In January, 1865, the regiment marched with its corps through the Carolinas to Goldsboro, North Carolina, participating in the battles of Bentonville and Fayetteville. From Goldsboro it moved to Raleigh with the advance of the army and engaged in a skirmish at Smithfield, which was the last action had with the enemy in North Carolina. After the surrender of Johnson's army it marched to Richmond, Virginia, and thence to Washington, D. C., where, on the 8th of June, 1865, it was mustered out of service. Returning to Indiana, with four hundred and thirty men and twenty officers, it was present at a public reception given to returned regiments, in the Capitol grounds, at Indianapolis, on the 14th of June. While in Washington the remaining recruits were transferred to the Forty-Second Indiana and continued to serve with that organization until its muster out of service, at Louisville, Kentucky, on the 21st of July, 1865.

Seventy-Fifth Regiment Infantry

(THREE YEARS' SERVICE)

Company H

First Lieutenant—WILLIAM McGINNIS
Sergeants—WILLIAM RILEY
    ABNER A. KELSEY
Corporals—SYLVESTER STROCK
    PETER MULRINE
    GEORGE W. ILER
    JONATHAN L. WILKERSON
Musicians—AMOS EARLYWINE
    JAMES LIGGET
Wagoner—KYLE GASKILL

PRIVATES

James Biggs
William Barett
Isaac Barnes
John Crow ,
Nathan Chaney
James Douglas
Andrew Garrett
David Hamilton
William Koontz
Ulrich J. Loop
Samuel Ligget
Benjamin F. Piatt
James Robinett
Isaac A Rinehart
Jackson Scott
John G. Thompson
Francis J. Wilson

Leroy Welch
Henry Biggs
John W. Chaney
Clark Dewitt
Thomas L. Dewitt
Michael Dennis
Isaac N. Kinnan
Daniel K. Shoup
Hiram Slain
John Sites
John Arick
Wesley Andrews
Henry C. Bowman
Robert B. Gatewood
John H. Lowman
Joseph Robinson
Isaiah Wilkerson

Seventy-Seventh Regiment

(FOURTH CAVALRY)

The Fourth Cavalry (Seventy-Seventh) Regiment was organized at Indianapolis on the 22d of August, 1862, with Isaac P. Gray as Colonel. On the completion of its organization the aspect of affairs in Kentucky was so threatening that the regiment was divided, four companies being sent under command of Major John A. Platter to Henderson, Kentucky, and the remaining companies to Louisville, from whence they were ordered into the interior, where they were joined by Col. Gray.

The battalion under command of Major Platter had a skirmish with the enemy at Madisonville, Kentucky, on the 26th of August, and again at Mount Washington on the 1st of October, in which a number were killed and wounded. On the 5th of October it engaged the rebels at Madisonville, suffering some loss. In the spring of 1863 this battalion joined the other companies, and after this the regiment served together, with the exception of Company "C," which became the escort for Gen. A. J. Smith, and followed the fortunes of that officer's command.

During the invasion of Bragg, a portion of the battalion under the command of Col. Gray, went into camp for a brief period near Madison, Indiana, and moved from thence to Vevay, near which place it crossed the Ohio river and moved, on a tour of duty, through Owen, Henry and adjoining counties in Kentucky, reaching Frankfort about the 24th of October. Soon after the companies of this battalion were stationed at Gallatin, from whence they moved after John H. Morgan's forces towards Green river. On the 25th of December the battalion fought Morgan near Munfordsville and defeated him, suffering a slight loss. Moving into Tennessee in January, 1863, it reached Murfreesboro in February, in which vicinity it operated for some months, fighting the enemy at Rutherford's Creek, on the 10th of March. On the 28th of March it was actively engaged in feeling the enemy near Murfreesboro. At this time the battalion was commanded by Col. L. S. Shuler.

The regiment, now united, moved with Rosecrans in the campaign toward Tullahoma and Chattanooga, participating in the battle of Chicamauga, on the 19th and 20th of September, and again engaging the enemy on the 23d of September. Crossing the Tennessee, it fought the rebels at Fayetteville, Tennessee, on the 1st of November, losing a few of its members.

The regiment marched into East Tennessee early in December, where it remained during the winter of 1863 and 1864. During this campaign it held the advanced position in all the cavalry movements, and was conspicuously engaged in the battles at Mossy Creek, Talbot's and Dandridge, for which it was highly complimented in the reports of the brigade and division commanders. On the 27th of January, 1864, a severe fight occurred at Fair Garden, between the division to which it was attached and two rebel divisions, the latter having been driven during the day eight miles. Captain Rosencrantz, with the second battalion of the Fourth Cavalry, dismounted as skirmishers, charged with the Second Indiana and First Wisconsin Cavalry (also dismounted) on the enemy's skirmishers. Major Purdy, with the first battalion, supported by Lilly's Eighteenth Indiana Battery, and the remaining four companies of the Fourth Cavalry, were ordered to a "sabre charge" on a rebel battery. This charge was led by Lieut. Col. Leslie, and resulted in the capture of the battery, one battle flag and more prisoners than the charging party had men engaged. The enemy were completely routed, and fled in disorder to the mountains. Lieut. Col. Leslie fell while gallantly leading his men on to victory, pierced through the breast with a rebel bullet. The other losses to the regiment were but few.

In March the regiment arrived at Cleveland, Tennessee, and in May moved with the cavalry of Sherman's army in the campaign against Atlanta. On the 9th of May it fought the enemy at Varnell's Station, Georgia, and on the 2d of June it had a skirmish near Burnt Church. It next moved on the McCook raid, participating in the fight at Newman, on the 31st of July, and in all the movements of that expedition.

After the capture of Atlanta it marched into Tennessee, and engaged the enemy at Columbia, Tennessee, in October. In November it was stationed near Louisville, serving with the Second Brigade of the First Cavalry Division of the Cavalry Corps of the Military Division of the Mississippi. In January, 1865, it was in the vicinity of Nashville, and in the following month at Waterloo, Alabama. Moving into Alabama with Gen. Wilson's forces, it participated in the active campaign in that state and Georgia, engaging in the battles of Plantersville and Selma. Leaving Macon, Georgia, in May, it reached Nashville, and went into the Provisional Cavalry Camp at Edgefield, where it remained until mustered out of service on the 29th of June, 1865. After its muster out the regiment remained at Nashville a few days until it was finally discharged and paid, when the organization was broken up, and the officers and men returned to their respective homes without coming to the State Capital in a body.

Company "C" was detailed to serve as escort to Gen. A. J. Smith, and engaged in all the operations of the command of that officer, including the campaign and siege of Vicksburg, and the Red River expedition. During the year 1864 it returned to the regiment, and served with it until its final discharge.

Seventy-Seventh Regiment

(FOURTH CAVALRY)

Farrier—William F. Brown
William H. Ferguson

PRIVATES

Hiram H. Hughes
James Brown (*Company I*)

Eighty-Seventh Regiment Infantry

(THREE YEARS' SERVICE)

The companies composing the Eighty-Seventh Regiment were recruited in the Ninth Congressional District. The regiment was organized at South Bend on the 28th of August, 1862, and at once moved to Indianapolis, where, on the 31st of August, it was mustered into the three years' service, with KLINE G. SHRYOCK as Colonel. On the day of its muster it left Indianapolis and proceeded to Louisville, Kentucky, where, on the 1st of September, it was assigned to Gen. Burbridge's Brigade. On the 1st of October it was transferred to the Third Brigade, Third Division, of the 14th Army Corps, and with it took part in Gen. Buell's campaign through Kentucky. It was under fire at Springfield on the 6th of October, and on the 8th of that month engaged in the battle at Perryville.

After marching and countermarching, through Kentucky, the regiment encamped near Mitchellville, Tennessee, in November. During this campaign the loss to the regiment was light, not exceeding six killed and wounded. After this the Eighty-Seventh occupied camps at Tunnel Hill, Pilot Knob, and Gallatin, Tennessee, and on the 29th of January, 1863, it moved to Concord Church, south of Nashville. On the 4th of March it engaged in a skirmish at Chapel Hill against Gen. Forrest's command, after which it moved to Triune. On the 28th of March Col. Shryock resigned, whereupon Lieut. Col. Newell Gleason was promoted Colonel, which rank that officer held until the close of Sherman's last campaign, when he was brevetted a Brigadier General.

On the 23d of June, the Eighty-Seventh moved with the Army of the Cumberland, and engaged in the summer campaign against Tullahoma, being under fire at Hoover's Gap, and being with that part of the Army which entered Tullahoma. It then marched to Winchester, Tennessee, and thence over the mountains to Battle Creek, on the Tennessee river. In the fall campaign against Chattanooga the regiment participated, crossing the Tennessee and marching over several high mountain ranges. It bore a conspicuous part in the bloody battle of Chicamauga, on the 19th and 20th of September, losing of its number forty killed, one hundred and forty-two wounded, and eight missing, among whom were eight officers killed and four wounded—being more than half of all the officers and men engaged. The regiment remained in Chattanooga during the siege of that place, and upon the reorganization of the Army of the Cumberland, it formed a part of the Second Brigade, Third Division, Fourteenth Army Corps. On the 25th of November the regiment was in the front line of its brigade in the storming of Mission Ridge, and lost, in killed and wounded, sixteen men. After the victory it engaged in pursuit of the enemy to Ringold, Georgia. On the 22d of February, 1864, it participated in an expedition against Dalton, and skirmished with the enemy in front of Buzzard Roost, near that place. Returning from this expedition it went into camp at Ringold, where it remained until the 7th of May.

In the laborious campaign against Atlanta, the Eighty-Seventh participated in all the principal battles and skirmishes, confronting the enemy at Rocky Face, Resacca, Cassville, near Dallas, Kenesaw, Peach Tree Creek, and before Atlanta. In a charge upon the enemy's works at Utoy's Creek, in front of Atlanta, on the 4th of August, the loss of the regiment was seventeen killed and wounded. It also participated in the battle of Jonesboro, on the 1st of September, and then moved into Atlanta, where it went into camp for a brief period.

Moving with its corps from Atlanta on the 3d of October, it participated in the campaign in pursuit of Hood through Northern Georgia, marching to Resacca, and thence through Snake Creek Gap to the Chattooga Valley. From thence it marched to Gaylesville, Alabama, and then returned to Atlanta, going by way of Rome and Kingston, Georgia. On the 16th of November the regiment left Atlanta with the Fourteenth Corps, and marching through Decatur and Covington, took the road to Milledgeville. Passing through Shady Dale and Eatonton Factories, it went into camp on the 23d, in the vicinity of Milledgeville. On the 24th the march towards Savannah was resumed, the regiment moving by way of Black Spring, Fair Play, and Long's Bridge to Saundersville, which was reached on the morning of the 26th. The advance guard of Wheeler's cavalry was met near that place and skirmished with, but offered no serious opposition. Marching to the left of the Georgia Central Railroad, and crossing the Ogeechee, the regiment reached Louisville on the 28th, where it rested until the 1st of December. It then moved toward Jacksonboro, going by way of Reynolds, Thomas' Station and Waynesboro, destroying a portion of the railroad and skirmishing with Wheeler's cavalry near the latter place. From Jacksonboro it marched to Hudson's Ferry on the Savannah river, reaching there on the 6th. On the 9th Ebenezer Church was reached, and on the 10th the immediate defenses of Savannah were approached, and the siege began. After the evacuation of Savannah, on the 21st of December, the Eighty-Seventh marched into the city and remained there until the 30th of January, 1865.

The regiment participated in the campaign made through the Carolinas, marching with the Fourteenth Corps to Goldsboro, North Carolina, where it remained in camp until the 10th of April, 1865. It then moved to Smithfield, and took part in the capture of that town. From thence it proceeded to Raleigh and then to a point near Holly Springs, where it camped until after the surrender of General Johnston's rebel army. From North Carolina the regiment marched to Richmond, Virginia, and thence to Washington City, where it participated in the grand review of Sherman's army. On the 10th of June, 1865, the Eighty-Seventh was mustered out of service at Washington and proceeded to Indianapolis, where, on the 21st of June, it was publicly welcomed home by Governor Morton, in behalf of the State, at a reception meeting held in the Capitol grounds, at which addresses were also made by Generals Hovey and Gleason.

The remaining recruits, whose terms of service would not expire until after the 1st of October, 1865, were, on the 10th of June, transferred to the Forty-Second Indiana, in which organization they continued to serve until its final muster out of service at Louisville, Kentucky, on the 21st of July, 1865.

The total casualties of the regiment have been as follows—Killed in action, forty-seven; wounded in action, one hundred and ninety-eight; died from wounds and disease, two hundred and fourteen.

Eighty-Seventh Regiment Infantry

(THREE YEARS' SERVICE)

Company K

PRIVATES

Samuel M. Hench

Eighty-Eighth Regiment Infantry

The Eighty-Eighth Regiment was recruited from the Fourth Congressional District, rendezvoused at Fort Wayne, and was mustered into the service on the 29th of August, 1862, with GEORGE HUMPHREY as Colonel. At this time great excitement existed in Louisville, Kentucky, in consequence of the approach of the rebel army under E. Kirby Smith, and every effort was being made by the Governor and military authorities to dispatch troops to the threatened points. The Eighty-Eighth was at once ordered to Louisville, and arrived there on the 30th. Here it was assigned to a position in the defenses of that city, and remained until the 1st of October, when it was assigned to the Seventeenth Brigade Rousseau's Division, and marched with the Army of the Ohio in pursuit of Bragg. At the battle of Perryville, October 8th, its brigade formed the right of Rousseau's division and against this the rebels directed their fiercest assaults. The brigade though suffering a frightful loss held the enemy in check until night closed the battle. The regiment was complimented by General Rousseau for its steadiness under fire.

The enemy retreated during the night following the battle, and the regiment joined in the pursuit as far as Crab Orchard. It then returned by the way of Lebanon, and marched to Tyree Springs and Nashville, Tennessee.

During the month of November the army was reorganized, and the Eighty-Eighth assigned to the Second Brigade (Beatty's), First Division (Rousseau's), Army of the Cumberland. The regiment moved with the main army, on the 25th of December, in the advance upon Murfreesboro, which resulted in the battle of Stone River, on the 31st of December, 1862, and 1st and 2d of January, 1863. In this battle it was severely engaged. Its division moved to the support of the right at its most critical moment, and meeting the exultant rush of the rebels with a withering fire, successfully checked his advance. Among the heroic deeds which crowned that battle none surpassed the grand efforts of Rousseau's splendid division. On the evening of the 3d Beatty's brigade advanced, drove the enemy from cover and carried his entrenchments, being the final charge of the battle of Stone River. That night the rebels abandoned Murfreesboro. The Eighty-Eighth lost in this battle eight killed and forty-eight wounded, a total loss of fifty-six. On the 5th of January, the regiment marched with its division into Murfreesboro.

The regiment remained in camp in the vicinity of Murfreesboro until the 24th of June; at this time the Army of the Cumberland commenced a forward movement, marching by the Shelbyville and Manchester roads. The rebel pickets were encountered a short distance from Murfreesboro, and fell back before the advance of the center to Hoover's Gap, where they held a strong position in a narrow, winding hollow, through a chain of hills. Here a brisk fight took place, and the rebels were handsomely whipped. The regiment was engaged in this fight, and also in the severe skirmishes at Tullahoma, Hillsboro and Elk River. The command crossed the Cumberland, Sand and Lookout ranges of mountains, and on the 11th of September its division had a severe engagement with the rebel General Polk at Dug Gap, Georgia.

On the 18th of September the regiment moved with its corps along Chicamauga creek to Crawfish Springs, and thence to Kelley's farm, arriving there at daylight on the 19th. This movement resulted in the battle of Chicamauga, September 19th, 20th and 21st. Our division advancing upon what was supposed to be an isolated force of the enemy, at first drove it some distance, taking many prisoners; but soon, with overwhelming numbers, the enemy forced us back, and the battle raged furiously along the whole line. For two days the corps of General Thomas, to which the regiment was attached, fought gallantly against the charging columns of the enemy, and on the third day formed the rear guard, and fell back toward Chattanooga, where the army concentrated.

On the night of the 24th of November the Eighty-Eighth moved with the command of Gen. Hooker, scaled Lookout Mountain and "fought among the clouds." On the following day it was engaged in the charge of Mission Ridge, being among the first to plant the Union flag on the rebel works. On the 27th the regiment was engaged at Graysville and Ringold, and assisted in capturing a rebel battery. On the 22d of February, 1864, the regiment marched with a reconnoisance in force, under General Palmer, towards Dalton, and took possession of Tunnel Hill, Georgia.

Early in the month of May, 1864, Sherman's army, which had been grouped around Chattanooga, confronting the rebel army under the rebel Gen. Johnson, moved on its campaign against Atlanta. The Eighty-Eighth marched with the army, and participated in the many battles, severe skirmishes and fatiguing movements, which crowned that campaign with success, and resulted in the occupation of Atlanta. The regiment was engaged at Buzzard Roost, Resacca, Dallas, Kenesaw Mountain, Peach Tree Creek, Atlanta and Utoy Creek, and accompanied the main army when it made its triumphal entrance into Atlanta.

On the 3d of October, the rebel General Hood, grown frantic with repeated defeats, made one of the most stupendous military blunders, swung his army in Sherman's rear, struck the railroad at Big Shanty, and, as Hood said, "fixed his claws upon the State Road," with a promise to never let go his hold." And on the same date, a portion of Sherman's veterans moved to drive Hood gently north into the kind embrace of Thomas. The regiment joined in the pursuit, and after a march of over three hundred miles, returned to Kingston, Georgia, on the 12th of November. Upon arriving there, Gen. Sherman at once cut loose from his communications with the North, and commenced the famous "march to the sea." The Eighty-Eighth marched with the column that penetrated the enemy's country by the way of Milledgeville, Louisville and Millen, and, upon the 21st of October, the "lost army" entered the city of Savannah, having marched three hundred and sixty miles without serious resistance.

On the 26th of January, 1865, the Eighty-Eighth marched with its corps from Savannah, moving up on the Georgia side of the Savannah river, by way of Springfield, and on the 7th of February the crossing was completed with great difficulty and labor, owing to the "bottom" being

Eighty-Eighth Regiment Infantry—Continued

three miles in width. It then marched for the Charleston and Augusta railway, passing through Blackville and destroying the railway west of Branchville. Crossing the South Edisto on the 13th, and the North Edisto on the 14th, the regiment marched to Lexington, and from thence moved to Winnsboro, crossing the Saluda river west of Columbia on the 17th, and the Broad river, near Allston, on the 19th. The Spartansburg railway was then destroyed for fourteen miles to the northward of Allston, and on the 20th Little river was crossed, and on the 21st Winnsboro was reached. On the 22d the regiment marched in the direction of Charlotte as far as Blackstocks, and then, facing to the right, marched for the Catawba river, which was reached the same evening. Owing to the swelling of the river from heavy rains, the regiment was compelled to remain on the left bank of the Catawba for several days. Hanging Rock was reached on the 1st of March, from whence the Eighty-Eighth moved to Horton's Ferry on Lynch's Creek, and on the 5th crossed the great Pedee at Sneedsboro, North Carolina. On the 6th it moved by Love's Bridge, over the Lumber river, in the direction of Fayetteville, crossing it on the 7th of March, and marched to within twenty miles of Fay-

etteville on the 9th, ten miles nearer on the 10th, and on the 11th entered the town. Here it remained until the 14th of March, when it moved in the direction of Goldsboro, taking Averysboro on the march. The regiment was present at the sanguinary battle of Bentonville, on the 19th of March. The command reached Goldsboro on the 22d of March, having marched five hundred and two miles since leaving Savannah. On the 10th of April the regiment left Goldsboro, and marched by way of Raleigh to Cape Fear river, and was at the latter point at the time of Johnston's surrender to Gen. Grant. The regiment marched from Cape Fear river, by the way of Richmond, Virginia, to Washington City, making the distance marched from Goldsboro, North Carolina, to Washington, four hundred and fifty-two miles.

Upon the 7th of June, 1865, the regiment was mustered out of the service of the United States at Washington, D. C., and at once left for Indianapolis. Upon the 13th of June it was greeted with an ovation in the State House Grove, and welcomed by eloquent and able addresses from Governor Morton and others, and its members dispersed to their several homes.

Officers

Colonel—GEORGE HUMPHREY
Lieutenant Colonel—CYRUS E. BRYANT
Adjutants—HARTMAN B. DUBARRY
        ALLEN H. DOUGALL
Quartermaster—IRA RUPERT

Company B

Captain—CHARLES S. TRUE

Company C

Captain—NELSON P. GUFFY
First Lieutenant—PHILIP W. SILVER
Second Lieutenant—LOUIS NEILL
First Sergeant—CHARLES A. WHITAKER
Sergeants—WILLIAM B. HENDERSON
        CHARLES DAVIS
        EDWARD KICKLEY
        WILLIAM S. JONES
Corporals—DORSEY SCUDDER
        WILLIAM C. HOLLOPETER
        WILLIAM DOUGLASS
        JOHN JONES
        JAMES WAUGH
        LEWIS SWEET
        OSCAR S. BARNEY
        JULIAN BEQUETT
Musicians—ANDREW BESACK
        JOHN H. COOK
Wagoner— DAVID H. PLUNK

Company C

PRIVATES

William H. Barnes
Russel A. Copp
Anthony Dreker
John Douglas
Edwin Felts
John H. Flemming
Oliver C. Graylass
Jeremiah Gorham
Abraham Henderson
Elias Heir
Samuel N. Ingraham
Frank Kickley
Joseph Kickley
Daniel D. Krebs
Robert T. Lepper

John L. Lepper
Osborn Mooney
Noah Nepper
Jacob H. Notestine
Adam Presser
Nicholas Rear
Charles R. Read
Joshua Sweet
David Simons
William F. Waugh
William H. Wallace
Samuel Zimmerman
Elbridge Bark
Alfred A. Davis

John Deal
Joseph Forsythe
Martin Goodwell
Jeremiah Goodwell
Marion E. Griswell
John U. Henderson
Isaac Hull
William H. Hull
James Judge
James McCormick
James Morton
Eli Neiser
James Morris
Frank McKinzie

Martin Miller
Moses Paff
John E. Pillars
Frank M. Patterson
David Shoup
Elijah Spencer
John Throp
John Wisel
Edward Wilson
Ellis Butterfield
John Butler
Jacob Bricker
John Bishop
Samuel Konkright

Henry Difendorfer
Moses Snider
Alvin Thacher
Hiram W. Thomas
Elijah Wells
Allen Archer
George H. Butler
William Devlin
Henry Ever
Henry W. Franks
Ezra Funk
Hiram Ward
William Zenenfus
Charles Zenenfus

Company D

Captain—CYRUS E. BRIANT
First Lieutenant—ISAAC BATEMAN
Second Lieutenant—JOS. D. STOPHER
First Sergeant—SCOTT SWANN
Sergeants—ISAAC A. SLATER
  AARON NOTESTINE
  MILTON THOMPSON
Corporals—DANIEL SHORDEN
  HENRY SHOBE
  ALLEN DOUGALL
  CHAS. W. McKEE
  THOMAS M. STEVENS
  HERBERT BELL
  BENJAMIN F. MILLER
  HENRY WYATT
Musicians—ZACHARIUS MILLER
  ERASTUS J. GODFREY
Wagoner—LEVI H. MILLER

PRIVATES

Charles Buegnot
George W. Bowers
Michael Browand
William Browand
Adam Bowers
Wilson S. Bell
Mathias Conrad
Joseph Cummings
Lafayette Coomer
James Donaldson
Joseph Ginther
Milton Horn
James Hall
David Halter
Amos Hilkey
William Johnson
Isaac Kendrick
James Kees

George Keith
Isaac Nesbitt
Theodore A. Pattee
Richard Price
Christian Parker
Joshua Parker
Henry C. Parker
Isaac Rhodes
Morris Rose
Felix Rose
Isaac Snider
Sofara Snider
Alfred Snider
John C. Stafford
Joseph Stafford
George Shordon
James A. Wilkinson
Nathan Wyatt
Scott Arney

David Browand
Hiram Button
Benjamin P. Bausser-
man
George Brown
John Dingman
George W. Hilkey
Andrew Hettinger
Henry Hettinger
Uriah Johnson
Emanuel Kile
James Loveall
Monroe Loveall
James H. Mitchell
Isaiah Notestine
David W. Snider
Josiah Snider
Milo Thompson

George F. Throp
Alexander Votra
Elisha Wilson
John Webb
Henry Butler
Abraham Carine
John Fratenbergh
David Going
Isaiah Haifley
Joseph H. Henderson
Samuel Harnish
John Hood
Edward Johnson
Job Kennison
Josephus T. Marsh
Amariah Parker
Washington Perkins
Cromwell C. Powers

John Turner
William Ward
Hiram Wise
Eli Wise
John B. Waters
William F. Alderman
William M. Cutter
Cyrus Davis
Edwin Horn
Joseph H. Nesbit
John K. Snyder
George W. Shores
Howard Wright
William Wyatt
Sydney Ginther
Joseph Heath
Jacob B. Powers
John R. Patterson

Company E

Captain—CHAUNCEY B. OAKLEY
First Lieutenant—RICHARD WILLIAMS
Second Lieutenant—JOHN G. GOHEEN
First Sergeant—AUGUSTUS C. BROWN
Sergeants—ELBRIDGE G. PAIGE
CHARLES S. TRUE
JERRY HEFFELFINGER
HENRY BENDER
Corporals—HARVEY J. KNISS
JOHN HENNING
SYLVESTER A. CARVIN
SYLVESTER GRIST
ABSALOM G. C. BENNET
HENRY M. MILLER
JAMES HEFFELFINGER
Musician—WARREN M. BEARD
Wagoner—WILLIAM A. KINCADE

PRIVATES

Joseph Bennet
William Carbaugh
John Cro
Milton W. Freeman
Robert L. Freeman
Amon Farmer
George W. Firestine
Eli Falkenberg
Harvey Geiger
Martin G. Heffelfinger
Joseph Hood
John Hathaway
Joseph Hyndman
Simon P. Jones

John Jackson
Andrew Karriger
Samuel Karriger
Isaac M. Krise
John K. Lyon
Christopher McBride
Wm. H. McClelland
Alex. C. McCurdy
Samuel Reed
Enos Reed
George W. Robinson
Harvey W. Ross
Samuel H. Smith
William Snyder

Seth M. Sipe
Martin Schram
Timothy Tyler
Henry Brown
John Ely
George Geiger
Charles Johnston
John Johnson
Samuel R. Erwin
Amos Miller
Henry C. McClelland
John Manning
James McBride
Smiley M. McCurdy

Thomas Neal
Samuel H. Shoaff
Daniel Shutt
Peter J. Watterson
Robert K. Brown
Charles E. Dugley
Martin D. Green
Solomon Johnson
Robert Jones
John Kagle
John Maxwell
Francis M. Mooney
Nathan McGuire

Herman McClintock
Elisha A. Richardson
David River
Jacob River
Mahlon Sipe
Gotlieb Summer
David Stoner
William Carter
John Curtis
Moses Hammersly
Oregon Hanes
William Henry
George Frets

Company F

Captain—ISAAC H. LEFEVER
First Lieutenant—JOHN O'CONNELL
Second Lieutenant—F. F. BOLTZ
First Sergeant—AMOS SINE
Sergeants—JOHN D. CARTWRIGHT
DAVID CASTON
GEORGE W. STITES
PAUL F. KING
Corporal—JAMES S. TYLER

Corporals—JOSIAH KING
ANTHONY MCCRONE
ROBERT W. HOPS
JOHN CLOSE
DAVID R. PALMER
PETER KISER
Musicians—CHARLES T. MORRIS
FRANK M. JOHNSON
Wagoner—JOHN MCBRIDE

PRIVATES

Martin Boggs
William H. Ball
William E. Bailey
Frank M. Braddock
William Boone
Charles Dolan
John A. Dolan

John H. Ferguson
John Y. Ferguson
Michael Hass
Thomas Hood
Marcellus Justus
Peter King
George Kreigh

Patrick Molloy
Granville Powell
Amos Robart
Alfred Summers
Jehu Shannon
John Schuckman
Daniel Walters

James H. Ball
Jacob A. Butler
Hugh B. Cotrill
Joshua Crawford
Nathaniel Duckworth
Thomas R. Davis
Josiah Gell

Thomas Grey
James W. Hood
Wesley Higgs
Daniel Holycross
Thomas Kintz
Robert Lenning
Volney C. Leonard
Isaac Miller

Eighty-Ninth Regiment Infantry

The companies composing the Eighty-Ninth Regiment were recruited in the Eleventh Congressional District, rendezvoused at Wabash, and organized at Indianapolis. The regiment was mustered into service on the 28th of August, 1862, with Charles D. Murray as Colonel. Proceeding to Louisville, Kentucky, in command of Lieut. Col. Hervey Craven, the regiment was, on the 2d of September, sent to Munfordsville, to reinforce the garrison at that place. In the attack made upon the place by the advance of Bragg's invading army, under Gen. Chalmers, it bore an honorable part, losing two killed, fifteen wounded and one missing. After a long and stubborn resistance the garrison was compelled to surrender to vastly superior numbers, on the 16th of September, and on the next day the captured officers and men were paroled and marched within General Buell's lines, from whence they proceeded to Brandenburg, on the Ohio river, and thence to Jeffersonville, reaching there on the 30th of September.

After a furlough to their homes the officers and men of the regiment reassembled at Indianapolis, on the 27th of October. The order for their exchange being received, the regiment, on the 5th of December, proceeded to Memphis, arriving there on the 8th of December. It was at once assigned to the Brigade of Gen. Burbridge in the Division of Gen. A. J. Smith, and on the 21st of December was placed on duty at Fort Pickering, near Memphis, where it remained, doing guard and fatigue duty until the 18th of October, 1863. It was then transferred to the city of Memphis, where it was engaged on picket duty until the 26th of January, 1864. During this time, however, the regiment marched on an expedition to Hernando, Mississippi, leaving on the 16th of August, 1863, and returning on the 20th. A detatchment of two hundred men, under command of Major Henry, also left Memphis on the 24th of December, 1863, skirmished with the rear of Gen. Forrest's command, at Lafayette on the 25th, marched in pursuit to Coldwater, and retnrned on the 31st of December.

On the 26th of January, 1864, the Eighty-Ninth left Memphis on transports, with the First Brigade, Third Division, Sixteen Corps, of Sherman's command, for Vicksburg, reaching there on the 31st of Jauuary. From this point it moved on the Meridian Raid, marching through Jackson, Hillsboro and other towns, and arriving at Meridian on the 14th of February, after having skirmished with the enemy at Quan's Hill and in the vicinity of Meridian, without casualty to the regiment. After tearing up the Mobile and Ohio Railroad track in that vicinity, it proceeded to Marion, where it went into camp and remained until the 20th, waiting the expected arrival of the cavalry force under Gen. W. S. Smith, by land, from Memphis. It then broke camp and marched by way of Canton for Vicksburg, reaching there on the 4th of March. The regiment lost, during the expedition, one killed, one wounded and captured, and three missing.

The Eighty-Ninth left Vicksburg on the 10th of March, with Gen. A. J. Smith's command, on steamers, for the mouth of Red river, reaching Semmesport on Atchafalaya Bayou on the 12th, and on the next day started for Fort De Russey. Here it joined in the assault on that Fort, which was captured on the 14th, the regiment sustaining a loss of one killed and nine wounded. Resting at the Fort during the next day, and embarking on that night, it moved up the river and arrived at Alexandria on the 16th. On the 21st the regiment moved with Gen. Mower's command to Henderson's Hill, and there participated in the capture of two hundred and seventy rebels, and four pieces of artillery. Returning to Alexandria, it remained there until Bank's army came up, when it moved with the united armies to Grand Ecore, which place was reached on the 3d of April. Remaining there in camp until the 7th, it again moved with the balance of Gen. A. J. Smith's command. On the 9th it rested in line of battle awaiting the approach of the rebel army under Gen. Richard Taylor, then in pursuit of the Thirteenth and Nineteenth Army Corps, which he had, the day before, met and defeated at Sabine Cross Roads. In the battle of Pleasant Hill, which was fought by A. J. Smith's command on the 9th, the Eighty-Ninth bore a conspicuous part, losing seven killed and forty-seven wounded, making a total loss of fifty-four.

On the 10th of April the regiment fell back towards Grand Ecore, arriving there on the 14th, where it remained until the 20th, awaiting the return of the gunboats and transports. It then marched to Nachitoches, and there lay in line of battle until the Army of the Gulf marched by, and then, from day to day, engaged in covering the retreat of that army to Alexandria, which place was reached on the 26th of April. From thence, on the 1st of May, it marched to Bayou Roberts, Gov. Moore's Plantation and Bayou La Moore, all within a few miles of Alexandria. On the 7th of May the regiment met the enemy at Bayou La Moore, and after a sharp engagement charged and repulsed him, with a loss to the Eighty-Ninth at four killed and eleven wounded; total, fifteen.

The dam to raise Red river, at the Falls at Alexandria, having been completed so as to allow the transports to pass below, the command of Gen. A. J. Smith resumed its march towards the Mississippi, the Eighty-Ninth leaving Moore's Plantation on the 14th of May, and reaching Yellow Bayou, three miles from Semmesport, on the Atchafalaya, on the 17th. During this march it engaged the enemy on the prairie, near Marksville, on the 16th, with but little loss on either side, the enemy retreating at the opening of the engagement. On the 18th the regiment recrossed the Yellow Bayou, and with other troops marched up Bayou De Glaise, to Smith & Norwood's Plantation, and there had a severe contest with the enemy under command of Gen. Poligniac, who was repulsed with great slaughter. The regiment lost eight killed and forty-five wounded; total, fifty-three. On the 19th of May the regiment reached Red River Landing on the Mississippi, and embarked the same evening for Vicksburg, which place was reached on the 24th of May. During the Red River Expedition the regiment was commanded by Lieut. Col. Hervey Craven.

The Eighty-Ninth remained in the vicinity of Vicksburg until the 4th of June, when it embarked for Memphis. arriving there on the 9th, and leaving there on the 23d, for

Eighty-Ninth Regiment Infantry—Continued

Collierville. From there it marched, as escort to a wagon train, to Moscow, and then moved to Lagrange, Tennessee. Here it remained until the 5th of July, and then marched to Pontotoc, Mississippi, reaching there on the 11th. From thence it moved to Harrisburg, near Tupelo, where, on the 14th of July it participated in the battle with the rebel troops under Generals S. D. Lee and Forest, called the battle of Tupelo. The regiment in this engagement, lost one killed and twelve wounded.

Returning from this expedition, the Eighty-Ninth reached Memphis on the 23d of July, where it rested until the 8th of August. It then marched with Gen. A. J. Smith's command to look after Gen. Forrest in Northern Mississippi, passing through Holly Springs to Oxford, where news was received that Forrest had entered Memphis. The command was at once marched back to Memphis, arriving there on the 30th of August, where it lay in camp until the 8th of September. At that date the regiment proceeded on steamer up the Mississippi, landing at Jefferson Barracks, Missouri, on the 19th of September. From thence it made a brief expedition to De Soto, returning on the 1st of October. On the following day the regiment started with Gen. A. J. Smith's command in pursuit of the rebel Gen. Price, then invading Missouri. It marched into the interior of the State, passing through the towns bordering the Missouri river to Independence, and from thence to Oxford, Kansas. From there it moved to Harrisonville, Missouri, where the pursuit was abandoned, after which the regiment marched to St. Louis, going by way of Lone Jack. Lexington, Glasgow, Columbia, Warrenton and St. Charles, During this expedition it marched seven hundred and twenty miles, nearly all of which was on foot. The regiment was not in any engagement during the march, but had the misfortune to lose Major Henry, Assistant Surgeon Porter and Quartermaster Ashley, who were murdered by guerrillas on the 1st of November, at Greenton, ten miles south of Lexington.

The Eighty-Ninth remained with Gen. Smith's command at St. Louis until the 25th of November, when it proceeded by steamer to Nashville, Tennessee, reaching there on the 30th. Here it went into camp, and on the 15th and 16th of December participated in the battle near that place.

On the first day of the engagement the regiment suffered no loss, but on the second, when it was conspicuously engaged, it lost two killed and fifteen wounded. On the 17th it started in pursuit of Hood's army, and arrived at Clifton, on the Tennessee river, on the 1st of January, 1865, from whence it proceeded on transports to Eastport, Mississippi. Here it remained until the 9th of February, when it proceeded by steamer to Vicksburg, and thence to New Orleans, arriving there on the 21st of February.

From New Orleans the regiment moved on transports to Dauphin Island, near Mobile, reaching there on the 8th of March. On the 19th it moved up Mobile Bay by steamer to the mouth of Fish river, and thence up Fish river to Don's Mills, where it disembarked and remained till the 25th of March. It then marched to a point between Spanish Fort and Blakely, where it lay, participating in the siege until the rebel fortifications were taken. The regiment lost during the siege two killed and eight wounded. On the 13th of April the Sixteenth Army Corps, under command of Gen. A. J. Smith, marched for Montgomery, Alabama, arriving there on the 27th of April. Here the regiment lay in camp, doing some picket duty, until the 1st of June, when it marched to Providence, on the Alabama river, and there took transports to Mobile, where it did patrol and guard duty until the 19th of July, 1865, when it was mustered out of service. Proceeding homeward, it reached Indianapolis on the 4th of August, where, after being publicly received by Governor Morton in the State House grove, it was finally discharged.

The remaining recruits of the Eighty-Ninth were transferred to the Fifty-Second Indiana and continued to serve with that organization until the 10th of September, 1865, when they were mustered out with the regiment.

During its term of service the Eighty-Ninth has suffered losses as follows: Thirty-one killed, one hundred and sixty-seven wounded, and four missing; making a total loss of two hundred and two. It has marched two thousand three hundred and sixty-three miles on foot, traveled by steamer seven thousand one hundred and twelve miles, and by rail one thousand two hundred and thirty-two miles; making the total distance traveled ten thousand seven hundred and seven miles.

Company H

First Sergeant—Martin M. V. Spencer

Company K

Sergeant—Sylvester L. Gorsline
Corporal—Elias W. Coverdale

PRIVATES

Charles Ehrman	Daniel P. Reynolds
Jackson E. Heavland	Benjamin H. Wood
Perry McDaniel	George Riley
George W. Riley	David Warling

Ninetieth Regiment

(FIFTH CAVALRY)

(THREE YEARS' SERVICE)

The Fifth Cavalry, Nintieth Regiment of Indiana Volunteers, was organized at Indianapolis in August and September, 1862. Four companies were mustered into service in August, five in September, and three in October of that year. Capt. Felix W. Graham was on the 2d of October commissioned Major, and on the 10th of December promoted to the Colonelcy. In October Companies "C" and "F" were sent to Carrolton, Kentucky, and Company "I" to Rising Sun, Indiana. These companies remained on duty at those places until December, when they moved to Louisville, and afterwards to Munfordsville and Glasgow, joining the regiment at the latter place in March, 1863. The other companies were, in December, sent to the counties of the First and Second Congressional Districts bordering on the Ohio river, and were distributed as follows: Companies "A" and "G" at Newburg, Company "B" at Rockport, Companies "D" and "L" at Mauckport, Companies "E" and "H" at Cannelton, Company "K" at Mount Vernon, Company "M" at Evansville. On the 28th of February, 1863, these companies moved to Louisville, Kentucky, and on the 4th of March left that place for Glasgow, where they arrived on the 11th. The other companies that had been serving on detached duty, joined the regiment at Glasgow, and the whole command was kept busy in scouting the country in the direction of the Cumberland river, until the 17th of April. On the 18th it marched to the Cumberland river and skirmished with the enemy, and on the 19th crossed over and drove the rebels three miles. It then returned and burned the town of Celina, Tennessee, after which it recrossed the river and reached Glasgow on the 20th. From the return of the regiment until the 22d of June, it did heavy scouting and skirmishing with the enemy, capturing many prisoners and driving many beyond the river.

The regiment then marched to Scottsville, and thence to Tompkinsville. Leaving there on the 4th of July, it started in pursuit of the rebel Gen. John Morgan's cavalry, reported to have crossed the Cumberland. The regiment was commanded by Lieut. Col. Thomas H. Butler, and marched through southern and central Kentucky. On reaching Louisville the command was placed on steamers and transported up the Ohio to Portsmouth. On the 19th of July it headed Morgan's forces at Buffington Island, and

attacked and drove them from the river and adjacent hills in every direction, killing and capturing many, and also capturing five pieces of artillery. After this the regiment returned to Louisville, reaching there on the 27th of July, from whence it marched to Bardstown, Lebanon and Glasgow, going into camp at the latter place on the 9th of August.

On the 18th of August, the Fifth Cavalry started for East Tennessee, making the tedious march across the Cumberland Mountains and entering Knoxville, with Burnside's army, on the 1st of September, being the first regiment of Federal troops to enter that city. It then moved upon an expedition across the Smoky Mountains, returning from which to Sevierville, it again took up its line of march for Greenville. Here it was placed on outpost duty, and during several days was constantly engaged in picket firing. After this the regiment joined its brigade on an expedition to Bristol, and on the 19th of September it had heavy skirmishing with the enemy. Near Zollicoffer, on the 20th, it engaged the enemy over two hours, and then fell back to Jonesboro. On the 22d a forward movement was commenced in the direction of Blountsville, where a battle was begun. Near sundown the enemy's line gave way, when Lieut. Col. Butler, at the head of a portion of the Fifth Cavalry, charged, capturing many prisoners and one twenty-four pounder howitzer.

The regiment next moved to Loudon, and back again towards Bull's Gap, and while on the return march near Henderson's Mill, on the 11th of October, the regiment met the enemy retreating from the forces of General Burnside and alone fought three thousand of them, with no hope of aid from any quarter. The enemy charged at every available and weak portion of the line, but, by the spirit and cool bravery of the officers and men, the rebels where held in check for a while. The regiment being nearly surrounded, it was compelled to fall back, and in an effort to extricate it from its perilous position, a desperate hand-to-hand conflict ensued, the belligerents intermixing with each other, many of both sides being killed and many of our men being captured from the rear, where the hardest fighting was done. Finally the regiment cut its way through the strong line of the rebel forces, and joined the brigade. It at once moved in the direction of Rheatown, where it came upon the rear

Ninetieth Regiment—Continued

of the enemy, when the fighting was renewed, the rebels retreating slowly, until night closed the scene. For two days after the command camped seven miles east of Rheatown, and then moved towards Blountsville. On the evening of the 13th of October, the advance met the enemy near Blountsville, and early on the morning of the 14th, another engagement was commenced. The Fifth Cavalry fought the rebels all day until dark. After this it was moved to near Abington, Virginia, from whence it soon after returned to Jonesboro, in which vicinity it remained on active outpost duty until the 6th of November. It then marched by way of Henderson's Mill, Greenville and Bull's Gap to Cheek's Cross Roads, encamping there on the 8th. On the 18th it moved to Bean's Station, and on the next day crossed the Clinch river to Tazewell, where it remained until the 29th. Marching to Powell river, near Cumberland Gap, it then moved by a circuitous route, to Maynardsville, near which place it met a division of rebel cavalry, and during the evening of November 30th, and the whole day of December 1st, it kept up heavy skirmishing with the enemy. Falling back to Walker's Ford on the 2d, the command was there attacked, and from 5 o'clock in the morning till two o'clock in the afternoon, the regiment retreated three miles, fighting all the time. Reinforcements coming to its relief the regiment was enabled to cross Clinch river.

On the 5th of December the Fifth Cavalry marched to Log Mountain to harass Longstreet's retreating column. After this it moved to Blain's Cross Roads, and from thence to Bean's Station, where, on the 14th of December, another hardly contested battle was fought, almost hand to hand, from noon on the 14th until three o'clock A. M. on the 15th. Retreating towards Rutledge, the regiment was engaged in skirmishing all day, and at night took up its line of march, reaching Blain's Cross Roads next day and going into camp. On the 23d of December the regiment marched in the direction of Mossy Creek, arriving there on the 24th, remaining there until the 14th of January, 1864, during which time skirmishing and sharp fighting was of daily occurrence. On the 17th of January the regiment, commanded by Major John Woolley, participated in the battle of Dandridge, fighting from ten o'clock in the morning until three in the afternoon. Then Major Woolley, at the head of his command, made a charge upon foot in advance of the main line of battle some three-fourths of a mile, driving the enemy before him until reaching the summit of a hill, where a rebel line of battle was discovered, reaching as far as the eye could see, of dismounted cavalry or infantry. The regiment was immediately marched back, reaching its original base safely. At midnight the whole command commenced retreating by way of

New Market, Kinney's Fork and Strawberry Plains, toward Knoxville, which place was reached on the 19th of January, 1864. On the 24th the horses of the regiment were turned over to the Fourteenth Illinois Cavalry, and on the 26th the regiment made a scout on foot to Pigeon Creek, near Sevierville. Returning to Knoxville, it received orders to march on foot to Cumberland Gap, which place was reached on the 10th of February. After a scout on the Virginia road, it resumed its march on foot, leaving Cumberland Gap on the 17th of February, and arriving at Mount Sterling, Kentucky, on the 26th.

The companies of the Fifth Cavalry remained at Mt. Sterling, Paris and Nicholasville, until the 1st of May, during which time it was remounted and refitted. Under command of Col. Butler, it then began its long and tedious march across the mountains to Tunnel Hill, Georgia, reaching there on the 12th, and joining the command of Gen. Stoneman. On the 13th it entered upon the active campaign against Atlanta, and was constantly engaged in all the cavalry operations of that army from Dalton to Decatur, Georgia. On the 27th of July it marched on the "Stoneman Raid" toward Macon, reaching the enemy's lines near that place on the 30th, and attacking their main body, driving them about two miles. Finding that the river could not be crossed, and having accomplished the work of destroying the railroads, the whole command made a retrograde movement, marching that afternoon and night. When near Hillsboro, on the 31st, a large body of Wheeler's cavalry, under command of Gen. Iverson, was met and an engagement at once ensued. The enemy was at first checked, but at two o'clock in the afternoon the whole command except the Fifth Cavalry left the field, Gen. Stoneman giving Col. Butler orders to hold the enemy until the last. This was done until the force that had ingloriously left the Fifth Cavalry was entirely out of danger, when the regiment was surrendered by Gen. Stoneman to the enemy, under the solemn protest of Col. Butler.

The portion of the regiment which had, from hard service, been dismounted, remained in the rear, near Decatur, Georgia, under Major Leeson, and were, shortly after the surrender of the regiment, put upon duty by order of Gen. Sherman, who exchanged their carbines for muskets. After the fall of Atlanta they remained there doing guard duty until the 13th of September, when they were transferred to Kentucky, where they were kept on guard and other duty until the regiment was remounted.

On the 17th of January, 1865, the regiment being mounted, armed and equipped, marched from Louisville for Pulaski, Tennessee, arriving there on the 12th of February.

Ninetieth Regiment—Continued

In this vicinity it remained, scouting the country, capturing bushwhackers and outlaws, until the 16th of June, 1865, when it was mustered out of service, and proceeded to Indiana. On the 21st of June it was publicly welcomed home at a reception meeting held in the Capital grove, at Indianapolis, and greeted with speeches by Governor Morton and General Hovey.

Companies "G," "L" and "M," having been mustered into service after the 1st of October, 1862, under the orders of the War Department, were not entitled to be mustered out with the regiment. These, with the remaining recruits, were transferred to the Sixth Indiana Cavalry, and served with it until the 15th of September, 1865, when that regiment was mustered out at Murfreesboro, Tennessee.

The Fifth Cavalry has been in twenty-two battles and skirmishes, and during the month of June, 1864, in Georgia, it was engaged in skirmishing nearly every day. It has marched twenty-four hundred miles, and been transported one thousand miles by water. It has captured six hundred and forty prisoners during its term of service, and its casualties have been as follows: Killed in action, thirty-four; died from wounds, thirteen; died in rebel prisons, one hundred and fifteen; died in hospital, seventy-four; wounded in action, seventy-two; taken by the enemy as prisoners, four hundred and ninety-seven; officers wounded, six; officers killed, one; officers taken prisoners, seventeen; total casualties, eight hundred and twenty-nine.

Ninetieth Regiment

(FIFTH CAVALRY)

(THREE YEARS' SERVICE)

Company D

Captain—HARRY A. WHITMAN
First Lieutenant—WM. W. ANGEL
First Sergeant—ANDREW W. STEVENS
Co. Com. Sergeant—JAMES PIPPINGER
Sergeants—ALBERT L. BROWNSON
    CALVIN L. THOMAS
    BARNEY HOPPER
    JOHN BENGNOT
    WARREN MONTGOMERY
Corporals—HENRY G. FRANK
    MOSES N. NILES
    JOHN FRASS
    ROBERT KEOWN
Buglers—WM. SUDBRING
   ORION THOMAS
Farrier—DANIEL HILL

PRIVATES

William H Archer	Lewis Young	William H. Stickler	William Overly
David C. Bleam	Frederick Block	George Brooks	Thomas Overly
David Crouse	Jacob Fink	James D. Brooks	David C. Owens
Peter Demarty	Hiram Graves	Daniel Donovan	Charles A. Paige
William Eyrick	Harrison Judah	Henry Emerick	Perry O. Rice
Samuel Folts	Calvin H. Jones	Jackson Holmes	Jacob Rine
Charles Fossleman	Charles Lake	Uriah W. Hinton	Nathaniel S. Risden
Frederick Hebring	Thomas G. Reed	John Kimbal	Christopher Swank
Henry Lanknaw	John Stills	Peter A. Liniger	Calvin Thomas
Wm. Limecolley	John B. Seinfort	Gustavus McClanahan	Ransom Workman
Ami D. Nuttle	George M. Crouse	John Nebb	John Eley
Harry Nill	Frederick Ezenthal	Cyrus A. Niles	Caleb Falkenberg
Thomas Reilly	Wilson H. Johnson	Isaac Overly	Louis Gillion
F. M. Sunderland	Philip Lash	Isaac Overly, Sr.	Wm. H. Hutchins
Frederick Weston	Henry Reiley	Daniel Overly	John Smalts
George Woodford	Christopher Search		

Ninety-First Regiment Infantry

(ONE YEAR'S SERVICE)

The Ninety-First Regiment was recruited from the First Congressional District during the month of August, 1862, and rendezvoused at Evansville. Only seven companies were raised, and these were formed into a battalion, and mustered into service, with JOHN MEHRINGER as Lieutenant Colonel, on the 1st of October, 1862. On the 10th the battalion started for Henderson, Kentucky, and, upon its arrival there, detachments were sent to Madisonville and Smithland, where they remained, performing guard duty, and protecting that section of Kentucky from guerrilla raids, until the 15th of June, 1863, when the detachment joined the battalion, and marched to Russellville, and from thence to Bowling Green and Burksville, in pursuit of the rebel chieftain John H. Morgan, then making a raid through Kentucky. Being unable to march as fast as the fleet-footed horses of John Morgan's command traveled, the pursuit ceased, the battalion marched to Russellville, and went into camp.

In the summer of 1863, authority having been given to recruit four regiments of six months' men, for infantry service, forty-three companies were raised, which left an overplus of three companies, and, on the 11th of September, these companies, designated "H," "G" and "K," were assigned to the Ninety-First and joined the command at Russellville, thus making the regiment complete. Lieut. Col. Mehringer was promoted Colonel. On the 25th, the regiment moved to Nashville, and, after a short stay at that point, returned to Russellville, arriving there on the 20th of November. On the 23d, the regiment moved to Camp Nelson, and from thence to Point Burnside, Kentucky, where it remained until January, 1864.

On the 3d of January, 1864, the Ninety-First broke camp and marched toward Jonesboro, East Tennessee, and from thence moved to Cumberland Gap. On the 22d of February, Company "A," under command of Captain Wise, had a sharp fight with a rebel force, twelve hundred strong, near the Gap. On the 17th of May, the regiment marched for Knoxville, and from thence moved to Cleveland, and then to Kingston, Georgia, to join Sherman's army, then moving upon the Atlanta campaign.

On the 3d of June, the regiment was assigned to the First Brigade, Second Division, Twenty-Third Army Corps, (General Schofield), and left Kingston to join its corps, then near Acworth. On the 15th, the regiment was engaged in the fight that caused the enemy to abandon his strong position on Pine Mountain. Generals Thomas and Schofield advancing, found the enemy again strongly posted along a line of hills, connecting Kenesaw and Lost Mountains. Our army pressed forward, constantly skirmishing in dense underbrush and forests, until the 22d, when two rebel corps sallied forth at New Hope Church and precipitated themselves upon a part of Hooker's and Schofield's corps. A desperate battle ensued, the enemy being finally repulsed, leaving his dead and wounded in our hands. The regiment took an active part in this battle. Until the 1st of July the regiment was constantly engaged in skirmishing with the enemy in his strong position on Kenesaw Mountain. On the 7th, the regiment crossed the Chattahoochee river, with its corps, and effected a lodgment on its east bank, the advance of the corps capturing a gun and surprising the rebel guard while laying a pontoon bridge. The enemy, being thus threatened on his line of communications, crossed the Chattahoochee on the night of the 9th, burning the bridges in his rear. Atlanta was now only eight miles distant, and our whole army safely on the right bank of the Chattahoochee. The men needed rest. So Sherman dispatched a cavalry force to strike the enemy's communications at important points. This was accomplished. On the 19th, the regiment was engaged at Decatur, Georgia, the whole line skirmishing heavily. On the 20th, the enemy made a sudden assault, resulting in the battle of Peach Tree Creek, in which the regiment was engaged. Another battle took place near Atlanta on the 22d, the enemy being repulsed.

The siege of Atlanta was vigorously pressed, our forces constantly advancing by parallels, until within easy artillery range of the besieged city. On the 3d of August demonstrations were made along the whole line, and on the 6th a severe engagement took place near Utoy Creek, the Ninety-First being engaged. On the 12th, the regiment was transferred from the 1st to the 3d brigade, in the same division and corps, in which it had served since June 3d, 1864. On the 27th, the regiment marched with the army in executing the grand movement by the right, which caused the evacuation of Atlanta. Gen. Schofield's corps struck the railroad a mile below Rough and Ready, and destroyed it for a great distance. The corps then moved toward Lovjoy's station, and, upon arriving in front of that position, received definite intelligence that Atlanta had been abandoned by the enemy on the night of the 1st of September. The regiment then marched with its corps toward Atlanta, and, on the 8th of September, went into camp at Decatur, a few miles east of Atlanta. The parallel line of the rebellion had been broken by the force of the perpendicular blow struck by Grant at Vicksburg. Another perpendicular blow was struck upon part of the line by Sherman at Atlanta. It now only remained to strike with vigor the shattered remnants of the line.

On the 4th of October the regiment started with its corps in pursuit of Hood. It marched by the way of Kingston, Rome, Resaca, Snake Creek Gap, to Galesville and Cedar Bluffs, when the pursuit ceased and the corps was detached from Sherman's army, and ordered to report to Gen. Thomas. Moving north the regiment arrived at Chattanooga on the 5th of November, and moved from thence to Nashville, Columbia and Centerville, and then back to Nashville. The regiment took part in the battle of Franklin on the 30th of November, and in the battles in front of Nashville on the 15th and 16th of December.

From Nashville the regiment marched to Clifton, Tennessee. On the 17th of December it left Clifton, by steamer, for Cincinnati, Ohio. From thence the troops were conveyed by rail to Washington, D. C., where they arrived on the 28th of January, 1865. From Washington the regiment moved, by steamers, to Wilmington, North Carolina, and reached the mouth of Cape Fear river, February 9th, where its corps landed upon the peninsula, near Fort Fisher, and after a few engagements captured Wilmington.

The regiment marched thence with its corps to Goldsboro and Raleigh, reaching the latter place on the 14th of April. Here it remained in camp until the 3d of May, when it moved to Salisbury, where it arrived on the 8th.

The Ninety-First remained in camp at Salisbury until the 26th of June, 1865, when it was mustered out of the service of the United States, at that place, and left for Indianapolis. Its remaining recruits were transferred to the 120th, 124th and 128th Indiana regiments, with which organizations they continued to serve till their muster out.

The Ninety-First left for the field with an aggregate of 635 officers and men. The three companies of six months' men, assigned to the regiment in September, 1863, were discharged upon the expiration of their term of service. The regiment then numbered but seven companies until the winter of 1864, when three companies were recruited for one year's service, and assigned as companies "H," "I," and "K." These companies were among the remaining recruits that were transferred to other regiments upon its final muster out. The regiment has lost eighty-one in killed and wounded, and returned to the State with nineteen officers and three hundred and fifteen men. Upon its arrival at Indianapolis, the regiment was greeted with an ovation in the State House Grove, and welcomed with addresses by Governor Morton and others, partook of a sumptuous dinner at the Soldier's Home, and retired from "war's stern alarms."

Company H

Captain—CHARLES EMERY
First Lieutenant—MARION E. GRISWOLD
Second Lieutenant—NAHTNA CROUSE
First Sergeant—WILLIAM J. REED
Sergeants—WILLIAM H. ALSHOUSE
WILLIAM P. HUFTY
JEROME POTTER
ANDREW MIDDLETON
Corporals—JOHN BAIER

Corporals—WILLIAM H. WORDEN
ROBERT M. LYWARD
UPTON NOLL
DANIEL FRISBY
SAMUEL BACON
JOHN L. BARKAS
GEORGE W. OPLIGER
Musicians—THEODORE F. McDOUGAL
THOMAS McCORMICK

PRIVATES

Samuel Allen	James Essex	Anthony Heit	Francis Parker	Henry Webka
Jesse W. Brown	August Flitterow	Christian Hendricks	Frank Rudolph	Oliver P. Walters
Lewis H. Bowers	William France	Elijah Lamar	Mathias Rabus	George H. Wilson
James Brown	James Fry	James McGamgha	Christian Richards	Hiram Watson
Francis Bischoff	Samuel Falkenberg	Conrod Mosser	William Russell	Loran Bethel
Thomas Bradbury	Joseph George	David W. Marquet	Joseph Schrack	John Griffith
Lewis Badial	George Grotairs	Isaiah Magner	Joseph Shivers	William Henderson
Zyra A. Conley	Taylor Grover, Jr.	Mathias Mashamer	Frank Sherwood	William A. Johnson
Cornelius Cook	Andrew Grover	Ayers P. Nash	Samuel Gilbert	Lawrence Power
Thomas Cadwalader	John Gailey	Henry Ortstedt	Frank Savoit	Joseph Stark
John Donahoe	Franklin Garver	Darius M. Preble	Peter M. Smith	Charles Staurt
Wm. H. Dougherty	Charles Gribler	Samuel Payne	W. C. Vandewater	Peter Eckley
William H. Eagy	George Hood	Horatio Pool	Jacob B. Williams	

Company K

Captain—JOSEPH H. KEEVER
First Sergeant—WILLIAM MYERS
Sergeants—NEWCOMB RANK
WILLIAM H. HUNTING
JAMES S. BAKER
EPHRAIM SPANGLER
Corporals—WILLIAM FREY
SAMUEL D. COLE

Corporals—E. C. GODFREY
JOHN ALBRIGHT
MARK HERRINGTON
LEWELLEN H. PRICE
AMOS HARTMAN
JACOB SMITH
Musicians—CALEB ZOOK
HENRY POWERS

PRIVATES

Frederick Beckman	R. J. Dingman	David W. Miller	Perry Davis	Daniel Leary
Lafayette M. Bratten	Joseph Denner	Henry M. Mason	Albert H. Cassada	Peter Lynch
Christian Bishop	Jackson Gibson	William C. Payne	Samuel Ernsperger	William McAuench
Henry E. Brandenberg	Elias Hoover	Patrick Ryan	Jeremiah Garl	Frederick Mullenhour
Oliver Blystone	Casper Hawkey	Lewis Riting	George Houston	John M. Swisher
Arthur M. Brackenridge	Elijah Hook	Ephraim Redman	David Hoover	James E. Thomas
Adam J. Bennett	Thomas Hubbs	Henry Simon	George Majors	William Thomas
George Carto	William R. Johnson	William Simon	Calvin C. Robbins	Joseph Zorg
William T. Cress	Jacob Johnson	Philander Allen	David Stewart	Hiram Ehminger
Henry Champion	Peter Long	David Corpening	Jacob R. Thomas	Lewis Regetz
	Peter Lovine			

One Hundredth Regiment Infantry

The One Hundredth Regiment was organized in the Tenth Congressional District during the month of August, 1862, and rendezvoused at Fort Wayne. The two companies, recruited for the Ninety-Eighth regiment in the Eighth Congressional District, were assigned to the One Hundredth Regiment, completing its organization, and the regiment was mustered into the service on the 10th of September, 1862, with Sanford J. Stoughton as Colonel. On the 11th of November the regiment left for Memphis, Tennessee, and arrived there on the 16th. The regiment was assigned to the Second Brigade, First Division, Army of the Tennessee, and on the 26th moved with an expedition through Northern Mississippi, having Vicksburg for its objective point. The movement, however, was unsuccessful, owing to the surprise and capture of Holly Springs by the rebels. The column then returned to the vicinity of Memphis, and the regiment was assigned to garrison duty at Collierville, and as guards along the Memphis and Charleston Railroad.

On the 9th of June, 1863, the regiment embarked on transports, and joined the army of Gen. Grant at the siege of Vicksburg, arriving in front of the rebel works on the 14th. The regiment took part in the siege of Vicksburg, and after its surrender, moved with Sherman's army upon Jackson, Mississippi, arriving in front of that place on the 11th of July. Five days were occupied in the siege of Jackson, the regiment being constantly engaged. On the 16th the rebel army evacuated and our forces entered the place and destroyed its military resources. During these movements, the regiment was commanded by Lieut. Col. Albert Heath, and formed part of the First Brigade, First Division, Sixteenth Army Corps. From Jackson the regiment marched to the Big Black river, where it remained in camp during the summer.

On the 28th of September the regiment marched to Vicksburg, embarked on transports, and sailed to Memphis, arriving there on the 9th of October. The regiment, at this time, belonged to the Fourth Division, Fifteenth Army Corps. The regiment moved with its division, on a rapid march across the country, to Stevenson and Bridgeport, Alabama; thence over Sandstone Mountain, and down Lookout Valley to Trenton, Georgia, and succeeded in turning the left flank of Bragg's army, then in position upon Lookout Mountain. This column secured a foothold on the Mountain, and drove the enemy from position, but without following in pursuit, pushed for Chattanooga, and after a rapid march, reached that place on the 23d of November. On the 25th the column moved upon the enemy's stronghold on Mission Ridge, and took part in that severe battle. Its division gained the crest of the hill and held the position, notwithstanding the concentric fire of the enemy's ar-

tillery and his repeated assaults. The fight lasted from 10 o'clock in the morning until dark, and the attack on the enemy's left was so persistent as to draw vast masses of the enemy to that flank, and enabled Gen. Thomas to break through the enemy's center. In this battle the regiment lost one hundred and thirty-two killed and wounded. Lieut. Col. Heath was severely wounded early in the action, and Major R. M. Johnson assumed command of the regiment. The next morning the command moved in pursuit of Bragg's army as far as Graysville. It then moved toward Knoxville, for the purpose of relieving Gen. Burnside. This was accomplished, the head of our column reaching Knoxville on the 6th of December. The regiment then returned with its division to Scottsboro, Alabama, arriving there on the 26th of December. But a few weeks before this army had left the banks of the Tennessee river, with only two day's rations, and no extra clothing, and during that time had fought a severe battle, and marched over eight hundred miles, through mud, rain and snow, part of the command barefooted, and yet all was endured without a murmur. The regiment remained in camp at Scottsboro until the 1st of May, 1864.

The entire army of General Sherman moved from Chattanooga early in May, 1864, on its campaign against the "Gate city of Georgia"—Atlanta. The two hostile armies were separated by Rocky Face Ridge, cloven by Buzzard's Roost Gap, through which runs the railroad. This pass was so fortified as to render it unapproachable. Sherman decided to turn the position. The army of the Tennessee moved through Snake Creek Gap, and threatened the enemy's rear at Dalton. The regiment was attached to this army and took part in all its movements and battles, being engaged at Dalton, Snake Creek Gap, Resacca, Dallas, New Hope Church, Big Shanty, Kenesaw Mountain, Nickajack Creek, Chattahoochee River, Decatur, Atlanta, Cedar Bluffs, Jonesboro, and Lovejoy's Station. The regiment then moved with its corps to Atlanta, and camped at East Point, after marching and fighting nearly one hundred days.

On the 3d of October the regiment marched with its corps in pursuit of Hood, and after forced marches through Northern Georgia and Alabama, drove Hood across the Tennessee river, left Gen. Thomas to meet and check his further career, and returned to his old camping ground near Atlanta.

At daybreak on the 14th of November the regiment moved with the column for Savannah and the sea. Atlanta lay behind, a mass of smoldering ruins—before was an untrodden path, an unknown enemy and adventure. The march of that army was marked by destroyed railroads and a ruined country. The regiment was assigned to the Sec-

One Hundredth Regiment Infantry—Continued

ond Brigade (Walcott's), First Division, Fifteenth Army Corps, in this march. On the 22d of November, near Griswoldville, Georgia, its brigade was engaged in a desperate fight. Our position was defended by a slight barricade. The enemy made an assault with a largely superior force, and four pieces of artillery; he was, however, completely repulsed. The action continued four hours, and the enemy made several assaults, only to be met with severe loss. Gen. Walcott was wounded, and Col. Catterson, of the Ninety-Seventh Indiana, took command of the brigade. Forty-nine prisoners were captured, and the regiment complimented by the commanding General. After a perilous march through almost impassible swamps, morasses and over swollen streams, the column debouched in front of Savannah on the 10th of December, which city our army entered on the 23d.

From Savannah the regiment moved with its corps, by steamer, to Beaufort, South Carolina, and thence through the Carolinas, capturing successively Branchville, Columbia, Georgetown and Cheraw, South Carolina, and met the enemy at Bentonville, North Carolina, where a severe battle ensued, and the enemy were defeated and driven from the field. The column then moved to Goldsboro, reaching that place on the 26th of March, 1865, having marched thirteen hundred miles and fought seventeen battles since leaving Chattanooga in May, 1864.

The regiment remained at Goldsboro until the 10th of April. It then moved with the army to Raleigh, where it remained until after the surrender of Johnston's army. The regiment then marched by the way of Richmond, Virginia, to Washington, District of Columbia, reaching that place on the 20th of May, 1865. The regiment remained in camp near Washington until the 9th of June, 1865, when it was mustered out of service, the remaining recruits being transferred to the Forty-Eighth Indiana, with which organization they continued to serve until its muster out at Louisville, Kentucky, on the 15th of June, 1865.

The regiment left for the field with an aggregate of nine hundred and thirty-seven men, and returned with six hundred and eighteen men for muster out. It has lost in killed in action and died from wounds, eighty-nine; discharged for disability by reason of wounds, or otherwise, two hundred and twenty-five; died from disease, one hundred and fifty; total casualties, four hundred and sixty-four.

The One Hundredth has marched, during its term of service, four thousand miles, been engaged in twenty-five battles, and has been engaged as skirmishers nearly one-third of the time it has been in the field. After its muster out it started for Indianapolis, and upon its arrival there was present at a public reception in the State House grounds on the 14th of June, and welcomed with addresses by Governor Morton and others. Its members then dispersed to their respective homes.

Officers

Colonel—CHARLES CASE   Adjutant—HENRY WILLIAMS

Company K

First Lieutenant—JEREMIAH M. WISE
Second Lieutenant—HENRY WILLIAMS
Musician—MELVIN M. BEALS

PRIVATES

Jacob Allwine	John T. Stouffer
Thomas Bickle	Bartholomew Smith
Matthias Cramer	Solomon Swisher
William A. Logan	Columbus Duke
David N. Pugh	John Kepeler
Moses N. Pugh	John K. Nerhood

Company A
RECRUITS

Lemuel W. Moe   George S. Phelps

One Hundred and First Regiment Infantry

The One Hundred and First Regiment was organized in the Eleventh Congressional District during the month of August, 1862, rendezvoused at Wabash, and was mustered into service on the 7th of September, 1862, with WILLIAM GARVER as Colonel. Troops were at that time being rapidly thrown into Kentucky to repel the invasion of Kirby Smith, and the regiment, as one of the new levies, moved at once to Covington, Kentucky, where it was assigned to a brigade, took position in the defenses, and remained until the threatening column of the enemy withdrew. On the 23d of September the regiment sailed on a steamboat to Louisville, Kentucky, and from thence marched with the command of Gen. McCook, on the 1st of October, in search of the retiring forces of Gen. Bragg. The column marched through Jefferson, Taylorsville, Bloomfield and Berryville, reaching Maxwell, Kentucky, on the 7th. There the regiment took charge of the Tenth Division train and escorted it to Springfield, Kentucky. Thence moved with the train to Crab Orchard. From thence the regiment marched to Lebanon; thence to Munfordsville, and was employed in guarding the railroad bridge at that place until the 30th of November. The regiment then moved to Glasgow, and from thence to Castillian Springs, Tennessee, where it remained until the 26th of December, 1862. The regiment then marched in pursuit of John Morgan, who was making a raid through Kentucky. The march was rapid, but unsuccessful, and, after a week's journey through mud and rain, fording rivers and creeks, the command returned to its camp at Castillian Springs, on the 2d of January, 1863. From thence the regiment moved to Murfresboro, Tennessee, arriving there on the 11th and going into camp. While stationed here the regiment was assigned to the Second Brigade (Colonel Hall), Fifth Division (Reynolds), Fourteenth Army Corps (Thomas). The regiment marched with a reconnoisance in force to Lebanon, on the 3d of February, and, again, on the 4th of March, to Woodbury, accomplishing the object sought for, and returning to camp at Murfreesboro.

On the 18th of March our brigade marched from Murfreesboro for the purpose of beating up certain rebel hiding places, and dispersing guerrilla bands infesting Wilson county, Tennessee. Moving by the way of Gainesville and Milton, at the latter place the rebel General John Morgan was encountered with a force of 3,700 men. Col. Hall resolved to give battle. He therefore posted his brigade on Vaught's Hill, near Milton, placing the One Hundred and First on the left. The rebels made several desperate assaults upon our position, and, after six hours' severe fighting, were repulsed with loss. The regiment lost in this fight forty-three killed and wounded. Lieut. Col. Doan was in command of the regiment. After defeating Morgan, the regiment marched with its brigade back to Murfreesboro.

On the 20th of April the regiment moved with its division to McMinnville, captured seventy prisoners, some stores, and destroyed the railroad in that vicinity. The division then returned to Murfreesboro, where the regiment remained in camp until June. On the 31st of May, Lieut.

Col. Doan assumed command of the regiment, Col. Garver having resigned.

On the 24th of June the whole army made a forward movement. At Hoover's Gap, at 4 p. m., Wilder's brigade became engaged. The Second Brigade moved to its support, under a heavy artillery fire, and for two days were on the skirmish line. After driving the enemy from the Gap, the regiment moved with its brigade to Manchester, Tullahoma and Elk river. The army halted at Decherd, and the regiment went into camp on University Hill, and remained there until the 17th of August. It then marched by the way of Battle Creek, Jasper and Sequatchie Valley to Shell Mound Ferry, crossed the Raccoon and Lookout Mountains, and reached the battlefield of Chicamauga on the morning of the 19th of September, having marched all night.

The Second Brigade at once became engaged with the enemy. It took position on General Palmer's right, and the battle raged with great fury. Twice the enemy were repulsed; but, being reinforced, rallied and forced us from position. Our brigade fell back to a strong position, and bivouacked. On the morning of the 20th, the battle commenced far to our left, and reached our front about noon. The enemy surged upon our line with greatly superior numbers, and with obstinate fury, but, protected by slight breastworks, our line repulsed every assault, and firmly held the position. The enemy's loss in the immediate front of the Second Brigade, largely exceeded ours. At sundown the enemy had broken the extreme right of our army, and was threatening the Chattanooga road. The division to which the regiment was attached, was ordered to cut its way through to Rossville. The charge was successfully made, but with considerable loss, our line being raked by grape and canister. Our division then halted for rest. The Fourteenth Corps were filing past for Rossville. General Thomas ordered two regiments to cover the retreat. The One Hundred and First and Sixty-Eighth Indiana, were selected. After marching one mile and a half toward the enemy, the command reached Brannan's Brigade, which was holding the front with fixed bayonets, having no ammunition. The enemy were in force over the crest of a hill within speaking distance. Our movements were covered by darkness. Taking ground in front of Brannan's line, he quietly withdrew, and ordered us to follow, which was done, the command reaching Rossville at midnight. The gallant Col. Edward A. King, commanding our brigade; was killed. The regiment lost thirteen killed, eighty-five wounded, and sixteen missing. A total loss of one-hundred and fourteen. The regiment remained at Rossville during the next day, and, at night, moved to Chattanooga; thence went on picket, and, on the 22d, had a sharp picket fight, losing nine wounded and two prisoners. The regiment then retired to Chattanooga.

On the 9th of October, the regiment was assigned to the Second Brigade, Third Division, Fourteenth Army Corps. On the 22d of November, it moved out of camp, and prepared for the assault on Mission Ridge. The regiment took part in the storming of Mission Ridge on the 25th, and moved with our pursuing column to Ringgold, Georgia, losing in the battle thirty-four in killed and wounded. Until the first week in May, 1864, the regiment remained near Chattanooga.

Upon the 7th of May, the regiment moved with Sherman's army, on its Atlanta campaign. The command of Gen. Thomas occupied Tunnel Hill. A demonstration was then made upon Buzzard's Roost. After two days' fighting, the regiment moved with its corps through Snake Creek Gap, and thence to Resacca, where it was engaged. It then moved with the pursuing column to Adairsville and Cassville, participating in fights at each place. Then moved to the right, forded the Etowah river, and moved by the way of Burnt Hickory to Dallas; then took position in line of battle near Pine Hill; then changed to the left near Lost Mountain, and then to Kenesaw Mountain, skirmishing from day to day. The regiment was in support of the Second Division in the assault on Kenesaw Mountain on the 27th of June.

On the 3d of July, the enemy having withdrawn from Kenesaw, the pursuit was pressed, and on the 18th the regiment crossed the Chattahoochee river. On the 22d, crossed Peach Tree Creek and engaged in skirmishing until the 28th of August. Then marched with the army, on the flank movement around Atlanta, and took part in the battle of Jonesboro, on the 1st of September. The regiment then marched to Atlanta. On the 3d of October it joined in the pursuit of Hood. Reaching Gaylesville, the pursuit ceased. The regiment then marched to Kingston, and thence to Atlanta.

On the 17th of November, the regiment started from Atlanta with the left wing of Sherman's army, on its march to Savannah. Marching by the way of Decatur, Oxford, Covington, New Eatonton, and Milledgeville, with but a few skirmishes with the enemy's cavalry, the column reached and entered Savannah on the 23d of December.

On the 20th of January, 1865, the regiment moved with its division, on the campaign through the Carolinas, and reached Goldsboro on the 23d of March. From thence moved to Raleigh, arriving there on the 14th of April. On the 30th, marched by the way of Richmond, Virginia, for Washington, D. C., reaching there on the 19th of May. On the 14th of June it left Washington for Louisville, and arrived there on the 19th. On the 24th of June, 1865, the regiment was mustered out of service at Louisville, Kentucky, and proceeded to Indianapolis, arriving on the 25th, and was greeted with a public ovation in the State House Grounds, after which it was finally discharged and its members returned home.

During its term of service the regiment has marched three thousand five hundred and seven miles, traveled by railroad seven hundred and fifty-nine miles, and by steamer six hundred and fifty miles, being a total of four thousand nine hundred and sixteen miles.

Company B

Sergeant—Foncaunon Harrison

PRIVATE

John W. Hunter

Company G

Sergeant—Lorenzo D. Wilson

PRIVATE

Jeremiah Smith

One Hundred and Twenty-Fourth Regiment Infantry

The One Hundred and Twenty-Fourth Regiment was formed by the consolidation of three companies raised for the One Hundred and Twenty-Fifth Regiment (which was originally intended as an infantry organization), in the Sixth Congressional District, and seven companies recruited from the Fifth Congressional District. The regiment rendezvoused at Richmond, and was mustered into service on the 10th of March, 1864, with JAMES BURGESS as Colonel. The regiment left Indianapolis by rail on the 19th, and arrived at Louisville the same day. From Louisville the regiment moved by rail to Nashville, reaching that place on the 24th. At Nashville the regiment was assigned to the division of Gen. Hovey, consisting of six regiments from Indiana.

On the 5th of April the regiment left Nashville for the front, and marched by the way of Murfreesboro, Shelbyville, Tullahoma, Stevenson, Bridgeport, Chattanooga, Cleveland and Charleston, to Athens, Tennessee. Upon arriving at Athens, the left wing of the regiment was detached and sent to Columbus, Tennessee. For a short time the regiment remained at Athens. Early in May the regiment moved with its corps toward Red Clay, Georgia, and, on its march, was joined by its left wing at Columbus. The Twenty-Third Corps, to which the regiment was assigned, arrived in front of Buzzard's Roost on the 8th of May. A demonstration was made by Gen. Schofield upon that formidable position, the regiment losing one killed and two wounded. A portion of Sherman's army having penetrated Snake Creek Gap, the regiment moved with its division through the Gap, and crossed the Oostanaula river, near Tilton.

Our column then passed to the left of Resacca. On the 18th the regiment marched to Calhoun. The next day it moved to the right of Kingston, skirmishing along the railroad. On the 21st the regiment moved to the right, encountered the enemy, and brisk skirmishing ensued. The two subsequent days were also passed in feeling the enemy and pressing his retiring columns, the regiment reaching a point near Cassville, on the 24th, and bivouacking. The country was very rugged, mountainous and wooded, with but a few obscure roads.

On the 25th the regiment moved to the left of Cartersville, and, throwing up temporary works, remained three days. On the 29th the regiment crossed the Etowah river, and marched to Burnt Hickory, where it again constructed works. On the first of June the regiment moved by the way of Alatoona and Pumpkin Vine Creek, and, after sharp skirmishing, took position opposite to and near Lost Mountain. Temporary works were constructed, and, for two days, sharp fighting was had with the enemy. The skirmish line then moved close to the formidable works of the enemy, the regiment advancing in support under a heavy fire of artillery and musketry. The next morning at daylight the regiment moved upon the enemy's works and found them evacuated. The regiment then took position on the right of Kenesaw Mountain. During these operations the rain fell almost continuously, rendering the narrow roads mere mud gulleys, and making a general movement of the army impossible. The men, however, daily worked closer to the entrenched enemy, and kept up an incessant picket firing, greatly annoying him. On the 23d the regiment advanced close up to the enemy's works on Kenesaw Mountain, and skirmished with his sharpshooters. The picket firing and skirmishing continued until the morning of the 3d of July, when the rebel General Johnson, finding his left turned, and, being in danger of being cut off from Atlanta, suddenly abandoned his strong position on Kenesaw Mountain, and fell back to Smyrna Church.

On the 4th of July the regiment moved toward the Chattahoochee river, and, on the 8th, effected a crossing of that river, fifteen miles above the Atlanta railroad bridge, and at once built defensive works.

On the 9th Col. Burgess resigned, and Lieut. Col. John M. Orr was promoted to the Colonelcy. On the 15th the forward movement was continued, the regiment taking the road to the right of Decatur. Before reaching that point the enemy was encountered, and brisk skirmishing ensued, resulting in the enemy being driven through Decatur, and the capture of that town. Until the 21st the usual skirmishing was carried on, obstinate resistance being encountered from the enemy. On the 21st the regiment reached a position where the hills and steeples of Atlanta were plainly in view.

On the 22d Gen. Dodge's Sixteenth Corps was moving toward the left flank of the army in order to strengthen it, when the rebel army, under Hood, made a sudden onslaught. Hardee's rebel corps penetrated a portion of our lines, and the battle raged furiously along the whole front. Gen. Dodge received and held in check the rebel corps of Hardee, and finally repulsed him with great slaughter. The regiment moved with its division to the support of Gen. Dodge, and aided materially in the repulse of the confident enemy.

The siege of Atlanta progressed vigorously. Digging and skirmishing were the labors of the day and night. Our men, always on the alert to accomplish a movement, found themselves opposed by a vigilant and untiring enemy. The crack of our rifles elicited answering replies. The smoke of our artillery brought forth shot and shell from the enemy's gunners. Thus, day followed day, until the 30th of August, when a new and bold movement developed, result-

One Hundred and Twenty-Fourth Regiment Infantry—Continued

ing in obtaining possession of the communications of Atlanta, and forcing its evacuation. The regiment marched with its division on this movement, crossed the Macon railroad near Rough and Ready, aided in destroying the railroad for several miles. Then moved in the direction of Lovejoy's, taking position on the left of Jonesboro, skirmishing and fortifying. The regiment then withdrew with its corps to Decatur, arriving there on the 8th of September. Here, in clean, pleasant camps, the men rested for a few weeks, proud of having aided in the capture of Atlanta.

The uneasy enemy did not let us rest long. The rebel General Hood, whose sole object seemed to be to have his army destroyed as soon as possible, moved north on the 1st of October, and struck our line of communications. On the 4th the regiment marched with its corps in pursuit. The column moved by the way of Marietta to Alatoona, and thence through Cassville and Kingston to Rome; and, crossing the Oostanaula river at that place on the 12th, a sharp skirmish was had with a portion of the enemy's forces, his main body having marched with great rapidity toward Resacca and Dalton. The column then headed for Calhoun and Resacca, but the rebel army had disappeared before our arrival. The pursuit was continued through Snake Creek and White's Gap to Summerville, and down the Chatooga Valley to Gaylesville, Alabama, where the pursuit was discontinued.

On the 23d of October the regiment moved with its division to Cedar Bluffs. On the 28th the march was taken up through Cave Springs, Rome, Calhoun, Resacca and Tilton, to Dalton, where the regiment embarked on railroad cars, and was transported to Nashville, arriving there on the 9th of November. The Twenty-Third Corps was now part of the command of Gen. Thomas.

On the 10th the regiment moved by rail to Thompson's Station, and from thence marched to Pulaski, reaching that place on the 15th. The rebel army under Hood was now advancing toward Nashville, and General Schofield commenced falling back toward Columbia. On the 21st the regiment marched to Linnville, and on the 23d arrived at Columbia. Temporary breastworks were constructed, and for two days the regiment was engaged in brisk skirmishing with the enemy. On the night of the 26th the regiment crossed to the north bank of the Duck river, and took position at Rutherford's creek. During this time the enemy's infantry was pressing Gen. Schofield's line, and frequently threatened an assault.

Communications with our cavalry having been cut by the enemy, and the line of retreat toward Franklin being imperiled, Gen. Schofield commenced falling back. The regiment, with its brigade, covered the roads by which our army was marching to Franklin. At Spring Hill, the enemy's cavalry was encountered, and severe skirmishing ensued. After a brisk fight the regiment forced its way through, losing Company "C," which was captured by the enemy. The regiment reached Franklin on the morning of the 30th, and immediately took position in line of battle on the southern edge of that town. Slight breastworks were hastily constructed. The enemy soon appeared in force, and made several attempts to carry the position by assault. His successive attacks were met and most decisively repulsed. During the night the regiment fell back with the army to Nashville, and took position to the right of Fort Negley, where it was employed in erecting defenses until the 15th of December.

On the 15th of December the army of Gen. Thomas advanced from its fortifications around Nashville, upon the rebel army of General Hood, and, after two days' severe fighting, inflicted a ruinous defeat upon the rebel foe. The regiment took part in this battle, and joined in the pursuit of Hood's demoralized army. Marching down the Granny White Pike, the regiment reached Franklin on the 18th, crossed the Harpeth river the next day; then marched to Spring Hill, and, crossing the Duck river, arrived at Columbia. The remnants of the rebel army having escaped across the Tennessee river at Bainbridge, the pursuit was discontinued.

On the 3d of January, 1865, the regiment left Columbia and marched by the way of Mount Pleasant to Clifton, where it embarked on transports and proceeded to Cincinnati; thence, by rail, it was carried to Washington City, arriving there on the 30th. Again embarking on transports, the regiment sailed to Morehead City, North Carolina, and landed at that place on the 27th of February. The next day the regiment reached Newbern.

On the 6th of March the regiment marched with Gen. Schofield's column along the railroad toward Kingston. Upon reaching Wise's Forks, the enemy was encountered in a strong position in force. Heavy skirmishing was kept up during the first day. On the 9th, the enemy, being largely reinforced, made an assault upon our left and center, and, after a severe battle, was repulsed, and retreated in much confusion. The regiment took an active part in this battle. On the 15th the regiment crossed the Neuse river and marched to Kingston. Thence to Goldsboro, reaching there on the 21st, where the junction was formed with the victorious columns of Sherman, who had marched from Atlanta to the sea, and from the sea through the strongholds

One Hundred and Twenty-Fourth Regiment Infantry—Continued

of the rebel hiding places, halting in the "Old North State" only long enough to greet their old comrades of the Twenty-Third Corps, and press forward to final victory.

For a short time the regiment was stationed at Lenoir Institute. On the 3d of May the regiment marched to Greensboro, reaching there on the 7th. After remaining a few days at Greensboro, the regiment proceeded to Charlotte, and went into camp. On the 13th of July the regiment left Charlotte and returned to Greensboro, and on the 31st of August, 1865, the regiment was mustered out of the service of the United States at that place. Leaving for home, it arrived at Indianapolis on the 10th of September, with five hundred and thirty-two men and thirty-three officers, under command of Col. John M. Orr. The regiment was present at a reception given to returned soldiers in the State House Grove, and was addressed by General Mansfield and others. The regiment then received final payment and discharge, and with quiet satisfaction, at having done their whole duty, the members of the regiment returned to their homes.

One Hundred and Twenty-Fourth Regiment Infantry

Company A

PRIVATES

John Albright
Philander Allen
Joseph Denner

Llewellyn H. Price
Ephriam Spangler

Company B

First Lieutenant—WILLIAM MYERS

PRIVATES

James S. Baker
Frederick Bickman
Benjamin R. Glines

Henry C. Keever
William E. Martin
Ezra C. Tingle

Company C

Captain—CHARLES EMERY
Second Lieut.—NATHAN KRAUSE, JR.

PRIVATES

Joseph Bartmas
Christian Conklin
Edward Geiger
Ambrose Kutz

Samuel R. McLain
Alvin V. Mitchell
David C. Slagel
Joseph W. Smith

Jacob Smith
Silas Tillison
Charles Fisher

Company D

PRIVATES

William Frey

Erastus C. Godfrey

George W. Opliger

Company E

Second Lieutenant—JOSEPH H. KEEVER

PRIVATES

Peter Lynch
John R. Miller

Peter Long
Patrick Ryan

William McAuench

Company F

PRIVATES

William C. Alshouse
Loran Bethel
Francis Bischoff
John Donnahue

Andrew Grover
John Griffith
George Houston
William Henderson

Frederick Mullenhour
William Thomas
Janvier B. Thomas

Company G

PRIVATES

Samuel D. Cole

John W. Swisher

Company H

First Lieutenant—MARION E. GRISWOLD

PRIVATES

Albert Coats
John Harris
William H. Johnson

James McConaughy
Milton Meranda
Francis Parker

Lawrence Powers
Levi Rhodes
Christian Richards

Company I

PRIVATES

William H. Hunting
Daniel Leary

Joseph Stark
Frank Savoit
Julius C. Wood

Charles Stewart
Wm. C. Vandewater

One Hundred and Twenty-Sixth Regiment

(ELEVENTH CAVALRY)

The Eleventh Cavalry, One Hundred and Twenty-Sixth Regiment of Indiana Volunteers, was recruited under the call of September 14th, 1863, the several companies being raised and organized during the fall and winter of 1863. On the 1st of March, 1864, the regimental organization was perfected at Indianapolis, and the command given to ROBERT R. STEWART, who was taken from the Second Cavalry, in which organization he held the rank of Lieutenant Colonel, and promoted Colonel of the Eleventh Cavalry. On the 1st of May the regiment left the general camp of rendezvous at Indianapolis. and moved thence, by rail, to Nashville, Tennessee, but a small portion of the regiment being mounted. Arriving there on the 7th of May, it went into camp of instruction, and remained there until the 1st of June. It then marched into Northern Alabama, and was placed on duty along the line of the Memphis and Charleston Railroad, with headquarters at Larkinsville, Alabama. The regiment was kept on this duty until the 16th of October, when it marched back to Nashville, where it was mounted and sent to the front.

In the campaign in front of Nashville, in November and December, the Eleventh Cavalry was actively engaged, and, after the defeat of Hood's forces, joined in the pursuit, going as far as Gravelly Springs, Alabama, arriving there on the 7th of January, 1865. It was then dismounted and placed on duty in that vicinity until the 7th of February, when it crossed the Tennessee river to Eastport, Mississippi, and there remained until the 12th of May.

In obedience to orders to report to Major General Dodge at St. Louis, the regiment then embarked on steamers and proceeded to that city, arriving there on the 17th. After being re-mounted it marched to Rolla, Missouri, arriving there on the 26th of June and reporting to Col. Morell, commanding that District. From Rolla the regiment moved to Fort Riley, Kansas, arriving there on the 8th of July. From there it moved to Council Grove, Kansas, and was stationed along the Santa Fe route across the plains, with headquarters at Cottonwood Crossing. The Eleventh Cavalry was continued on this duty until the 1st of September, when it was ordered to march to Fort Leavenworth, where it arrived on the 11th. On the 19th of September, 1865, the regiment was mustered out at that place in compliance with telegram orders received from the General Commanding the Department of Missouri.

On the 26th of September, the regiment reached Indianapolis with thirty officers and five hundred and seventy-nine men, under command of Col. Abram Sharra, for final discharge and payment. On the 28th of September, after partaking of a sumptuous dinner at the Soldier's Home, the Eleventh Cavalry marched to the State House, where it was publicly welcomed by speeches from General Mansfield, Colonel Stewart and Surgeon Read, to which responses were made by Colonel Sharra, Majors Crowder and Showalter and Chaplain Barnhart. After the reception the regiment was marched out to Camp Carrington, where the men and officers were paid and discharged from the service of the United States.

One Hundred and Twenty-Sixth Regiment

(ELEVENTH CAVALRY)

Company C

PRIVATES

Perry Andrews
James W. Barnhart
Sylvanus Bolenbaugh
Mark M. Brown
John Bumgartner
John Burdge
Thomas Cloud
John Countryman
David Dellinger
William Golden
William Hilton
Jacob Horn
Moses McKinzie
Henry Magner
Samuel Major
Thomas Major
Henry McCune
James McGrath
Riley J. Miller
James Mooney

Andrew Slacher
Theodore Summers
Wilson Tague
Riley Thompson
Arthur Watson
Samuel Wert
Gilbert Wilson
Samuel M. Allen
Ethan Babcock
Mordecai Chilcoat
Joshua Chilcoat
John W. Ely
Dudley Gilford
George Johnson
Jonathan D. Kline
William Lynch
John W. Ray
William Slusser
Herod Wenz

Company I

PRIVATE

Thomas J. Shue

Company K

PRIVATE

David Eggiman

One Hundred and Twenty-Seventh Regiment

(TWELFTH CAVALRY)

The Twelfth Cavalry, One Hundred and Twenty-Seventh Regiment, was organized at Kendallville, Indiana, in the Tenth Congressional District, on the 1st of March, 1864, eight companies of which were recruited by Colonel Edward Anderson in the Ninth Congressional District, in the fall and winter of 1863, and were rendezvoused at Michigan City; and four companies were recruited in the Tenth Congressional District, in the fall and winter of 1863, and were rendezvoused at Kendallville; subsequently the companies which were at Michigan City, were removed to Kendallville, for the purpose of completing the regimental organization, and COL. EDWARD ANDERSON was made Colonel of the regiment. Early in May, 1864, it left camp at Kendallville, and proceeded to Indianapolis, and, on the 6th of the same month, the regiment left Indianapolis for the field, under orders to proceed to Nashville, Tennessee. But six companies of the regiment were mounted, and all of the companies were armed as infantry, for want of cavalry arms, until the regiment arrived at Louisville, where the infantry arms were turned over by the six mounted companies, and cavalry arms were issued instead. The mounted portion of the regiment, also the mounted portion of the Ninth and Tenth Cavalry Regiments, marched from Louisville to Nashville, under the command of Col. Anderson, while the dismounted portion of the regiment proceeded to Nashville by rail, under the command of Lieut. Col. Alfred Reed.

The regiment remained at Nashville in camp of instruction for about three weeks, when it was ordered to Huntsville, Alabama, for which place it started on the 29th of May, the dismounted portion proceeding thence by rail, under command of Col. Anderson, and the mounted portion marching from Nashville under the command of Lieut. Col. Reed. Col. Anderson was assigned to the command of the railroad defenses from Decatur, Alabama, to Paint Rock, Alabama, a distance of about sixty miles, and to the command of all that district of country lying between Huntsville and Paint Rock, and between the Tennessee river and the Memphis and Charleston Railroad, that portion of the country being, at the time, infested with several bands of guerrillas and "bushwhackers."

The dismounted companies were assigned to the especial defense of the railroad, and to the erection of blockhouses, under the command of Major Orris Blake, and the six mounted companies (which were the only mounted cavalry then at or near Huntsville), under command of Col. Anderson, were employed very actively in fighting and ridding the country of guerrillas and "bushwackers," in which numerous skirmishes and engagements were fought, and quite a large number of the regiment were killed and wounded.

For about a month after the arrival of the regiment at Huntsville, the headquarters of the regiment were at that place, when they were removed to Brownsborough, where they remained until the 15th of September, 1864, when the regiment was ordered to Tullahoma, Tennessee, to garrison that post, where it arrived on the night of the same day, and reported to Maj. Gen. Milroy. Col. Anderson was assigned to

the command of the post, and also retained command of the regiment. On the 23d of September, Col. Anderson was relieved by orders from the Secretary of War, and was ordered to Indianapolis to report to Governor Morton for special service, soon after which he joined his command in the field. In the absence of Col. Anderson, Major Blake was assigned to the command of the post of Tullahoma and of the regiment, during which time the regiment was constantly employed in watching the movements of the rebel General Forest, who, with a large force, was then threatening Tullahoma and several other points along the Nashville and Chattanooga Railroad. In the meantime the regiment had several skirmishes with a part of Forrest's command, and with bands of guerrillas. In the month of October, 1864, Major Blake was ordered by the Secretary of War to report for duty to the Acting Assistant Provost Marshal General at Indianapolis as assistant.

Three mounted companies, viz: "C," "D," and "H," stationed at Huntsville, under the command of Captain Major D. Williams, of Company "C," participated in the defense of that place, with the Thirteenth Cavalry, on the 1st of October, 1864, against the attack of a portion of the rebel Forrest's command. These companies subsequently joined the regiment at Tullahoma, and on the 26th of November, upon the evacuation of that post, the regiment proceeded to Murfreesboro, Tenn., and participated in the battle of Wilkinson's Pike and Overall's Creek, and was employed in the several skirmishes in the defense of Murfreesboro against the command of Forrest, in December, 1864, Lieut. Col. Reed commanding the regiment, and Col. Anderson commanding the brigade to which the regiment was attached. Soon after which the regiment proceeded to Nashville and went into winter quarters, and there received new arms, and was assigned to the Second Brigade, Seventh Division, Cavalry Corps.

On the 11th of February, 1865, the regiment embarked on board transports and steamers, under orders to proceed to New Orleans, Louisiana, which orders were subsequently countermanded, and the regiment disembarked at Vicksburg, Mississippi, by order of Major General Canby, to engage in a raid along the Mobile and Ohio Railroad. These orders were subsequently countermanded and the regiment was newly mounted, arms changed, and embarked again for New Orleans, where it arrived on the 12th of March, 1865, whence it proceeded to Navy Cove, Mobile Bay, reported to Major General Canby, and participated in the operations against the forts and defenses of Mobile, Alabama, a portion of the regiment acting as escort to Major General Canby, and the balance engaged, also, in running a courier line into Florida, from near Fort Blakely, Alabama.

After the fall of Mobile, the regiment reported, on the 17th of April, to Major General Grierson, and under the command of Major Wm. H. Calkins, participated in the raid of over eight hundred miles through Alabama, into Georgia, and then across the State of Alabama, to Columbus, Mississippi, where it arrived on the 20th day of May, 1865. The regiment was highly and specially compliment-

One Hundred and Twenty-Seventh Regiment—Continued

ed by Major General Grierson, in a letter to Governor Morton, for its gallant conduct and military discipline. Here the regiment remained under the command of Major Blake, until about the middle of July, when Col. Anderson rejoined his command after a temporary absence, and proceeded with a portion of the regiment to Grenada, Mississippi, establishing the headquarters of the regiment there. Three companies, viz: "D," "K" and "L," proceeded to Austin, on the Mississippi River, in command of Capt. D. M. Graves, where they remained about two months, employed in protecting Government cotton and other property, and again reported for duty to Col. Anderson, at Grenada, where that portion of the regiment remained until orders were received for muster out.

The remaining six companies remained at Columbus, Mississippi, and vicinity, engaged in protecting Government cotton, etc., under the command of Major Blake, until they were ordered to proceed to Vicksburg, Mississippi, to join the balance of the regiment which had preceeded them. These companies arrived on the 2d day of November, and on the 10th of November, 1865, the regiment was mustered out of the service at Vicksburg, and ordered to proceed to Indianapolis, where it arrived on the 16th of November, and on the next day was honored with a public dinner by the citizens of the city, and was welcomed home by a public reception at the State House Grove, where addresses were delivered by Governor Baker and Colonel Trussler, Secretary of State, and were responded to by Col. Anderson, Lieut. Col. Reed, Major Calkins and Major Blake. The regiment was finally paid off, and its members received their discharges on the 22d of November, 1865.

Company B

PRIVATES

Edward Burford   Andrew Klotz

Company I

PRIVATES

James W. Garner	Peter Russett
James W. Nuttle	Ezra Van Tassel
Valentine Power	Irwin Kern
Joseph Richart	Edwin Turnock

One Hundred and Twenty-Eighth Regiment Infantry

The One Hundred and Twenty-Eighth Regiment was recruited from the Ninth Congressional District, during the fall and winter of 1863, rendezvoused at Michigan City, and was mustered into service on the 18th of March, 1864, with RICHARD P. DE HART as Colonel and JASPER PACKARD as Lieutenant Colonel. On the 23d the regiment left Michigan City by rail, and proceeded, by the way of Indianapolis and Louisville, to Nashville, where the division, commanded by Gen. Hovey, was organized, and the regiment assigned to the First Brigade. On the 6th of April the regiment started on a march for the front, and, moving by the way of Stevenson, Bridgeport and Chattanooga—through a section of country famed for the beauty of its mountain scenery, where the hills kiss the clouds, and silver streams laugh in the sunshine—reached Charleston, East Tennessee, on the 21st. Gen. Hovey's division was then designated as the First Division, and assigned to the Twenty-Third Army Corps, under command of Gen. Schofield.

On the 4th of May the regiment marched with its corps from Charleston, and entered immediately on the campaign against Atlanta. Sherman's moving columns were concentrating in the vicinity of Chattanooga, preparatory to moving with determined vigor upon the forces of the rebel Gen. Johnson, who, apparently secure behind the inaccessible ridges of Rocky Face, challenged our advance through the dangerous defile of Buzzard's Roost Gap, leading to Dalton. But Sherman decided to take another route, and not expose his men to certain destruction from the fire of plunging shot, or the deep waters of the creek by which the enemy flooded the Pass. The Pass was unapproachable, and the "Great Flanker" turned to the left—and left the enemy in position.

On the 9th of May General Schofield moved with his corps close to Dalton, while General Thomas demonstrated with vigor against Rocky Face Ridge. Meanwhile McPherson reached Snake Creek Gap, surprised a force of the enemy, and held the Gap. On the 12th the whole army, save one corps, moved through the Gap on Resacca. The battle of Resacca resulted. Thus, constantly moving, threatening, flanking and fighting, the approaches to Atlanta were won, the One Hundred and Twenty-Eighth taking part in the principal movements, culminating in such battles as Resacca, Dallas, New Hope Church, Lost Mountain, Kenesaw Mountain, Atlanta and Jonesboro.

From the 8th of May until the 5th of September, under the broiling sun by day and the pestilential dews by night—through difficult ravines; skirmishing in dense forests; drenched by heavy rains; struggling through mud and mire—our troops pressed on. Some portion of the regiment was on the skirmish line nearly every day for four months.

On the 9th of June Gen. Hovey retired from the command of the First Division, and the First Brigade was assigned to the Third Division (Cox's) of the same corps. On the 6th of June, Col. De Hart having been disabled by wounds, Lieut. Col. Packard assumed command of the regiment. On the 9th of August the First Brigade was reorganized, and the One Hundred and Twenty-Eighth assigned to the Third Brigade of the same division, the brigade being under command of Col. I. N. Stiles of the Sixty-Third Indiana. After the fall of Atlanta the regiment marched from Jonesboro to Decatur, Georgia, where it went into camp with the rest of the corps.

On the 1st of October the rebel Gen. Hood crossed the Chattahoochee river with his army, and marched north, by the way of Dallas. Sherman's army, with the exception of the Twentieth Corps, moved in pursuit. The regiment left Decatur with its corps on the 4th, and, crossing the Chattahoochee, moved toward Dallas, threatening the flank and rear of the enemy's forces then assaulting Alatoona. The rebels being defeated at Alatoona, moved rapidly to the northwest, striking the railway at Resacca, on the 12th, and capturing Tilton and Dalton. The army of Sherman meanwhile made a march to Rome, where the Twenty-Third Corps crossed the Oostaunaula and drove a brigade of the enemy through the narrow entrance of the valley of the Chattooga, capturing two guns. Then learning that the enemy had moved for Resacca, the pursuit was continued through Resacca, Snake Creek Gap, Villanow, Dirt Town and Gover's Gap, to Gaylesville, Alabama, which place was reached on the 20th. The regiment marched, in this pursuit, over three hundred miles.

On the 30th of October, the Twenty-Third Corps was detached from Sherman's army, and ordered to proceed to Chattanooga and report to General Thomas. The regiment marched with its corps to Chattanooga, and was moved from thence by rail to Pulaski and Nashville. So soon as it was ascertained that Hood was moving to invade Tennessee, the regiment moved with its corps to Columbia. On the 24th of November, the skirmishers of the One Hundred and Twenty-Eighth encountered the advance of the enemy. For six days severe skirmishing was had with the enemy's line at Columbia, one-half of the regiment being alternately on the skirmish line. The enemy's line pressed our line strongly, but did not assault. Meantime Gen. Schofield made preparations to fall back to Franklin. During the night of the 29th, the regiment marched twenty-six miles, and reached Franklin at daybreak of the 30th. The enemy followed closely, and repeatedly assaulted our line at Franklin as soon as we had formed, but Gen. Schofield had chosen an excellent position, and repulsed the rebel onslaught with decisive results. The regiment lost several officers and men in this battle, which was fought with great fury and obstinacy, the enemy continuing his assaults until late on the night of the 30th. The battle of Franklin was the first severe check of Hood's invasion of Tennessee.

The regiment fell back the night after the battle to Brentwood Hills, and the next morning marched to Nashville and took position in its defenses. For two weeks the army of Gen. Thomas faced the rebel force of Gen. Hood, who occupied the southern approaches to Nashville.

On the 15th of December, Gen. Thomas' army moved upon the enemy in his chosen position, and, after two days' fighting, utterly defeated the boastful foe, and drove his demoralized command beyond the waters of the Tennessee. This battle closed the existence of Hood's army. From that time it ceased to exist as an organized body. The regiment was actively engaged in the closing up of Hood, and joined in the pursuit as far as Columbia, Tennessee, arriving at that place on the 26th. Here the command rested for a short time preparatory to another campaign which was to strangle the last army of the rebellion.

On the 5th of January, 1865, the regiment left Columbia and marched by the way of Mount Pleasant and Waynesboro, to Clifton, on the Tennessee river, where it embarked on transports and sailed to Cincinnati, Ohio. From thence the regiment moved by rail to Washington City, and thence to Alexandria, Virginia. On the 20th of February, the regiment embarked on the steamer Atlantic, and sailed to Fort Fisher, North Carolina, and from thence, without landing, sailed to Morehead City, North Carolina, where the regiment disembarked and was conveyed by rail to Newbern.

Early in March the regiment set out with its division, and marched along the Atlantic and North Carolina railroad in the direction of Kingston, repairing the railroad as the column moved. On the 8th of March, the enemy was encountered in force at Wise's Fork, four miles below Kingston. The enemy had met with success in capturing two regiments of Eastern troops by surprise, and was pushing on, confident of easy victory, when he was met and checked by Ruger's division just arriving on the field. For two days heavy skirmishing resulted, and on the 10th, the enemy made a heavy assault, but was repulsed and fled in great disorder from the field. The regiment took an active part in this fight, losing severely in killed and wounded. The whole command then moved to Kingston, which was occupied without resistence from the enemy.

On the 20th the regiment left Kingston, and after a march of thirty miles, reached Goldsboro, on the evening of the next day. On the 25th it left Goldsboro and marched to Le Noir Institute, where the regiment was employed in protecting the railroad until the 9th of April. The regiment then returned to Goldsboro, and was assigned to duty in that city. The regiment was yet stationed at Raleigh, North Carolina, in January, 1866, at the time this sketch was written. The regiment was commanded by Col. DeHart until the 6th of June, 1864, when being wounded, Lieut. Col. Jasper Packard assumed command and has led the regiment ever since. On the 29th of April, 1865, Col. DeHart being mustered out by order of War Department, Lieut. Col. Jasper Packard was promoted to the Colonelcy. Subsequently Col. Packard was promoted to the rank of Brevet Brigadier General of Volunteers, by the President, to date March 13, 1865.

Company K

PRIVATES

Benjamin Purdue
William S. Apple
Patrick Broderick
Jesse A. Cramer
Isaac Golliday

One Hundred and Twenty-Ninth Regiment Infantry

The One Hundred and Twenty-Ninth Regiment was recruited from the Tenth Congressional District during the winter of 1863 and 1864, rendezvoused at Michigan City, and was mustered into service on the 1st of March, 1864, with CHARLES CASE as Colonel, and CHARLES A. ZOLLINGER as Lieutenant Colonel.

On the 30th of March, the regiment left its camp at Michigan City, and was conveyed by rail via Louisville to Nashville, where it arrived on the 7th of April. Lieut. Col. Zollinger was in command of the regiment. Upon its arrival at Nashville the regiment was assigned to the Second Brigade, First Division, Twenty-Third Army Corps.

On the 5th of April, the regiment took up its line of march for Loudon, East Tennessee, but, before reaching that point, its orders were changed, and the regiment marched for Charleston, East Tennessee, arriving there on the 24th. Thus was accomplished a march of two hundred miles by a regiment fresh from the hamlets and towns of Indiana. As the column wound through the fertile valleys and over the rugged mountains that characterize the country through which it passed, the men were enthusiastic in their admiration of the natural beauty of the country. There was but little time for rest, however, for, so soon as the first division had joined its corps at Charleston, orders came to move on a campaign that was to strike a formidable blow at the rebel strongholds guarding Atlanta.

On the 3d of May, the regiment moved with its corps toward Dalton, reaching there in time to participate in the initiatory demonstration that opened the campaign against Atlanta. On the 12th, the regiment marched through Snake Creek Gap, and, breaking through a dense forest, took position near Resacca. On the 15th, a heavy battle ensued at Resacca, the enemy being defeated and driven across the Oostanaula river. The regiment joined in the pursuit, moving over blind roads on the left, and, crossing the Oostanaula river above Resacca, found the enemy strongly entrenched near Cassville. On the 20th, the rebel army fled across the Etowah river. The regiment reached the banks of the Etowah, and encamped for two days, waiting for supplies. On the 25th, the regiment crossed the Etowah river, and moved upon the enemy's position at New Hope Church. Before reaching there, however, the enemy, after a severe engagement with a portion of our army, had fallen back to Lost Mountain. The regiment, for several weeks afterward, was almost constantly skirmishing with the enemy, pushing through deep defiles and heavy underbrush. During this period the rain fell almost continuously, rendering the roads almost impassable. On the 15th of June, Lieut. Col. Zollinger was promoted Colonel, having had active command of the regiment ever since its departure for the field. Colonel Case resigned early in June.

On the 19th of July, the regiment was engaged in a severe fight near Decatur, Georgia, losing very heavily in killed and wounded. Sherman's army was now closing around Atlanta, and brisk skirmishing met our advances in every new movement. On the 5th of August, a brigade of Schofield's corps tried to break through the enemy's line about a mile below Utoy creek, but failed to carry the position. The next day Gen. Hascall, commanding the division to which the regiment was attached, attacked and turned the position, resulting in the engagement of Strawberry Run, in which the regiment lost twenty-five in killed and wounded.

On the 29th of August, the regiment marched with its corps round East Point, and came into position near Rough and Ready, on the railroad, which was at once destroyed. Other portions of Sherman's army were doing similar work, and, on the 1st of September, it was ascertained that the enemy had abandoned Atlanta. The regiment then marched with its corps to Decatur, and went into camp. Thus, after four months' campaign, our army gained possession of the mountain regions of the center of the rebel dominion, and the Atlantic and Gulf slopes were open to the movements of our veterans.

On the 4th of October the regiment moved with its corps in pursuit of Hood, who had cut Sherman's communications at Big Shanty, and was demonstrating on the garrisons guarding our supplies along the railroad that formed our only line of supply. Moving by the way of Marietta, Alatoona, Cassville, Kingston, Rome, Resacca, and Snake Creek Gap, the regiment arrived at Gaylesville, Alabama, where furthur pursuit of Hood's flying columns ceased. The Twenty-Third Corps was then detached to the command of Gen. Thomas, and the regiment marched with its corps to Chattanooga, and from thence was transported by rail to Nashville and Johnsonville, where it remained until the 20th of November. The regiment then moved to Columbia, and occupied the crossings of Duck River. For three days the enemy pressed our position at Columbia, and heavy skirmishing was carried on. On the 29th the regiment fell back across Duck River, burning the railroad bridge in its rear. The enemy's column having passed our flank, the regiment marched rapidly with its corps to Franklin. The enemy followed closely, and, on the 30th, assaulted our position at Franklin. Our ground was well chosen, and, after several severe assaults, the enemy was decisively repulsed with great loss. The regiment met with heavy loss in killed and wounded at the battle of Franklin. Our army fell back during the night to Nashville, and the regiment took position in the suburbs of that city, and threw up defensive works.

On the 15th of December the regiment moved from Nashville, and advancing with Gen. Thomas' army on the fortified position of the rebel army of Gen. Hood, participated in the two days' battle which resulted in the utter rout of the enemy, and his disastrous retreat across the Tennessee river. The regiment joined in the pursuit until it was discontinued.

On the 5th of January, 1865, the regiment marched with its division to Clifton, and embarking in transports, sailed to Cincinnati. Thence it was conveyed by railroad to Washington City, and from thence by steamer to Cape Fear inlet. Fort Fisher being already captured and Wilmington secured by Gen. Schofield, the regiment, without landing, sailed by sea to Morehead City, to reinforce the column about to move from Newbern. The regiment landed at Morehead City, and proceeded by rail to Newbern.

On the 6th of March the regiment moved with the main column from Newbern, and marched along the railroad in the direction of Kingston, repairing the railroad as it advanced. On the 8th the enemy encountered our advance and captured two regiments of Connecticut volunteers. Flushed with success his columns rapidly advanced, and endeavored to check our further progress; but he was met and checked by Ruger's division of the Twenty-Third Corps, to which the regiment was attached. Very heavy skirmishing at once ensued, the enemy making bold attempts to drive our line from position. On the 10th, the enemy being largely reinforced, the heavy skirmishing culminated in a battle. The enemy made several desperate assaults, all of which were met and repulsed, with great loss to the enemy, and during the following night the enemy fled in great disorder leaving his killed and wounded. Thus ended the engagement at Wise's Forks, in which the regiment took an active part, losing very heavily. Our way was now open to Kingston, and the regiment pushed on with the main column to Kingston, and from thence to Goldsboro, reaching there on the 21st. From Goldsboro the regiment moved to Mosley Hall, where it remained until the 5th of April. It then moved to Goldsboro, rejoined its corps, and marched to Raleigh. From Raleigh the regiment moved to Charlotte, reaching there on the 9th of May. Here the regiment was engaged in provost duty during the summer of 1865. On the 29th of August, 1865, the regiment was mustered out of the service of the United States at Charlotte, North Carolina, and started for home. The regiment reached Indianapolis early in September, with five hundred three officers and men, was present at a reception to returned soldiers in the State House Grove, and welcomed by addresses from General Mansfield and others. The regiment soon received final payment and discharge, and its members returned to the peaceful vocations of life.

Officers

Colonel—CHARLES CASE.
Lieut. Col.—CHARLES A. ZOLLINGER
Adjutant—HERMAN C. HAHN
Quartermaster—JOSEPH W. COPE

Company B

Captain—CHARLES A. ZOLLINGER
First Lieutenant—JAMES HARPER
Second Lieutenant—NAHAM TILBERY
Sergeants—BENJAMIN H. BROWN
OWEN DAVIS
Corporals—SAMUEL F. LEARD
ANDREW CRAMER
JAMES F. McCLURE
Musicians—JOHN F. TISRON
ANDREW TREEPE

PRIVATES

Jacob Baker	William T. Garver	John Rosenberger	Oscar T. Vanada	James McConnel
Wesley Bilderback	Joshua Hartzell	John Rich	Elisha Wilson	Josiah Salter
Sebastian Barnnard	Elias Hartzell	Isaac Sultz	John Scannell	Joseph Shuler
Levi Brollyer	Ambrose James	Ohio Smith	William McDorman	Phillip Shaffer
Casper Conrad	George H. Kime	Lewis Slandroff	Cyrus Her	Frank Vavier
Francis M. Coleman	Isaac Klinger	Milo Thompson	George Coles	John W. Webster
Albert Carter	Daniel Mercer	Jasper Tilberry	Wesley J. Eastwood	Thomas Cissell
John W. Deetrick	Frank McKinney	Oliver H. Wilson	James M. Fletter	Gabriel Dinkins
William H. Deetrick	Dennis Monahan	Joseph Warner	Frederick Felton	Patrick Doyle
Michael Daugherty	William B. McMakin	John S. White	Willis Green	John Drewey
David F. Deetrick	Henry Myres	Peter D. Bovie	Clark Hill	Albert Mosher
Henry Dreear	Joseph Peters	James C. Judge	Samuel Lowery	Samuel C. Scott
Cyrus Fike	Christopher Platter	Amasa S. Knapp	Michael Lucey	Raymond J. Spaulding
John W. Frankenberger	Adrain Rogers			

Company C

Corporal—BENJAMIN F. BETHEL

PRIVATES

Stratten Bennett	Evans Bennett	Dick Kreite

Company D

PRIVATES

William Finney	James Sinclair	Henry F. Smith	John Snyder	Ebenezer Rodenberger
Isaac Grimes	Thomas F. Spacy	Charles Hackett	William D. Clark	George T. Scales
George W. Krider	Samuel W. Scott	John W. Kline	William Cochran	John A. White
Isaiah W. Sipe				

Company F

Corporals—FRANCIS F. McCLELLAND   URIAH J. SHIRTS

PRIVATES

Andrew I. Kimes   George Kniss

Company I

PRIVATES

Whitmore Gardner	Henry Myres	Charles Wells	James A. Humphrey

One Hundred and Thirtieth Regiment Infantry

The One Hundred and Thirtieth Regiment was recruited from the Eleventh Congressional District during the winter of 1863 and 1864, rendezvoused at Kokomo, and was mustered into service on the 12th of March, 1864, with CHARLES S. PARRISH as Colonel. The regiment left its camp at Kokomo on the 16th, and moving by rail by the way of Indianapolis and Louisville, arrived at Nashville, where it was assigned to the Second Brigade, First Division, Twenty-Third Army Corps. On the 5th of April the regiment left Nashville, and took up its line of march for Charleston, East Tennessee, passing through Murfreesboro, Shelbyville, Tullahoma, Stevenson, Chattanooga and Cleveland, and arriving at Charleston on the 24th. On the 3d of May the regiment broke camp and took up its line of march for the front, passing through Cleveland, Tennessee, and Red Clay, Georgia, and on the 9th first came into the presence of the enemy at Rocky Face Ridge. The regiment was in front of a conical peak, surrounded by heavy guns, and surrounded by formidable works at its base. This elevation was known by the name of "Tater Hill." The regiment was engaged in support of a detachment, which advancing on this position of the enemy, drove him into his works. From that time until the 15th of May there was a continual series of skirmishes, terminating in the decisive battle of Resacca, during which the regiment received and repelled a charge of the enemy. After the battle the regiment joined in the pursuit, and crossed the Etowah river on the 24th. Skirmishing was almost constant, as day followed day. The rain fell in torrents, and the men were destitute of shelter, and for a long time short of rations. On the 17th of June the regiment was engaged with the enemy at Lost Mountain. On the 22d an engagement took place at Pine Mountain, during which the rebels were repulsed. On the 27th the regiment was engaged upon the left of Kenesaw Mountain, and the rebels driven into their works. The advanced position obtained by the regiment in this bold movement was held for several days. Upon being relieved the regiment moved with its division in pursuit o the enemy, who had fallen back to the Chattahoochee river. On the 11th of July the regiment crossed the Chattahoochee river, and fortified a strong position on its banks. On the 17th the regiment advanced toward Decatur, and, encountering the enemy, drove him through Decatur, and assisted in destroying the railroad.

The siege of Atlanta was now vigorously pressed. The regiment was constantly under fire. On the 6th of August, the regiment moved with its brigade upon a rebel battery, which was annoying our flank. The column moved through a dense woods. and, emerging into an open field, came in full view of the rebel guns, strongly supported by infantry, on the opposite side of the field. A charge was at once made, the enemy driven from his position, and a few prisoners captured. On the 29th of August the regiment moved with Sherman's army on its flank movement around Atlanta, and was engaged in the battle of Jonesboro. From thence it moved to Lovejoy's station, and, returning with its corps, went into camp at Decatur.

On the 4th of October, the rebel Gen. Hood moved north, in feeble imitation of Gen. Sherman's flank movement. The regiment marched with its corps in pursuit, and having followed his devious course as far as Gaylesville, Alabama, halted for a short time, while Hood, bent upon certain destruction, pushed on north.

On the 30th of October the Twenty-Third was assigned to the command of Gen. Thomas at Nashville, and the regiment marched with its corps to Chattanooga, and was conveyed by rail from that place to Columbia; thence it marched to Centreville, where the regiment was engaged in watching the fords of Duck river, threatened by the advance of Hood's army. On the 30th of November it was ascertained that the enemy had passed the left flank of our army, and was moving on Franklin. The regiment then abandoned its position at Centreville, and marching in the rear of Hood's army, by a rapid movement, reached Clarksville on the Tennessee river, and from thence moved to Nashville, where it took position with its brigade in the fortifications.

On the 15th of December the regiment moved with the army of Gen. Thomas, and took part in the two days' battle in front of Nashville, which resulted in the extinction of Hood's army. Joining in the pursuit, it pushed on rapidly, through mud and rain, until the 27th, when further pursuit ceased, and the regiment went into camp at Columbia.

On the 5th of January, 1865, the regiment marched from Columbia for Clifton, and upon reaching that place embarked on transports, sailed to Cincinnati, and from thence was transported by rail to Washington City. Embarking on a steamboat at Alexandria, the regiment sailed to Fort Fisher, North Carolina, and disembarked. From Fort Fisher the regiment moved to Fort Anderson. On the 1st of March the regiment embarked and sailed to Morehead City, and from thence went by rail to Newbern, North Carolina. On the 6th of March the regiment marched with its brigade from Newbern, and proceeded along the line of the railroad. On the 8th the enemy were encountered in force at Wise's Forks, about four miles from Kingston. Sharp skirmishing ensued for two days, resulting in a severe battle, the enemy being repulsed, and abandoning the field in great confusion. The regiment was actively engaged in this battle, and moved, immediately after its close, to Kingston, which was occupied without resistance from the enemy.

General Schofield at once put a large number of troops at work upon the railway, rebuilt the wagon bridge over the Neuse river, and brought forward supplies, preparatory to making another movement. On the morning of the 20th of March the regiment left Kingston with its division and entered Goldsboro, with but slight opposition, on the ensuing day. Thus a junction was formed with the main army under Gen. Sherman, and our forces having free communication with the sea, both by river and railway, one great object of the campaign was accomplished.

Sherman's army rested a short time at Goldsboro, preparatory to opening a new campaign. Meantime General Sherman turned over the command of his army to Gen.

One Hundred and Thirtieth Regiment Infantry—Continued

Schofield, and left for City Point, Virginia, for the purpose of having an interview with Lieut. Gen. Grant, and arranging the manner of co-operation for the coming campaign. Gen. Sherman, having received his instructions, returned and reached Goldsboro on the 30th of March. Soon afterwards orders were issued for the guidance of the army.

On the 10th of April, at daybreak, the heads of columns of Gen. Sherman's army were marching for Smithfield toward the enemy. A few miles from Goldsboro the rebel cavalry were encountered behind rail barricades, but the columns, pressing on, swept the rebel skirmishers before them, and entered Smithfield on the 11th. Here the news was received of the surrender of Lee's rebel army at Appomattox Court House, Virginia, which was hailed with glad shouts by the soldiers. Gen. Sherman at once gave orders to drop all trains, and the army marched rapidly in pursuit of the enemy to and through Raleigh, arriving at that place on the 14th of April in a heavy rain. The rebel army was retreating rapidly toward Greensboro, and Sherman prepared to follow, when a communication from the rebel Gen. Johnson arrested hostile movements.

From Raleigh the regiment moved to Greensboro, and from thence to Charlotte, North Carolina, where it went into camp with its division. During the summer and fall of 1865, the regiment was employed in guard duty at Charlotte. On the 2d of December, 1865, the regiment was mustered out of service at Charlotte, and started for home, arriving at Indianapolis on the 13th, with twenty-seven officers and five hundred and forty men. Upon its arrival it was greeted with a public reception in the State House grove, and, its members receiving final payment and discharge, left for home. Col. Charles S. Parrish, who had commanded the regiment during its entire term of service, was promoted by the President to Brevet Brigadier General, to date from March 13, 1865.

Company E

Corporal—Louis C. Gould

PRIVATES

Augustus Hair
David Montgomery
William Todd

Company F

PRIVATE

David Brown

Company G

Corporal—Adam Wolf

PRIVATE

John Bear

Company H

PRIVATES

John W. Snider
Norris E. Melott

One Hundred and Thirty-First Regiment

THIRTEENTH CAVALRY)

The Thirteenth Cavalry, One Hundred and Thirty-First Regiment, was the last cavalry organization raised in the State. Recruiting for the companies composing the regiment was commenced in September, 1863, and continued during the fall and winter of that year. On the 29th of April, 1864, the organization of the regiment was completed, by its muster into service, with GILBERT M. L. JOHNSON as Colonel. On the 30th of the same month it left Indianapolis, dismounted and with infantry arms and accoutrements, for Nashville, Tennessee. The regiment remained in camp of instruction at that place until the 31st of May, when it was ordered to Huntsville, Alabama, for the purpose of garrisoning that post. During the stay of the command at that place, it was engaged in several skirmishes with prowling bands of rebel cavalry, and on the 1st of October, held the place against the entire command of the rebel Gen. Buford.

On the 16th of October, companies "A," "C," "D." "F," "H," and "I," under command of Col. Johnson, proceeded to Louisville, Kentucky, for the purpose of drawing horses and equipments for the entire command. Upon their arrival there, the companies were ordered to Paducah, under command of Major Moore, to assist in repelling an attack of Gen. Forest. Leaving Paducah on the 1st of November, they returned to Louisville, where the object of their mission was completed, and the line of march was taken up for Nashville, at which point the remaining companies from Huntsville, reported to Regimental headquarters. On the 30th of November, companies "A," "C," "D," "F," "H" and "I," fully mounted and equipped, under command of Col. Johnson, proceeded to Lavergne, under orders from Gen. Thomas to watch the movements of Hood's army, then advancing on Nashville. These companies being cut off from the line of retreat, retired, in obedience to orders from Gen. Wilson, upon Murfreesboro, reporting to Gen. Rousseau, under whose direction they participated in the battles of Overall's Creek, Wilkinson's Pike and twelve different skirmishes with the enemy, with a loss of sixty-five men killed and wounded, and two men missing, from an aggregate present for duty of three hundred and twenty-five. During the same period companies "B," "E," "G," "K," "L" and "M," left at Nashville under command of Lieut. Col. Pepper, participated, dismounted, in the battle of Nashville on the 15th and 16th of December, immediately after which they were joined by the other six companies from Murfreesboro. After effecting an exchange of arms and procuring

an entire remount, the regiment was assigned to the 2d Brigade, 7th Division of the Cavalry Corps of the Military Division of the Mississippi, Col. Johnson commanding the brigade.

On the 11th of February, 1865, the Thirteenth Cavalry embarked on transports for New Orleans, but disembarked at Vicksburg, under the orders of Gen. Canby, to prepare for a raid on the Mobile and the Ohio Railroad. These orders being countermanded, the regiment left Vicksburg on transports, on the 6th of March, for its original destination, and, on arriving at New Orleans, re-embarked for Navy Cove, Mobile Bay, where it reported to Gen. Canby, and assisted in the operations against the forts and defenses of Mobile. It was also engaged in running a courier line to Florida, connecting with Gen. Asboth. After the fall of Mobile, under command of Gen. Grierson, the regiment was placed in condition for a long march, and, on the 17th of April, started on a raid of some eight hundred miles through the States of Alabama, Georgia and Mississippi, arriving at Columbus, in the latter State, on the 22d of May. From thence it proceeded to Macon, Mississippi, garrisoning that point and the line of railroad, sixty miles in extent, and taking possession of immense quantities of captured commissary, quartermaster and ordnance stores and ordnance. On the 6th of June, the regiment returned to Columbus, Mississippi, and remained there until orders were received for muster-out, when it proceeded to Vicksburg, where it was mustered out of service on the 18th of November, 1865. Proceeding homeward, it reached Indianapolis on the 25th of November, with twenty-three officers and six hundred and thirty-three men, for final discharge, and, on that day, partook of a substantial dinner at the Soldier's Home, after which the regiment marched to the State House, where it was publicly received by an assemblage of citizens. Lieut. Governor Baker, in an appropriate speech, welcomed the soldiers home. He was followed by Gen. Thomas W. Bennett, after which Gen. G. M. L. Johnson, Lieut. Col. Moore and Captain Walls responded in behalf of the regiment.

In June, 1865, Col. Johnson was assigned to the command of the sub-district of north-east Mississippi, and from that date until the muster-out of the regiment, Col. Johnson held this important command, the immediate command of the regiment devolving upon Lieut. Col. Moore. On the 25th of September, 1865, in consideration of meritorious services rendered, Col. Johnson was promoted to the rank of Brevet Brigadier General.

One Hundred and Thirty-First Regiment

(THIRTEENTH CAVALRY)

Commissary Sergeant—JEREMIAH BIGGS
Sergeant—ZACHARIAH ALLERTON
Corporals—HAMILTON HARPER
MICHAEL DEAN
EPHRAIM REYNOLDS
Farrier—JAMES BOWLES
Wagoner—WILLIAM REYNOLDS

PRIVATES

Oscar Curtis
Abraham Crabill
Alexander Dawkins
George W. Ferguson
Thomas A. Gilpin
Charles A. Graeber
Charles Hammond
Samuel Jones
John Lee
William H. Lopshire
Samuel Morningstar
Nicholas Memmert
Samuel Sackett
Albert Shell

John Yeager
Thompson Bronson
Joseph Gibson
Wyman Holmes
Thomas Henderson
Barnum Hutchins
Charles Bohlus
John A. Cash
Benjamin F. Cavins
William Horton
James B. Parker
John Riley
Dennis Winkler

One Hundred Days' Volunteers

The Governors of Ohio, Indiana, Illinois, Iowa and Wisconsin having offered to raise for the service of the General Government a force of volunteers to serve for one hundred days, Governor Morton, on the 23d of April, 1864, issued his call for Indiana's proportion of that force. The troops thus raised were to perform such military services as might be required of them in any State, and were to be armed, subsisted, clothed and paid by the United States but were not to receive any bounty. These troops were designed to aid in making the campaign of 1864 successful and decisive, by relieving a large number of veterans from garrison and guard duty, and allow them to join their companions in arms, then about entering upon one of the most active and important campaigns of the war. Their places were filled by the One Hundred Days' Men as fast as the latter could be organized into regiments and sent forward from the camps of rendezvous. The organizations from Indiana consisted of eight regiments, numbered consecutively from the One Hundred and Thirty-Second to the One Hundred and Thirty-Ninth, inclusive.

One Hundred and Thirty-Seventh Regiment

The One Hundred and Thirty-Seventh Regiment was organized and mustered into service at Indianapolis, on the 27th of May, 1864, with EDWARD J. ROBINSON as Colonel, and proceeded to Tennessee. Five of the companies were from the counties in the Third Congressional District; and five from other portions of the State, as follows: One from Kokomo, one from Medora, one from Zanesville, one from Sullivan county, one from Rockville and a consolidated company from Owen and Lawrence counties.

One Hundred and Thirty-Ninth Regiment Infantry

The One Hundred and Thirty-Ninth Regiment was organized and mustered into service, at Indianapolis on the 8th of June, 1864, with GEORGE HUMPHREY as Colonel, and soon after, proceeded to Tennessee. The companies composing the regiment were raised as follows: Elizaville, Lawrenceburg, Kendallville, Knightstown, Connersville, Newcastle, Portland and Vevay each furnished one company, while New Albany and Metamora furnished a consolidated company and Columbia City, New Haven and New Philadelphia furnished another.

Each of these regiments, on arriving at Nashville, was assigned to duty at different places along the lines of the Nashville and Chattanooga, Tennessee and Alabama and Memphis and Charleston Railroads, and, until the latter part of August, 1864, were kept constantly engaged in guarding these lines of communication, used by Gen. Sherman for the transportation of supplies to his army then advancing on Atlanta. The regiments all served beyond the period of one hundred days and returned to Indianapolis where they were finally discharged from service.

One Hundred and Thirty-Seventh Regiment Infantry
(ONE HUNDRED DAYS)

Company E

Captain—JAMES SEWELL
First Lieutenant—JOHN RILEY
Second Lieutenant—WILLIAM A. CRAWFORD

PRIVATES

Alexander W. Austin
Matthew B. Allen
Matthias W. Bohman
John Brundige
Wilson R. Brundige
Columbus Beaber
Benjamin Clark
John Crawford
Henry Coverdale
Isaac B. Dawes
Cyrus Dustman

James G. Foreman
James Foster
John W. Foughty
David Heathman
Judson Hyser
Elias B. Kore
William B. Kyle
Albert A. Knowlton
George H. Knowlton
Abraham Lennington
Abram J. Lopshire

John Ligget
John W. Lacey
Emanuel Matthias
Joseph Myres
Darius McGinnis
George W. Mills
George H. McLean
George Miller
Jesse Osman
John T. Patterson

Frank A. Robinson
Samuel Roberts
Edward Roberts
Daniel Stump
James K. P. Shepler
Adam Smith
Albert Shultz
Lawrence Sewall
Jacob J. Todd
George W. Weaver

One Hundred and Thirty-Ninth Regiment Infantry
(ONE HUNDRED DAYS)

Officers

Colonel—GEORGE HUMPHREY
Adjutant—CHAUNCEY B. OAKLEY

Company H

First Lieutenant—GEORGE W. BELL

PRIVATES

Joseph P. Anderson
Isadore A. Bryant
John L. Black
John Bengout
Justice Burns
Henry Bauer
Benjamin F. Botts
Henry Brubaker
George Brubaker
William H. Boyce
John Baber
Samuel Collet
Martin Crabill
Willis W. Case
Philip S. Cartill
Winfield S. Clark
Henry C. Clark
Winfield T. Durbin
Henry C. Durbin
Edward Dunnegan
William M. Durbin

William T. Ferguson
Emanuel K. Flory
John D. Feagler
Samuel W. Feagler
Theodore F. Gorden
Levi Garrison
Daniel Grover
George W. Gregg
Michael Huston
Jacob Heffelfinger
John W. Hartley
George H. Hoyne
Darius K. Houghton
George James
Enos Kuhlman
Marshal Keernan
William W. Labar
Franklin Lester
Alfred Martin
John W. Maley
James B. Maars

Warren W. Martin
George W. Myers
Miles Newby
Charles Overman
Drewery H. Oliver
Nelson Parker
Albert C. Pattee
James Provines
James B. Ramsey
Eugene V. Smith
David C. Stillwell
Samuel P. Sauers.
John W. Sellers
John T. Smith
John W. Shuster
Joseph Snodgrass
George Senkpiel
John C. Salmon
George Stultz
Edward H. B. Scriven

Benjamin F. Stalker
Benjamin F. Spurgeon
George Smith
William Snith
Henry Smith
Leonard Shull
William S. Thomas
James R. Voss
Henry Walker
William H. Warden
Horatio Wood
Christian Wells
John Wells
William H. Withers
Hiram Weirich
George Wineland
James Williams
Rezin M. Youtz
Levi Zumbrum
Charles E. Rush

One Hundred and Forty-Second Regiment Infantry
(ONE YEAR SERVICE)

The One Hundred and Forty-Second Regiment was recruited for the one year service, under the call of July, 1864, most of the companies being from the Tenth Congressional District, the recruiting rendezvous being at Fort Wayne. The companies and detachments having reported to the general rendezvous at Indianapolis, the regiment was there organized and mustered into service on the 3d of November, 1864, with JOHN M. COMPARET as Colonel.

On the 18th of November the regiment left Indianapolis for Nashville, and on its arrival there was assigned to the garrison of the post, and while so engaged was attached to the Second Brigade, Fourth Division of the Twentieth Army Corps—which division was left behind in Tennessee, at the time the Twentieth Corps marched with Sherman through Georgia.

During the battle of Nashville, on the 15th and 16th of December, the brigade to which the One Hundred and Forty-Second was attached was in the reserve, and occupied the left of the inner line of defense, extending from the Cumberland river to Fort Negley. After the battle the regiment was retained on duty at Nashville until its muster-out of service on the 14th of July, 1865.

On the 16th of July the regiment arrived at Indianapolis with thirty-two officers and five hundred and eighty-three men for final discharge and payment. On the 18th it marched to the State House grounds and was publicly received by the citizens, who had assembled to greet the return of three thousand soldiers, of five different regiments and two batteries of Indiana volunteers. From the reception stand the soldiers were addressed by Governor Morton, Generals Hovey, Chapman and Bennett, and others. A few days after the officers and men were paid off and discharged from service.

Officers

Colonel—JOHN M. COMPARET
Lieutenant Colonel—CHAUNCEY B. OAKLEY

Adjutant—PERCIVAL G. KELSEY
Quartermaster—THEODORE S. COMPARET

Company A
PRIVATES

Frederick Jimey
George McClannahan

Robert McEwen
Jerome Perry

Frank Ringler
William B. Warren

James Parmeter
Frederick Gobat

Company C

Captain—CHRISTOPHER HETTLER
First Lieutenant—WILLIAM B. WARREN
Second Lieutenant—CLOSSON WARREN
First Sergeant—FRANCIS M. RYLAND
Sergeants—ALFRED COOLMAR
   CHARLES W. POWELL
   DAVID MILES
   JOHN BUTT

Corporals—FRANCIS M. SAMS
   JOHN L. HANES
   RUDOLPH GRIPE
   TOBIAS RABUS
   JOHN STEIN
   JOHN A. BARKAS
   WILLIAM C. JONES
   AUSTIN LYON

PRIVATES

Franklin Arnold
John Auch
Theodore Bley
John Boshet
Daniel Beer
Albert W. Beatty
James L. Black
Frank Carry
George Craven
John G. Clark
Alfred Comstock
Joseph Clode
Samuel Dierstine
Antoine Dennis
William Dickey
Augustus Dourdick

Frederick Dirkas
Morris B. Dishong
Daniel Emerick
Charles Ehinger
Warner Ehinger
George Foster
John W. Farmer
Joseph France
Peter M. Grisley
Lewis Guilliam
Frederick Grannaman
Philip Geissenger
William Gorden
Peter Gabe
George Hessenauer
Henry Huffeister

David Kleindoust
John Kern
Frederick Kenneman
William Lang
Frederick Lower
Andrew Leeta
Frederick Meyer
George W. Moore
Dennis Madden
Anderson Martin
Gottleib Mullenbach
William Miller
Peter Mettert
Samuel Nickles
John Nill

David H. Overly
Napoleon Pompey
Charles Piquinot
August Rissing
Timothy Rallihan
Henry Schroeder
John Schulizer
Alexander Slater
John W. Shirts
Arthur S. Sisley
Eddem Saddlet
William Scoppman
Lewis Tinkham
Zophiral Voiral
Henry Weidbrok

Ellis Wert
Herman Walda
Benedict Welton
John Brown
Michael Herring
Casper Neep
Henry Oerting
Joseph Smith
Julius Saydot
John A. Slammer
Harrison Critchet
Christian Gable
William L. Gerard
Casper Krock
Lewis Mehre

Company D

Musician—JAMES SHEWEY
PRIVATES

Adam Amspacker
John W. Bowman
James Balentine
Jonathan H. Bryan

John G. Cunningham
John Devilbiss
James Dunivan
M. V. B. Funk

Lewis T. Jones
Celestine Marette
Thomas D. Overly

Jacob Shewey
Joseph Smith
James H. Smith

Peter W. Sipe
Peter Walburn
John Bailey

Company E

Captain—DAVID HOWELL
First Lieutenant—GEORGE P. SHAFFER
Second Lieutenant—ROBERT H. PARKER
First Sergeant—HENRY G. TAYLOR
Sergeants—JAMES BROWN
JEREMIAH WALLACE

Sergeants—RICHARD CHAMPION
WILLIAM B. DRAKE
Corporals—BASCOM C. ANDERSON
THOMAS J. SPURLING
JOSEPH KILHEY
JOHN THOMAS

Corporals—AUGUSTUS G. BOLTZ
HENRY PLOVER
JOHN WARNER
LEMUEL BALING
Musician—HENRY A. COBURN

PRIVATES

William C. Bloomhuff
Frank M. Bloomhuff
William S. Besser
Henry C. Baker
Samuel Baker
Daniel Bareus
Richard Bareus
Lewis Blyler
James I. Chilcote
John Connors
Joseph Clemens
Jonathan Coleman
Henry Dearman
Clarence E. Doane
William R. Drake

Henry Doutrick
Solomon Derome
William Dressler
Rufus F. Eby
Ira Friend
Frederick G. Hitsfield
Warren Hoke
Benjamin Hanes
William Hight
John A. Henry
Henry Hill
Adam Huff
James R. Howey
Ira Hardendorf
Thomas King

Joseph Klingaman
Gotleib Kromer
John Kern
Henry Lopshire
John Lopshire
Edward Lewis
Asbury Moore
George Mitchel
John Meyers
Barney McKenna
Samuel Mahon
Alexander McDowell
John Nierdemar
James Overly

Cornelius O'Connor
John M. Parker
Sanford R. Philley
Ezra Rank
Samuel Somers
William H. Somers
Peter Swager
Reuben Strout
Henry Stender
Edward H. Stein
Herman Stein
John Snider
George A. Simmons
Henry Story

George Throp
James Threadgall
Lawrence Tilford
John W. Truitt
Eri Williams
Christian Winkleman
Cornelius Weaver
Israel Young
John H. Young
Samuel S. Brown
Patrick Fitsimmons
Henry Hildebrand
Elias Kline
Leander P. Miner

Company F

Captain—ALONZO BIGELOW
First Lieutenant—ROBERT W. SWANN
Second Lieut.—WM. L. WESTERMAN
First Sergeant—NELSON PARKER
Sergeants—JAMES DONALDSON
ABRAM LOWERY

Sergeants—JOHN C. WHITELEATHER
ELIHU REICHELDERFER
Corporals—JAMES C. DUTCHER
ALEXANDER KENTNER
WILLIAM B. DANIELS
JOSEPH BRUDI

Corporals—JOSEPH A. BERRY
THOMAS S. TRUITT
WILLIAM W. LABAR
WILLIAM ORT
Musician—CHESTER C. HOLLINGER

PRIVATES

Samuel Albertson
Elwood J. Breece
Francis C. Banserman
Eleazer Briggs
Jonathan Bates
Jonathan G. Bennett
Christian F. Brudi
Benjamin F. Brelsford
John Banhill
Isaac G. Copp
Matthias Conrad
Wheeler Cutler
Samuel H. Crozier
Robert Castle
John Dagant
Charles Driver
Nathaniel C. Doctor

John Day
George R. Driver
David D. Driver
Amariah Daniels
Samuel D. H. Daniels
Joseph Deutzel
John W. Driesback
Harvey B. Foote
Amos C. Friece
Dennis Francis
Silas Felton
Martin Falk
Jacob Gable
William L. Gerard
Martin L. Henderson
Daniel Hatfield

Franklin Herrick
Porter Hill
John Hoover
Alfred Hollinger
William H. Hubecker
John Janes
William Klingerman
John Kelley
Peter LeClaire
John Lalow
Joseph S. Martin
Jacob Martin
Joel W. Morse
Elza Mariette
Peter Mettert
John Myers

Uriah Mitten
Lycurgus S. Mill
Samuel Oberholtzer
Henry L. Price
Lewis Perkins
Henry Powers
David R. Palmer
William Robinett
Jonathan B. Roberts
Scott Rugg
William A. Reichelderfer
Joseph D. Sweet
Sturgis C. Shaffer
Comfort Starr
Frederick Stambo

William Thomas
Ephriam B. Wartenbe
Samuel Walker
William J. Williams
James A. Whittington
William Wirebaugh
Isaac D. Warrington
William Welker
Seth Adams
John Compton
Jerome Davis
Leopold Evard
James Milledge
Alonzo O. Ober
Augustus A. Skinner
David Yoder

Company G

Corporal—JOHN M. MALEY   Musician—ARTHUR M. WALKER

PRIVATES

Richard Beck
Lewis Butner
John W. Crawford
Harvey Dye
John T. Fair
Hugh Harter

Caleb M. Houdyshell
John Hittenger
Adam Hughes
Casper Crock
George H. Points
Henry Sweet

Sidney B. Weeks
Daniel Sweet
Jefferson Wurtembe
Gilbert Shaw
Levi Zumbrum
William L. Beck

William Coleman
Nathaniel Cook
Henry Friend
William Gaskill
Daniel Hourigan
Skilman Houdyshell

Nathaniel Hilliard
Francis H. Johnson
Anderson Pence
James H. Scovell
Francis Stofiel
Daniel Ziegler

Company H

Corporal—THEODORE HELM   Musician—EDMOND HELM

PRIVATES

Royal Bugbee   Lewis Davis   John Ferguson   William Todd

Company K

Captain—ANDREW STEVENS

PRIVATES

Hiram B. Derr
William Charles

William Turner
William Derr

John F. Mooney

John Jones

Francis McMahan

One Hundred and Forty-Sixth Regiment Infantry

The One Hundred and Forty-Sixth regiment was recruited in the First, Third and Fourth Congressional Districts and organized at Indianapolis on the 3d of March, 1865. On the 9th it was mustered into service, with MERIT C. WELSH as Colonel, and left Indianapolis on the 11th for Harper's Ferry, Virginia. Arriving there on the 15th it was assigned to one of the provisional divisions of the Army of the Shenandoah. From that time until the 27th of July, it was engaged in performing post and guard duty at Charlestown, Winchester, Stevenson Station, Jordan's Springs and Summit Point, Virginia. It was then ordered to the Relay House from whence it moved to Baltimore where it was assigned to duty in the Military District of Delaware, Gen. Lockwood commanding. One company was at once detached and placed on duty at Hicks' General Hospital, Baltimore, one company sent to Havre De Grace, and, on the 1st of August, four companies were detached and placed on duty as follows: One company at Dover, and one at Wilmington, Delaware; one at Salisbury and one at Easton, Maryland. These companies were continued on this duty until the 31st of August, 1865, when the regiment was brought together and mustered out of service, at Baltimore. Arriving at Indianapolis on the 8th of September, with thirty-two officers and seven hundred and seventy-one men for final payment and discharge, it was publicly welcomed home, at a reception meeting held in the State House grounds, at which speeches were made by Governor Morton and Generals Mansfield and Washburn, which were responded to by Colonel Welsh, Lieutenant Colonel Morrison, Major Spillman and Adjutant Hill. The regiment then marched to Camp Carrington, where it was paid off and finally discharged.

One Hundred and Forty-Sixth Regiment Infantry

Company I

Corporal—LOTT LOGAN
Musician—JOSEPH KETCHUM

PRIVATES

Mathias Ghogle
John Heldendright
John Hohing
Charles McNair
Henry McNair

One Hundred and Fifty-Second Regiment Infantry

(ONE YEAR SERVICE)

The One Hundred and Fifty-Second Regiment was recruited in the Tenth Congressional District, and was organized at Indianapolis on the 16th of March, 1865, with WHEDON W. GRISWOLD as Colonel. It left Indianapolis on the 18th for Harper's Ferry, Virginia, and on arriving there was assigned to duty with one of the provisional divisions of the Army of the Shenandoah. It was stationed for a short time at Charlestown, Stevenson Station and Summit Point, and then moved to Clarksburg, in Western Virginia, where it remained until its muster out, on the 30th of August, 1865.

One Hundred and Fifty-Second Regiment Infantry
(ONE YEAR SERVICE)

Lieutenant Col.—JOSEPH W. WHITAKER   Surgeon—WILLIAM H. THACKER   Assistant Surgeon—HEMAN H. SHERWIN

Company B
PRIVATES
Alexander F. Brown   Daniel Murphy   Joseph L. Skinner

Company C
First Sergeant—GEORGE H. MINIARD   Sergeant—JOHN RAYPOLE
Sergeant—TIMOTHY M. ALBEE   Corporal—JOHN F. WELLS
PRIVATES

Calvin Conklin	George Sanders	James A. Watterson	Winfield S. Kestler	Amos Miller
Leonard Cooper	Jacob Slyter	Gardener Works	George Kiser	Henry V. Miller
Joel Delong	Charles D. Shyre	George Wilson	David McGrady	Ronald T. McDonald
Albert A. Demonsey	John W. Watterson	George Gardener	William G. McBride	Reuben Rerick
Isaac E. Evans	Samuel Watterson	John Julien	Andrew J. Miner	

Company F
PRIVATES
Jacob Marquart   Isaiah Magner

Company G
Captain—WILLIAM A. KELSEY
First Lieutenant—ORRIN D. ROGERS
Second Lieutenant—FRANK A. ROBINSON
First Sergeant—ROBERT S. ARMSTRONG
Sergeants—JOHN NAIL
    DANIEL J. RHOADS

Sergeants—MATTHEW SCHWARZ
    MILO H. BROOKS
Corporals—ENOCH CLARK
    HENRY BLACKBURN
    GEORGE RUSH
    ROBERT W. BRUNDIGE
Wagoner—JAMES B. HENDERSON

Corporals—BENJAMIN CLARK
    DANIEL C. GROVER
    WILLIAM CLARK
    MATTHIAS HOLLOPETER
Musicians—JOHN FAIRFIELD
    JOHN THEEMLER

PRIVATES

Earl Adams	Jacob Fouser	John A. Ivy	Frank Paragay	John Smalts
Thomas Ambler	Samuel Fogwell	Calvin Jones	Christian D. Parker	Heman H. Sherwin
Jonathan Byres	William Grieble	Braden Johnson	Isaiah Reddin	John F. Sherwin
Luther Birely	Patrick Golden	Jacob Kaufman	Gustavus Ross	Henry Vannardan
Thomas Carroll	John C. Grover	Frank Laronway	Samuel Roberts	Joseph York
Jesse Crouse	Julius Grojohn	Charles Mason	David Rhoads	John Ball
Peter Conrad	Zachariah T. Garrett	Israel Miller	Reuben Rousseau	William C. Stevick
John Craig	Isaac N. Harper	Levi Matthews	Henry Serits	Asa Smith
Levi Coleman	John Heinsche	George Miller	David P. Smith	Hamilton Scott
Henry Decker	David Heinsche	Stacion McDonald	Willlam Shaughnessy	Asa Turner
William Dawkins	James L. Hunter	Charles E. Morse	Henry Scott	Herschel Herring
Absalom Durbin	David Harbaugh	Alexander McClure	Lewis Snider	Thomas Oceleston
Joseph Davis	Sidney Hatfield	Charles Noyer	Louis Schlandorff	Elmore Scribner
John Ehringer	James A. Hollopeter	John B. Parisot	Nathan W. Sedgley	Martin Stills
Henry Elophe				

Company H
Captain—MARSHALL W. WINES
First Sergeant—JOSEPH E. G. HOLMAN
Sergeants—WILLIAM H. FOSS
    SAMUEL GAULT
    LEWIS CLARK

Corporals—JOHN S. SHEIK
    ARNOLD SMITH
    RILEY RICKETS
    WILLIAM H. NEAL

Corporals—NICHOLAS KINGER
    PETER SONNET
    EDWIN C. SMEAD
Musician—PERRY L. BAKER

PRIVATES

Amon Baes	Samuel Gohring	Thomas F. Kelly	Charles Richard	John Schneider
Francis Bailey	William Hazlet	Conrad Kuehlman	Owen W. Rummell	John I. Smithey
Timothy Baldwin	Nathaniel Haggerty	James Knight	Florentine Ray	Peter Scherschel
Michael Brucker	Daniel Hallaner	Gerhardt Lauer	John Roudebush	Charles Starling
Alexander Bailey	Joseph Herchenreider	John Lauer	Peter Russell	Samuel Tanner
Newton Bayles	Marcus Herchenreider	Ernst Long	Philip Schuckman	Christian Youse
Lyon Burford	Peter Hendler	Peter Michards	Nelson Smith	George D. Baker
Adam Cognet	Jason Hobbs	Benjamin Mapes	Christ Schranger	William N. Kennon
Patrick Cunningham	Calvin P. Hauser	Thomas McIntosh	Jason Schaffer	Rudolph Schwartz
Jacob Clark	George P. Hilkey	Benjamin McIntosh	Charles Smalley	John B. Sanford
Thomas Cutshell	Alexander Jobst	William Magner	Randall D. Sprague	James A. Winwright
Frank Englehart	Amand Jobst	Philip Nussdorfer		

Company I
Corporal—WILLIAM PHELPS
PRIVATE
Thomas Bird

One Hundred and Fifty-Fifth Regiment Infantry

(ONE YEAR SERVICE)

The One Hundred and Fifty-Fifth Regiment was composed of companies recruited in the Ninth, Tenth and Eleventh Congressional Districts and was organized at Indianapolis on the 18th of April, 1865, with JOHN M. WILSON as Colonel. On the 26th of April the regiment left for Washington and upon its arrival there it was sent to Alexandria and was assigned to the provisional brigade of the Third Division of the Ninth Army Corps. On the 3d of May it was transferred to Dover, Delaware, at which place companies were detached and sent to Centreville, and Wilmington, Delaware, and Salisbury, Maryland. On the return to the regiment of two of these companies a railroad accident occurred by which a number were severely injured. On the 1st of September it reached Indianapolis with seven hundred and seventy men and officers, where it was finally discharged.

One Hundred and Fifty-Fifth Regiment Infantry

(ONE YEAR SERVICE)

Company D

Captain—Joseph M. Silver
First Lieutenant—George R. Whitmore
Second Lieutenant—Richard H. Garland
First Sergeant—John H. Jacobs
Sergeants—Elbridge G. Paige
        Omer Stater
        Philip Sternier
        John Whinnery
Corporals—Lewis H. Bowers
        Oliver Hebert
        Amos Prindle
        Charles Smith
        John West
        David Walter

PRIVATES

Peter Aumstutz
John Barden
Frank Besancon
William Bryant
Oliver Benward
Joseph Besancon
George D. Beckman
Joseph Burchfield
John N. Broom
Isaac D. Barcus
John W. Calvert
Mahlon I. Connett
Jacob Cronmiller
Peter Dailey
Joseph Dailey
Joseph Dame
Hiram Dingman
Charles Friese
George Ford
William S. Garhart
Thomas Gorley
William R. Herrick

Arinda Herrick
Thomas Holt
David Henderson
August Hartman
John G. Hartshorn
Justice Humbert
Homer C. Hartman
Henry Herr
Freeman James
Anton Kayser
Frederick Kerns
James Kestler
George P. Lake
William Monroe
John Myres
Henry J. Mulholland
Samuel Mengus
Peter Mengus
Lyman O. Nye
William Putt
William H. Richey
Stephen Robinson

Franklin Reed
Jacob M. Snyder
William A. Snyder
Henry Smith
Salfedor Smith
Louis C. Shepherd
Peter Snowberger
Emil Swartz
William W. Tourgiee
George W. Williams
Lewis Zollinger
Eli Arnold
Lewis H. Barr
Strouse Benward
William D. Bloomhuff
Jonathan Bowman
Jacob Fair
John McNall
Charles E. Nichols
James Slater
Adam Schwegel
William Welsimer

Fifth Battery, Light Artillery

The Fifth Battery of Light Artillery was authorized to be recruited on the 16th of September, 1861. It was raised in Whitley, Noble, Laporte and Allen counties. On the 17th of September the men rendezvoused at Indianapolis, where the battery was mustered into service on the 22d of November, with PETER SIMONSON as Captain. Its armament consisted of two twelve-pounder howitzers, two six-pounder rifle and two six-pounder smooth-bores. On the 27th of November, it left Indianapolis with one hundred and forty-eight men, and arrived at Camp Gilbert, near Louisville, on the 29th. Here it was placed in a school of instruction, where it remained until the 20th of December, when it was assigned to General O. M. Mitchell's division of Buell's army, then stationed at Bacon Creek, Kentucky. On the 9th of February, 1862, it moved with its division to Bowling Green and Nashville. During the month of March it moved to Murfreesboro, and from thence to Fayetteville, Tennessee and Huntsville, Alabama. The guns of this battery being in the advance, before reaching Huntsville, were placed in position and opened upon the flying railroad trains of the enemy, and, by a few well directed shots, halted all but one, and aroused the slumbering citizens to find their city in the possession of the national troops, at daylight on the 11th of April. The same day two guns of the battery were placed upon platform cars and run ahead of locomotives, each way on the Memphis and Charleston Railroad seventy miles. On the return, bridges were destroyed, thus rendering the position secure. During the stay at Huntsville, many raids were made in different directions. in which the battery participated, the men being frequently used by Gen. Mitchel as cavalry, doing excellent service as scouts.

In June half of the battery, under command of Captain Simonson, were attached to the Nineteenth Illinois, under Col. Turchin, and marched by way of Winchester, Tennessee, and Paint Rock, Bellefonte, and Stevenson, Alabama, to Bridgeport, Alabama. Here they remained on the bank of the Tennessee river, in full view of the enemy's pickets, for two months, until August, when the balance of the company joined them. On the 24th of August, the battery was ordered to Stevenson to cover the removal of Government stores, hospitals, rolling stock, &c., from that post. On the morning of the 31st of August, the enemy, in strong force, attacked the post, and a spirited and determined artillery battle was kept up until two o'clock in the afternoon, when the enemy ceased firing. Everything being in readiness, the troops were withdrawn, the battery being with the rear guard. The only loss to the battery was of one man taken prisoner. About this time, Gen. Mitchell was assigned to a command at Beaufort, South Carolina, and Gen. Rousseau took command of the Third Division, which had been placed in Gen. McCook's corps. With the Army of the Ohio, under Gen. Buell, the division fell back before Bragg's army to Nashville, via Murfreesboro, and from thence, on the 8th of September marched toward the Ohio river, going by way of Bowling Green and Munfordsville to Louisville.

Remaining at Louisville about a week, it marched with its division on a new campaign after Bragg. On the 8th

of October it participated in the battle of Chaplin Hills, near Perryville, being hotly engaged for six hours, the battery maintaining its position, supported by the Thirty-Eighth Indiana, Thirty-Third Ohio and Tenth Wisconsin regiments, an hour longer than any other command on the field, and was highly complimented by the General commanding, for gallant and meritorious conduct during the engagement. The loss to the battery was two men killed and eighteen wounded, thirty-two horses killed and crippled, and one caisson chest blown up by the enemy's shell. From Perryville the Fifth Battery marched via Harrodsburg, Danville, and Stamford to Crab Orchard, and thence via Stamford, Greensburg and Glasgow, to Bowling Green, where the army was re-organized, Gen. Buell being relieved by Gen. Rosecrans. Moving southward, the battery reached Nashville on the 9th of November, and, on the 24th of December, it was transferred to the Second Division, under Gen. R. W. Johnson. On the 26th of December, the battery again moved, with its division, and became engaged with the enemy at Triune, on the 27th and skirmished with him until the 30th, when the battle of Stone river was begun. Early on the morning of the 31st, the Second Division was fiercely assailed by a superior force, and with the First and Third Divisions of the Twentieth (McCook's) Corps, was routed and driven back nearly two miles, losing heavily in men and material. The Fifth Battery was severely cut up, losing three men killed and sixteen men and officers wounded—one mortally. Thirty-two horses and two guns were lost. The division commander, in his official report, says: "Captain Simonson managed his battery with skill and courage, and with it did good execution. He lost two guns, but not until the horses had been killed, and the guns disabled." In the repulse of the enemy on the two last days of the engagement, the battery, with its remaining guns, did effective service.

After this battle the Fifth Battery went into winter quarters at Murfreesboro, and spent the succeeding five months in drilling and preparing for the succeeding campaign. On the 24th of June, 1863, the army was put in motion, the battery being still in the Third Brigade of the Second Division of the Twentieth Army Corps. On the same day it became engaged with the enemy at Liberty Gap, and heavy skirmishing continued for three days, when the enemy fell back and concentrated his force at Tullahoma. The whole army of the Cumberland advanced upon that position, which was evacuated as the national forces approached, and quiet possession was taken on the 2d of July. On the 16th of August, the army again moved southward, the Twentieth Corps forming the right wing. Proceeding via Winchester and Salem down the Paint Rock, and then up the Hurricane Fork of that stream, and thence across the Cumberland Mountains to Bellefonte, Alabama, it moved from there to Stevenson, and crossed the Tennessee river at Caperton's ferry, on the 31st of August. After passing over Sand Mountain, and Lookout and Pigeon-toe Ridges, to Hog Jaw Valley, Walker county, Georgia, it was discovered that the command had advanced too far, when it fell back across Pigeon-Toe Ridge to Winston Springs, and thence over the Lookout Ridge into Chicamauga Val-

Fifth Battery, Light Artillery—Continued

ley to Pond Springs, and formed a Junction with the main army, on the 19th of September. About noon on that day, the division became engaged and fought till after dark, the battery losing one gun and several horses. The next morning at sunrise, the battle was renewed with great fury, and the battery remained in position, heavily pressed, until two o'clock in the afternoon, when it was ordered to fall back, in doing which it lost another gun. It finally reached the main line, near Ringold, after dark. On the 22d it retired to the lines around Chattanooga, In this engagement the Fifth Battery lost one killed, nine wounded, and two prisoners. Twenty-six horses and two guns were lost.

In November the battery was ordered to Shell Mound, Tennessee, to guard the river and road from Bridgeport to Chattanooga. To reach that point the troops were obliged to cross the mountains bordering the Tennessee river called Waldron's ridge, up which the men were obliged to draw the guns and caissons with the picket ropes, one hundred men being required to haul one gun. The ascent of three miles was thus made in one and a half days. At Shell Mound the battery went into winter quarters, and there remained until February, 1864, when it moved to Blue Springs, Tennessee, and was attached to the First (Stanley's) Division of the Fourth Corps. During the winter fifteen men of the battery re-enlisted. In February a reconnoissance was made of the enemy's position on Buzzard Roost, under the command of Gen. Palmer, in which the battery participated, and was actively engaged, without loss.

On the 3d of May, began the memorable campaign against Atlanta, during which the battery occupied a constant position in the advance, marching with its division and participating in the following engagements: Tunnel Hill, Rocky Face Ridge, Resacca, near Adairsville, Kingston, Cassville, Pine Mountain, before Kenesaw Mountain, New Hope Church, Hurst's Station, Peach Tree Creek, before Atlanta, and at Jonesboro. At Pine Mountain, while engaged in placing the battery in position, the gallant Captain Simonson was killed and one man wounded. Other losses were sustained as follows: At New Hope Church, two killed and two wounded; At Hurst's Station, one mortally wounded, and two slightly wounded; before Kenesaw, one killed and one wounded; at Peach Tree Creek, one killed. On the 20th of September the battery turned over its guns, horses and equipments to the ordnance officer at Atlanta, and the non-veterans were ordered to report at Indianapolis for muster-out. Arriving at Indianapolis on the 18th of November, the non-veterans were mustered out on the 26th of November, 1864. The veterans and remaining recruits were transferred to the Seventh Battery, and on the 5th of April, 1865, they were permanently consolidated with that battery, and continued to serve with it until its final muster-out, on the 20th of July, 1865.

At Pine Mountain, the shot that killed Lieut. Gen. Polk, of the rebel army, was fired from one of the Rodman guns of the Fifth battery. The total losses to the battery during its term of service were as follows: Killed nine, mortally wounded three, wounded forty-eight, died of disease, twenty-one, prisoners of war, three; total eighty-four. It lost in battle four guns, and expended over sixty thousand rounds of ammunition. It has renewed its armament three times during its term of service.

Officers

Second Lieutenant—WILLIAM L. HULSE
Sergeants—JAMES FULLERTON
        SAMUEL P. C. FREEMAN
Corporals—JOSEPHUS ARMACK
        WILLIAM G. ROBERTSON
Buglers—CLAUD C. MILLER
        WILLIAM L. HULSE

PRIVATES

William L. Armstrong	Harrison Imbody
George Acker	Louis T. Vigina
Isaac Barr	Nicholas Brue
Harrison Crumer	Thomas Cole
David Cool	Otis Heath
Daniel Culver	Anthony Kramer
Samuel Culver	Patrick Ney
Jacob C. Clark	Alonzo K. Beale
John E. Douglass	Michael McCarty
Joseph Davis	Arthur Peabody

Eleventh Battery, Light Artillery

The eleventh battery was recruited at Fort Wayne, and mustered into the service at Indianapolis on the 17th of December, 1861, with Arnuld Sutermeister as Captain. Soon after its organization the battery proceeded to Louisville, and moved with General Buell's army to Nashville, arriving there on the 26th of February, 1862. From thence the battery moved with its division to Pittsburg Landing, arriving there at the close of the battle of Shiloh, and participated in the siege of Corinth which followed. Upon the evacuation of Corinth, the battery moved with the main army through northern Mississippi to Tuscumbia, Alabama, and thence to Huntsville, where it went into camp in July. The rebel General Bragg having transferred a large part of his army through Alabama and Georgia, reached Chattanooga in advance of General Buell's forces, turned his left, and, moving up the Sequatchie valley, crossed Tennessee, and entered Kentucky. General Buell's army fell back to Nashville, and then moved in pursuit of the rebel army. The battery moved with the main column, and, after the pursuit of Bragg had ceased, returned to Nashville, and, upon the re-organization of the army under General Rosecrans, was assigned to the Third Division, Twenty-first Army Corps.

After the battle of Stone River and occupation of Murfreesboro, the battery went into camp near that place. On the 24th of June, 1863, the battery moved with the main army upon the enemy's position at Tullahoma, which place was abandoned by the enemy, who fell back across the Tennessee river. The battery then halted at Cowan's Station. General Sheridan's division, to which it was assigned, was engaged, during the months of July and August, in guarding the railroad from Decherd, Tennessee, to Stevenson, Alabama. and sections of the eleventh battery were stationed at important points along the railroad. On the 16th of August, a general forward movement was made, and General Sheridan's division crossed the Tennessee river at Bridgeport upon a bridge which it had constructed on the 1st of September, and, moving by the way of Trenton, joined its corps near Winston's Gap. From thence the battery moved with its division to Steven's Gap. On the 19th of September, the battle of Chicamauga began. Sheridan's division moved to support the right of Crittenden's corps at Gordon's Mill. Here a sanguinary engagement took place, with great loss on both sides, but Sheridan's division held its position, and, at one time, gallantly charged the enemy, recapturing a battery. The following day the fight was renewed with great fury, and, the enemy having broken a portion of our line, our army retired to Rossville, and from thence to Chattanooga. The Eleventh Battery was severely engaged in this battle, and lost heavily in killed and wounded. Upon arriving at Chattanooga, the battery took position in the fortifications, and was engaged during the siege of that place. The battery took part in the battle of Mission Ridge, on the 25th of November, and remained at Chattanooga during the following winter.

On the 5th of March, 1864, a number of the members of the battery re-enlisted as veterans at Chattanooga. In May the battery moved with General Sherman's army upon the campaign against Atlanta, and took part in the principal engagements and movements that crowned that campaign with success. After the capture of Atlanta the Eleventh Battery returned to Chattanooga, where it remained stationed until, on the 21st of November, 1864, sixty-five of its members were transferred to the Eighteenth Indiana Battery, and consolidated with it, and the Eleventh Battery lost its designation, the new organization being known as the Eighteenth Battery. The consolidated battery remained at Chattanooga until orders were received to proceed to Indiana for muster out. On the 7th of June, 1865, the Eighteenth battery was mustered out of the service at Indianapolis.

Eleventh Battery, Light Artillery

(THREE YEARS' SERVICE)

Officers

Captain—ARNOLD SUTERMEISTER
First Lieutenants—HENRY TONS
    WILLIAM GREEN
    JOHN OTTO
    HENRY M. WILLIAMS
    JOHN H. JACOBS
Second Lieutenant—CHARLES R. SCOTT
Quartermaster Sergt.—JOHN H. EHLERS
Sergeants—GEORGE THOMPSON
    JOHN MCKINLEY
    H. H. BICKELL
    ELI RANK
    WALTER STRATTON
    GEORGE WALTMAN
Corporal—D. H. M. PHILLABAUM

Corporals—T. C. GILLOCK
    RICHARD BIDDICK
    GEORGE CRAIG
    FRANCIS KELLAR
    JOHN D. MCGRADY
    CHARLES DUDLEY
    PETER CAMPBELL
    ALBERT TOTTEN
    JOHN J. CONKLIN
Buglers—WILLIAM L. ANDREWS
    WILLIAM EDMONDS
Artificer—CHRISTIAN SEILER
    JOHN F. CROW
    MICHAEL B. RYAN
Wagoner—JOHN GRATHAM

PRIVATES

Henry W. Caldwell	Nathaniel Blane	John Corcoran	George Hussart	Hirah F. Jarvis
William M. Chapman	Louis H. Bowers	Henry I. Darling	James B. Henderson	Theodore Johnson
Ephriam Goodwill	Henry M. Brown	Philip Feters	William Hobbs	John Keller
Jabob Schmittley	Samuel M. Cairns	Robert Gill	John Hobbs	Gottlieb Kerchner
James Ballard	Wellington Clossen	Samuel Grider	John W. Hoke	John Koons
Louis Bewley	John Clear	Francis Grojohn	Dallas P. Holbrook	John Balmer
Adolph Lamont	Robert Green	A. J. Cotterel	William P. Kimball	Gottlieb Ueltschi
Joseph Lapshire	Elias Hobbs	William H. Cuttshall	Charles Leibritz	John W. Vodermark
Henry Laner	D. W. Johnston	Hiram Congelton	Jasper Ludwig	Lewis Voss
Francis Leavenway	Samuel Jones	John Carls	George Lampman	David Walters
John W. Morehouse	Jackson Jones	Samuel Dougherty	George W. Linden	Henry Weber
Stacy McDonald	Isaac Landers	Henry F. Drews	John McIntosh	Julius Young
William McGrady	Jasper Ludwig	Elijah Dolloff	Hugh McBratney	Andrew J. Zeak
Patrick McMahon	Rudolph Lusher	Richard Ehle	James McNally	Henry Zollinger ƚ
Philip Miller	John W. Mortsalf	John Englert	Addison McGuire	Daniel Barr
John L. Moore	Robert McKee	Daniel D. France	William Millard	William W. Ford
Daniel O'Grady	Thomas Robbitt	Charles S. Farris	Martin Monasmith	Barney Finnegan
Christian Ouk	David Ritter	Orville B. Farris	Herman Michalis	Alfred Gardner
Adam Phillabaum	Samuel Shoaff	Jacob Felger	John A. Mason	John Hobbs, Sr.
Charles Quantt	Thomas VanDusen	Almond H. Flint	Frederick Myers	William Holmes
Fabius Rupple	William H. Warfield	William Glenn	Elisha Marshall	Valentine Seitz
Lorenzo Schuler	Jacob Watson	Lewis H. Gardner	Henry J. Newcomer	Henry Slater
William Schuler	Charles I. Willis	Jacob Good	Herman Otto	Thomas Stokes
John Schuler	Clark L. Wilcox	Peter Grasely	George Rank	James M. B. Snyder
John Shofer	James Johnson	William Grotton	Charles E. Rogers	Henry Blaze
James Shofer	James W. Kilpatrick	Gottlieb Gribi	Laban J. Riley	A. J. Bird
William Shehan	David Flick	John Harner	Edward Schell	George W. Brooks
George Stall	Thomas J. Devlin	John Howenstein	John Shore	William J. Coles
Jeff H. Thompson	James K. Regan	John Hahn	Jacob Smith	Benjamin C. Challis
Jacob Waggnerman	William Ring	Perry Haines	James A. Snyder	John W. Demerest
Jacob Wilhelm	Philander Sprague	Rudolph Iseli	Patrick A. Stokes	Lovetus A. Ferris
J. C. Williams	Martin E. Rundel	Charles Ismer	John Stratton	Daniel Oplinger
George W. Ainsworth	Christian Annan	Jeremiah Irvin	Albert Smeed	Thomas Stafford
Loren Bethel	Ferdinand Ballou	Alexander Irvin	Elisha J. Smith	James W. Kilpatrick
Warren Clossen	Henry Beamer	Joseph P. Jerot	Joseph Sunderland	John Adam
John P. Dugan	Edward Bearss	Isaac Johnson	Woolsey H. Sawtell	Adin Black
John Eikoff	James Boden	John Joner	John Telly	James Brown
James Godfrey	Alexander Bowser	Samuel Kelker	William B. Tyner	Thomas Smith
William Graver				

Twenty-Third Battery, Light Artillery

The Twenty-Third Battery of Light Artillery was recruited during the fall of 1862, and was organized and mustered into service at Indianapolis on the 8th of November, 1862, with JAMES H. MYERS as Captain. From that time until the 4th of July, 1863, the battery did duty at Indianapolis, under the orders of Gens. Carrington, Hascall and Wilcox, who, respectively, had the command of the Military District during that period. Its duties consisted mainly in aiding in guarding the rebel prisoners. On the 10th of June, in obedience to the orders of Gen. Willcox, a section of the battery accompanied the Seventy-First Regiment, under Col. Biddle, on a brief expedition to Monroe, Sullivan and Green counties, to quell the disturbances in that quarter created by the interference with and killing of the government enrolling officers. On the 4th of July Gen. Willcox received an order from Gen. Buruside, commanding the Department, directing him to send to Kentucky all the available troops then at Indianapolis. Intelligence had been received that a large force of rebel cavalry, under Gen. John H. Morgan, had attacked Col. Moore's command at Green River bridge and been defeated, and was then marching on Louisville. Accordingly, all the infantry, cavalry and artillery that could be spared was sent to Louisville, with orders to report to Gen. Boyle, commanding that district. The Twenty-Third Battery formed part of this force. After Morgan crossed the Ohio into Indiana, at Brandenburg, the battery rendered good service in following him up, and ultimately helping to capture the raiders. It then returned to Indianapolis, and remained there until the six months' regiments were sent to the field, in September, 1863, when it proceeded to Camp Nelson. Kentucky, and became a part of Gen. Willcox's division, and with it marched through southern Kentucky to Cumberland Gap. From there it moved to Knoxville, and participated in the campaign in the mountainous regions of East Tennessee during the winter of 1863, including the engagements fought at Knoxville and vicinity under Gen. Burnside, and the operations in the region of country extending from Morristown to Greenville, and from Bull's Gap to Cumberland Gap, and thence to Blain's Cross Roads. During this campaign Willcox's command was obliged to cross several ranges of mountains and broad rivers, and was often away from its base of supplies and severed from all support.

In May, 1864, the battery was assigned to the Twenty-Third Army Corps, under command of General Schofield, and with it took part in the campaign against Atlanta. After the occupation of that place, the battery moved with its corps northward, through Georgia and Middle Tennessee, engaging the enemy at Columbia and Franklin. On arriving at Nashville it rested until the 15th and 16th of December, when it participated in the battle before Nashville, and then followed in pursuit of Hood, going to Clifton, on the Tennessee river. At that place it embarked on transports, and proceeded, with the Twenty-Third Corps, to Cincinnati, and from thence, by rail, to Washington, D. C. From Washington the battery moved to Alexandria, Virginia, and from there sailed to Wilmington, North Carolina. From thence it marched to Goldsboro, Raleigh and Greensboro, participating in the campaign made by Schofield's forces in that State. After the surrender of Johnston's rebel army the battery was ordered to proceed to Indiana for muster out. Arriving at Indianapolis on the 27th of June, 1865, with three officers and one hundred and twenty-three men for final discharge, it was present at a public reception given to returned soldiers at the Tabernacle on the 30th, at which speeches were made by Governor Baker, General Hovey and others. On the 2d of July, 1865, the battery wss formally mustered out, and the officers and men discharged from service.

Twenty-Third Battery, Light Artillery

Officers

Captain—JAMES H. MYERS
First Lieutenants—LUTHER S. HOUGHTON
      AARON A. WILBUR
Orderly Sergeant—JOHN G. BRIGHT
Quartmaster Sergt.—JOHN KNAPPENBERGER
Sergeants—ABRAM L. STONER
    CHARLES M. GILLETT
    JOSEPH BOWERS
    WILLIAM SHEEHAN
    FREEMAN F. BELL
    LOUIS A. GRIFFITH
Corporals—WALLACE W. CORBETTE
    FREDERICK BOTTERON
    WARREN JUMP
    LAFAYETTE S. NAIL
    MANASSA RUPERT
Harnessmaker—GEORGE W. HOLLINGER
Wagonmaster—DANIEL PERKINS

PRIVATES

William J. Bright
James C. Chamberlain
Albert A. Doremus
Jacob Freese
Joseph Gillingham
Joseph Gruber
Hiram Heney
Henry Hoskins
John Kaylor
George Longley
James Mayhew
Anson Miller
Edward Miller
Daniel Mullen
Harris Ruth

William Ringwalt
Hiram Slater
Osborne Treepe
Isaac Patterson
Thomas Hazelett
Jacob Gorrell
John Minnick
Joseph Minnick
John R. Helmick
Jehial Gustin
Alfred Bushy
Joseph Treepe
John L. Nichols
Leonard Burrier